THE
Richard
Wesley
PLAY ANTHOLOGY

THE
Richard Wesley
PLAY ANTHOLOGY

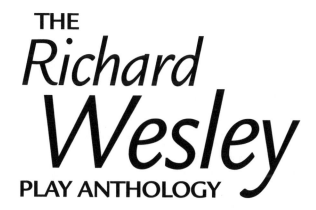

APPLAUSE
THEATRE & CINEMA BOOKS

An Imprint of Hal Leonard Corporation

Published in 2015 by Hal Leonard Books
An Imprint of Hal Leonard Corporation
7777 West Bluemound Road
Milwaukee, WI 53213

Trade Book Division Editorial Offices
33 Plymouth St., Montclair, NJ 07042

Printed in the United States of America

Book design by Lynn Bergesen

Library of Congress Cataloging-in-Publication Data

Wesley, Richard, 1945-
  [Plays. Selections]
  The Richard Wesley play anthology.
     pages cm
  Includes bibliographical references and index.
  ISBN 978-1-4803-9499-5 (alk. paper)
  1. African Americans—Drama. I. Title.
  PS3573.E8147A6 2015
  812'.54—dc23
                    2015011140

www.applausebooks.com

Contents

Introduction

We are unfair
And unfair
We are black magicians
Black arts we make
In black labs of the heart…
　　　　　　　　—LeRoi Jones, 1965

One weekend during my sophomore year at Howard University, Owen Dodson, the chair of the Department of Drama, returned to campus from a weekend spent in New York seeing various Broadway and Off-Broadway stage productions. He was gushing in class that following Monday—fired up in a way his students had never seen before. The excitement in Professor Dodson's voice was like that of a prospector who has discovered a mother lode of rich, wonderful ore. The "rich, wonderful ore" he had encountered in New York that weekend was the play *The Dutchman*, authored by an exciting new playwright, then named LeRoi Jones but known throughout the world today as Amiri Baraka.

The Dutchman was only the latest, and perhaps the most explosive, in a series of black-themed dramas that had emerged on New York stages, beginning with Lorraine Hansberry's *A Raisin in the Sun* in 1959, and continuing with such plays as *Purlie Victorius* by Ossie Davis, *The Cool World* by Warren Miller and Robert Rossen, James Baldwin's *Blues for Mr. Charlie*, and Jean Genet's *The Blacks*. But *Dutchman* represented a boldness and blunt depiction of the unspoken rage that had roiled the psyche of African Americans for decades. If *Raisin* can rightfully be considered a historical breakthrough for African-American playwriting and theater in America, *The Dutchman* was a game changer, an announcement of the arrival of a new generation of African-American cultural artists. This was the play that generated nationwide conversation. Whenever and wherever the young people of the mid-1960s encountered *Dutchman*, minds were changed, and all of us immediately began to imagine new possibilities about what could and could not be said onstage.

LeRoi Jones transformed the cultural/political landscape in much the way that DuBois's *Souls of Black Folk* announced a new generation of black thinkers at the turn of the twentieth century, Alain Locke's *The New Negro* led to the famed Harlem Renaissance, Richard Wright's *The Negro and the Racial Mountain* fired the imaginations of black intellectuals in the '40s and '50s, and James Baldwin's *Notes of a Native Son* reflected the emergence of the civil rights generation. But those were books and essays whose contents were consumed over long periods of time, with readers reclining in chairs—with time to stop and think, mull and reconsider, riding in the subways and buses. *Dutchman*, on the other hand, was a play, performed by living, breathing human beings, where everything—passions, dreams, desires, fears, and most of all, the deep secrets and unexpressed emotions that underlie so much of the racial discourse in the United States—was visible, expressed, and *immediate*.

I'd come to see that the finest playwrights across two thousand years of Western theater, from Euripides to Shakespeare to Miller and Albee, had created dramas that did more than make powerful commentary on the ages and societies in which they were living. These writers also demanded that their audiences peer into their mythology, their histories, their expectations and assumptions, their moral compasses, and their very souls. The playwrights wanted their audiences to ask themselves whether or not their culture—their society—was working the way it should be and, if not, whether they should think about effecting some kind of change. These writers were not creating mere entertainments; they were throwing intellectual, moral, and spiritual *bombs*. That was why their work made a difference; that was why their plays endured over time.

The theater is powerful, and therefore dangerous. *Actors*—human beings, right there in front of us—moving around in three-dimensional space, sometimes so close to us we can feel their breath upon us, see the wrinkles in their skin, witness the spittle flying from their mouths. There is no escape, no shutting the book, no running off to do another chore. Everything—the good, the bad, the uncomfortable—is right there before us, demanding that we *pay attention*.

Trojan Women was the first great antiwar play in the Western theatrical canon, and demanded that Greek society face up to the moral implications of the genocide that had been committed in its name during the sacking of Troy. Athens was not happy. *Richard III* (most likely wrongly) painted Richard Plantagenet as a vicious villain and usurper of the throne, and also made Henry VII, the first Tudor, a glorious hero and rescuer of England. Henry VII's granddaughter, Elizabeth I, was very happy. *A Doll's*

House, with its implicit criticism of the role of women in traditional marriage and its exploration of their unhappiness with their station, was said to cause fistfights outside the theater on its opening night in Stockholm. *The Crucible*—ostensibly a drama about the infamous Salem witch hunts in the Massachusetts colony of the early eighteenth century, but also a not-very-thinly-disguised criticism of the anti-Communist "witch hunts" of the McCarthy era in the postwar United States—very nearly brought its author, Arthur Miller, before the House Un-American Activities Committee after its premiere in the 1950s.

Little wonder, then, that artists of all kinds have always found themselves viewed with suspicion and even fear, to the point that city governments, religious authorities, self-appointed guardians of the public good, and activists on both the right and the left prepared to censor, regulate or otherwise control the content of artistic works in the public sphere. "The pen is mightier than the sword" is not mere poetry.

Dutchman, absurdist/surrealist in structure, was not only deeply influenced by jazz but also filled with a poetry of prose born out of Jones's years-long involvement with writers and poets who were part of the Beat generation. Savoring such an "artistic gumbo" encouraged a budding playwright like myself to articulate as fully as I could all of the ideas and passions then churning within my soul.

Between the ages of seventeen and twenty-three, I had lived through the murders of the civil rights activists Andrew Goodman, James Chaney and Michael "Mickey" Schwerner; the assassination of the Mississippi NCAAP Field Secretary Medgar Evers; the bombing deaths of four little black girls attending Sunday School in a church in Birmingham; the shooting deaths of the civil rights workers Jimmy Lee Jackson and Virginia Liuzzo; the assassination of President John F. Kennedy; the assassination of Malcolm X; violent and deadly rebellions by black citizens during long, hot summers in Los Angeles, Cleveland, Milwaukee, New York, Philadelphia, Baltimore, Newark, Detroit, and other major cities; the assassination of Martin Luther King Jr.; and the assassination of Robert Kennedy.

On a very personal level, there was also the loss of my father to terminal cancer. With my younger brother already in the army, I became the sole support for my mother, and that circumstance led the local draft board to grant me a deferment from military service. The urban rebellion in Newark, New Jersey, that summer resulted in police action that led to the deaths of one young man I had known since childhood and another who had been a high school classmate. One week later, while the debris was still being cleared in Newark, Detroit erupted. I had an uncle living in

Detroit at the time. Days passed during which no one knew whether he was alive or dead.

Eight former high school classmates served in Vietnam. The Suarez brothers (not their real names) returned home physically changed by their tour overseas: their hair was prematurely gray and, like so many veterans, they were unable to speak with depth about what had happened to them "over there." One look into their eyes, however, might have told us all we needed to know. There were two others, whom I'd known since kindergarten. Justin, a Marine, was decorated for valor and returned home a hero. Sadly, as I write this, I am still dealing with the news of his recent death, attributed to years of suffering from the debilitating effects of exposure to cordite and Agent Orange. Everett returned home badly wounded and years later died in a VA hospital because of the lingering effects of those injuries. Lionel, who served as a radioman in his squad, was on patrol when he was killed. The news that he died only ten days before he was to return home just made everything more depressing. Greg, a classmate at Howard, had become homesick and wanted to return to New Jersey, so he decided to transfer to the Newark campus of Rutgers University. But there was a delay in the processing of his paperwork, and my friend was declared eligible for the draft as he was no longer enrolled in college. Shortly before my graduation, I learned that he had been killed in action.

Young people the world over were agitating for a change in the status quo of the societies they lived in. People my age, of all races, were in the streets across the United States—and also in London, in Tokyo, in what was then West Berlin, in Nicaragua, in El Salvador, in Saigon, in Prague, in Phnom Penh, in Johannesburg, in the bush in Angola, in the swamps of Mozambique, on the coast of Guinea-Bissau, in the depths of what was then known as Rhodesia. The issues that moved most of us were anti-Colonialism, anti-Imperialism, income inequities, and racial, ethnic, and gender oppression. There was also the overwhelming fear that the utopian future so many of us had been hearing about all of our lives would not be a democratic one, but instead would come to be dominated by a corporate-centered, monopolistic, capitalistic elite. Orwell's world of *1984* was just ahead, we believed, but worse, Aldous Huxley's *Brave New World* would be there to complement it. The conformist, consumerist 1950s that the baby boom generation spent passing from kindergarten to high school had given way to the 1960s: an era in which we saw a young president— hero to many of us and a man who encouraged us to dream of doing great things for our country—murdered before our very eyes. We learned that our government, acting in our name, had, in the previous decade, arranged the overthrow of democratically elected heads of state in Iran, in Venezuela, in Guatemala. We also learned that the kindly, grandfatherly President Eisenhower of our childhood had acquiesced to and authorized the murder of Patrice Lumumba in the Congo and had deliberately undermined a democratic election to unify Vietnam because Washington did not like the outcome. We learned that liberation movements in Africa and Asia were all being undermined through sustained interference by the United States, which included intelligence sharing, supply of military weapons (missiles, aircraft, bombs, chemical warfare) and political and diplomatic interference in the United Nations. The Cold War rhetoric of the time—the idea that America had to do unpleasant things against Communism in defense of the "free world"—ceased making sense to us. As fifth graders, we were taught to abhor the Soviet Union sending tanks into Budapest to put down the Hungarian revolt against authoritarian rule and oppression. Now, as young adults, we were expected to support our government propping up a corrupt dictator in Vietnam who openly espoused an admiration for Adolph Hitler. There were American soldiers risking and, in too many cases, giving their lives in Vietnam—kids my age who were the sons and daughters of men and women who died fighting Hitler in World War II. What the hell was going on?

Barely a month before my graduation from college, a classmate, a young woman who was truly loved by all of us who knew her, died as the result of a botched abortion attempt. She was an only child. The *Roe v. Wade* Supreme Court decision was still three years away. In 1967, a pregnancy without marriage brought not only social stigma but also probable expulsion from the university. But for those of us who were her friends, my classmate was a young woman with a big heart, a warm smile, and a wonderful ability to get things done—someone who was smart and who had everything to live for. And suddenly, she was dead.

All of these tragedies, the national as well as the more personal, shaped my thinking at the time. Young people across America were gripped by a similar feeling: that death was stalking all of us. Even though I may have sometimes felt the world was coming to an end, the thinking artist in me knew full well nothing could be further from the truth. All of the loss, all this blood and pain, had to mean something. There was a purpose to what we were going through. And each of us, in our own way, began the search for that meaning.

The post-Civil Rights era also gave rise to the anti-war movement, the Weather Underground, the Chicano resistance, the American Indian

Movement, and the feminist movement. All of these combined to provide me, as a young artist, with an ideal arena in which to channel my energies. I remember thinking that I was born at just the right time, came of age in just the right place, and was part of the perfect instrument for social change. In short, this was what every artist lived for.

I found my sense of meaning through ever deepening involvement in the Black Arts Movement. In Black America at large, there were as many opinions about the role of black artists in the black community as there were artists to practice the craft and audiences to see the work. There was not even agreement on whether or not there was any such thing as a "black theater." The majority of the African-American public was committed to the vision of civil rights leaders who had, for generations, risked life and limb for the inclusion of black Americans into mainstream American life—in housing, in public accommodations, in jobs, in education. But there was also wide dissent from that view—or at the very least, a feeling that "protesting" our right to humane treatment in American life was a fool's errand. "Why on earth are we constantly expected to be suppli-cants?" this dissent asked. "Why are we always begging for something? And why is America always so comfortable with this down-on-our-knees approach to protesting our rights as free and full citizens?"

The Black Power movement was the reemergence of a centuries-long internal debate among African Americans that had been suppressed for at least two generations. For centuries—from the time of the free men of color era of the earliest colonial days, through the Civil War, the Recon-struction, the advent of Jim Crow, and down to the early 1920s— the black community was buffeted by an internal debate among its intellec-tuals, leaders, and educators over two points of view about the direction of the struggle against the oppression black people faced.

During the antebellum period there were the enslaved who were ready to revolt and the enslaved who wanted to wait, to remain patient and trust in the judgment of time and providence. Those who advocated patience hoped that faith, enlightened reason, or perhaps even the shifts in economic fortune might cause whites in America to take away the chains and do away, once and for all, with "the peculiar institution" of slavery.

The differences in attitudes were characterized by the differences in circumstances of many of the blacks themselves. "Free men of color" were largely the mixed-race sons and daughters or descendants of slave owners who had either raped enslaved women or kept them hidden away as par-amours. Intermarriage was strictly forbidden by law, so white men who had taken black women as lovers moved with them to the far edges of the territories. There they lived in common-law relationships, away from prying eyes and largely ignored by white settlers who had far more serious matters on their minds, like sheer survival. Some of these free blacks were farmers; or traveling tradesmen, seamstresses, handmaidens; or had small businesses such as general stores or livery. While their status may not have been as high as that of many whites, they had some status nevertheless, and therefore a stake in the society of which they were a part.

Not so the enslaved Africans who toiled under the lash. They had no stake, no hope. And they knew they would remain that way unless they seized their freedom, wresting it from the hands of their masters. There were slave revolts, large and small, in every generation, from Jamestown right into the Civil War. History, of course, does not recount all of them, save for the largest and bloodiest. Revolts led by Gabriel Prosser, Denmark Vesey, and Nat Turner immediately come to mind—the ones that sent chills down the spines of the plantation owners and those who supported them in deed and in spirit.

These forces would pull black consciousness in America in one direction and then another for the remainder of the nineteenth century and well into the twentieth. Advocates for both points of view were as eloquent in debate as Clay and Webster, or Douglas and Lincoln. There were some black groups that advocated a return to Africa, while others demanded that black Americans remain in the only land they'd ever known and fight for their rights in a country they'd helped to build. There were black Americans who were interested in learning trades, working to establish apprenticeships and small businesses in order to build their communities from within; while others advocated for an end to the laws of segregation, they also agitated against job discrimination and for access to public accommodations for every American, everywhere. One side was dedicated to the idea that whatever salvation African Americans were going to achieve would be driven primarily by energies and ideas from within the Race, while others sought alliances from outside the community. Those leaders who wanted to build alliances beyond the black community were motivated by a sense that blacks could not afford to hold themselves separate from the rest of the country, particularly at a time when racism and the idea of separate but equal were so rampant and had already done so much damage to the African-American community.

These debates effectively ended in the early 1920s. The United States government deported Marcus Garvey, a native of Jamaica and the most effective advocate of Black Nationalism. The NAACP, a biracial organization dedicated racial justice, almost immediately became the primary advocate of equality and freedom for black Americans, and Black Nationalism was pushed to the margins of black society for the next forty years until the emergence of Malcolm X effectively inspired a new generation of youth who were growing disillusioned with the slow progress toward racial justice in America.

The Black Power/Black Arts Movement defined itself as a young person's game. Its leadership, its strongest voices, was young men and women (mostly men) who were in their thirties. Huey Newton, Eldridge Cleaver, and Bobby Seale were all in their early to mid-thirties. Kathleen Cleaver, Angela Davis, and Elaine Brown were slightly younger. Black Nationalists like Ron Karenga were of a similar age. The more traditional Civil Rights Movement was deemed the territory of the "old heads." Roy Wilkins, executive director of the NAACP, was already well into his sixties; Whitney M. Young Jr. of the National Urban League was in his mid- to late forties; Dorothy Height, president of the National Council of Negro Women, was in her late sixties. These black leaders rejected virtually every position the young militants were prepared to take.

The Southern Leadership Conference, founded in 1957 by a group of black ministers who were in their mid- to late thirties at the time, was an exception. Martin Luther King Jr., the SCLC's founder and president, was thirty-nine years old at the time of his assassination in 1968, the same year I joined the Black Theater Workshop (a subsidiary of Harlem's New Lafayette Theater). He was just five years older than Amiri Baraka, six years older than Ed Bullins (after Baraka, perhaps the most influential playwright of the Black Theater Movement and certainly the most prolific). But after Dr. King's murder, the SCLC was taken over by an older, more traditional, and less charismatic leadership, and its influence with younger people began to decline.

Roy Wilkins of the NAACP and Dorothy Height of National Council of Negro Women were both old enough to remember Garvey. As young adults in the 1920s and '30s, they had rejected his positions, and they worked very hard over the years to bring their views of assimilation to dominance in the African-American community. With Garvey deported and no other nationalist spokesperson on the scene with the necessary charisma or broad-based vision and organizational skill, nationalism soon became marginalized inside black America and very nearly forgotten. But now, some forty years later in the 1960s and '70s, Wilkins, Height, Young and an entire generation of black ministers, community activists, social leaders and mainstream politicians were confronting a new cohort of young, angry firebrands holding up as heroes the likes of Garvey and

Monroe Trotter, a tough-minded intellectual and political activist of the early twentieth century. Old-school leftists like the novelist Richard Wright or the great actor and concert singer turned activist, Paul Robeson—a man who extolled the Communist Soviet Union as treating black Americans better than they'd ever been treated in the United States—also emerged as icons among the young artists and revolutionaries. Forty years of struggling to achieve integration and acceptance into the American mainstream was now being challenged, even rejected, by young people who had yet to learn many of the lessons their elders had not only absorbed but built whole new lives and aspirations upon.

It would be a mistake, however, to think that the elders were universally rejected. The young Black Power leadership was very much aware of its limited practical experience and was never averse to seeking advice from a wide range of older artists, thinkers, historians, religious leaders, educators, and community activists whose writings and teachings had laid the groundwork for much of what the young people of the 1960s and early 1970s were trying to do.

Historians Chancellor Williams, Richard B. Moore, George Padmore, J. A. Rodgers, and John Henrik Clarke; scholar and poet Sterling Brown; political activist Ella Baker; religious leader and social activist Albert Cleague; author and educator John Oliver Killens; scholars Hoyt Fuller, Addison Gayle Jr., and William Branch; writers Dudley Randall, Darwin T. Turner, and Lofton Mitchell; and educators and theater pioneers Margaret Walker Alexander, Randolph Edmonds, and Theodore Ward ranged in age from their late forties to well into their seventies and early eighties at the time they were accessible to us. They were among the most brilliant thinkers of their time, and their work greatly influenced the emerging black intellects and artists of the mid-1960s. These young people included poet and founder of the Third World Press, Haki R. Madhubuti; activist and educator Angela Davis; writer and editor Kalamu Yaa Salaam; and poet and playwright Sonia Sanchez. It was their work and the work of so many others, some now gone, that gave the Black Arts Movement its heft and sense of direction.

The other half of the debate inside the black community was now fully restored: Nationalism vs. Integration. An emphasis on the development of black-owned businesses, the greater study of black history and cultural awareness, as well as the development and implementation of black political power, contrasted with, and on an equal footing with, the prevailing ideas of complete assimilation into the "American mainstream." And this was vitally important to the young at the time. The Black Arts Movement would become an exploration of who African Americans thought they were. Integration is impossible between one group of people who feel inherently "superior" and another who, historically, have been made to feel they are "inferior." People who believe their history is defined by their former enslavement, or that they have contributed nothing to the growth of the country beyond protest marches and George Washington Carver's experiments with the peanut cannot have a truly substantive interaction with their peers because they have no real idea of who they are. The younger generation wanted to push back against this. Though few of us voiced the opinion at the time, we were committed to expanding the definition and image of what it meant to be an American.

We don't want to have a higher form of white art in blackface. We are working toward something entirely different and new that encompasses the soul and spirit of Black people, and that represents the whole experience of our being here in this oppressive land.

—Ed Bullins, 1968

By 1965, the Ford Foundation had been actively engaged in providing seed money to help establish new, or alternative, theater companies in New York. This was an outgrowth of the new national energy to redress racial and social discord in the country, influenced not only by the success of the Civil Rights Movement, but also by the efforts of Lyndon Johnson's Great Society Programs, particularly the National Endowment for the Arts and the National Endowment for the Humanities. Federal dollars flowed to the states, and states' dollars flowed into the communities. Almost immediately, new theaters began to appear across the country. In New York City's Greenwich Village, for example, small theaters that had been struggling for years suddenly found funds available that had never been there before. These developments on the part of the government sparked interest from private funding institutions. And this interest led the Ford Foundation to fund activist white producers like Joseph Papp—who was able to bring the New York Shakespeare Festival/Public Theater to life in that same year (1967)—and Wynn Handman, who developed the American Place Theater in Hell's Kitchen.

But the Ford Foundation had also concluded that the time had come to expand a black presence in the American theater. So Douglas Turner Ward, a black writer, actor, and director, and former member of the esteemed

Harlem Writers Guild (one of his fellow members was Lorraine Hansberry), received enough funding to join with actor Robert Hooks and lawyer Gerald Krone to found The Negro Ensemble Company in the East Village, not more than a quarter of a mile from the Public Theater. The American Place Theater, the Negro Ensemble Company, and the Public Theater would all play major roles in the development of black playwrights over the next decade. And they were not alone.

There had not been such an explosion of theater development since the Federal Theater Project during the days of the New Deal some thirty years before. And it could be argued that the growth of theater activity in the sixties was greater, more expansive, and in the end, more diverse.[1]

By 1969, there were twenty-five theaters in the New York metropolitan area, eight in Harlem alone. In 1971, there were 250 black theater companies scattered across the continental United States that offered seasons of at least four productions. For a while, many of these theaters formed a support organization known as the Black Theater Alliance, and they opened an office in midtown Manhattan to serve as advocates for their interests.

Those years—1966 through 1973—were the halcyon times of the Black Arts Movement. In addition to Amiri Baraka, Ed Bullins, and Douglas Turner Ward, many other playwrights emerged as voices in the new Black Theater. These included Ben Caldwell (*Million Dollar Psych-Out*), Steve Carter (*Nevis Mountain Dew*), Philip Hayes Dean (*The Sty of the Blind Pig*), Lonnie Elder III (*Ceremonies in Dark Old Men*), J. E. Franklin (*Black Girl*), "Sonny Jim" Gaines (*What If It Had Turned Up Heads*), Jimmy Garrett (*And We Own the Night*), Charles Gordone (*No Place to be Somebody*), Bill Gunn (*Johnnas*), Elain Jackson (*Toe Jam*), Adrienne Kennedy (*Funnyhouse of the Negro*), Leslie Lee (*First Breeze of Summer*), William Wellington Mackey (*Family Meeting*), Ron Milner (*Who's Got His Own*), Aisha Rahman (*A Bird Sings in a Gilded Cage*), Charles Russell (*Five on the Black Hand Side*), Sonia Sanchez (*The Bronx Is Next*) and Joseph A. Walker (*The River Niger*). The Negro Ensemble Company in Greenwich Village; the New Federal Theater on the Lower East Side; the New Heritage Theater, the National Black Theater, the Afro American Studio for Acting and Speech, and the Soul and Latin Theater, all in Harlem; the Billie Holiday Theater in Brooklyn; the Theater of Universal Images in Newark; the Congo Square Theater in Chicago; the Concept East Theater in Detroit; the Free Southern Theater

---

1. Theaters serving Asian Americans, like the Pan Asian Repertory Theater in Los Angeles; Latinos, like the Nuyorican Café in New York; and Native American communities in the Northwest also sprang forth.

in New Orleans; the Karamu Theater in Cleveland; the Inner City Cultural Center in Los Angeles—these were just a few of the aforementioned 250 black theaters across the United States. All provided stages where new writers' work was presented to audiences eager to see images of themselves, interpreted by people like themselves. The characters in these plays were nothing like the images of blacks seen in the movies or on television. The stories the playwrights told tended to be more hard-hitting, political, and intellectually challenging than the traditional fare coming out of Hollywood, and this included the then popular "Blaxploitation" action dramas and their thin plots based on the idea of "sticking it to the man."

It seemed as though there was no shortage of new playwrights, poets, and essayists, just as there seemed to be no shortage of spaces for them to present their work to a public eager to hear them. And that was what drove so many of us into writing workshops all over the country, and what brought me to Harlem and the Black Theater Workshop in the fall of 1967. The workshop, an adjunct of the New Lafayette Theater, was headed by Ed Bullins, who had been brought east from Oakland, California, by New Lafayette founder Robert Macbeth to become playwright-in-residence.

Charles Wright, a former classmate at Howard, who was then the accountant at the New Lafayette Theater, saw me in Harlem one day and told me about the workshop. As soon as he mentioned Ed's name, I knew I wanted to attend. I was familiar with Ed's work from seeing productions of his short plays at the Spirit House cultural center in my hometown of Newark, New Jersey, where native son LeRoi Jones (Amiri Baraka) had returned after time spent in the Bay area on the West Coast. Ed's short plays were often agit-prop dramas—trenchant depictions of street life in the black community, or satirical spins on the politics of the day, exhortations to revolutionary political action; these were the kinds of plays I wanted to write. Baraka was also very good with these types of plays, which were seldom more than half an hour in length, pointed, witty, and urban and always contemporary, and usually involved no more than four characters. Plays like these were highly mobile. They could be performed almost anywhere—in storefront theaters, on doorsteps, on street corners, on rooftops,—and they were relatively inexpensive to mount. Done well, they could have a powerful effect on audiences, provoking conversation, argument, *thought*.

This was manna for a twenty-two-year-old playwright who had not only studied and fallen in love with Maxim Gorky and Bertolt Brecht while in college but, having grown up on television and B-grade action movies, was accustomed to fast-paced dialogue, easily identifiable character types, and quickly digestible story lines that were layered with subtle and many times subversive meaning. I was aware of a great many deficiencies in my work, and I was eager to learn. I knew that a chance to study with Ed was akin to going to a weekly master class in graduate school. Professor Dodson had implored me to go to his alma mater, Yale University School of Drama, to pursue a master's degree, but in 1967 I was all "schooled" out. I wanted to get onto the streets. I wanted to *work*. And now, here I was, about to join a workshop led by one of the strongest young writers in New York. I felt as though I was going to receive an advanced education that would go far beyond the limited confines of a classroom.

At its height, the workshop grew to nearly forty attendees, but more accurately, there was a core group of about eleven writers who gathered week after week from the workshop's inception until its end four years later. Among them were Martha Evans Charles, Charles "OyamO" Gordon, Milburn Davis, Keith Harris, and Sharon Cappell—all of whom would go on to develop careers as playwrights in the local black theater scene.

The workshop met once a week, in a rented hall on 112th Street, near St. Nicholas Avenue. The New Lafayette Theater normally used it as a rehearsal space, but on Saturday mornings from nine a.m. until about one in the afternoon, the hall belonged to the writers. When some of us groused about having to get up so early on a Saturday morning, Ed would tell us that he set the hour because only "serious" writers would be willing to get up so early on a Saturday morning to attend a workshop. Ed lived way up on Gun Hill Road in the Bronx in those days. His commute on the subway was as long as mine from Newark (ninety minutes). Sessions were rarely cancelled. If Ed could make it there at that hour, then so could the rest of us. We met in all kinds of weather. Rain, sleet, snow, it didn't matter. If transit was running, Ed was meeting. I think a blizzard got us one time, but that was about it.

We listened to each other's work and exchanged ideas and opinions about a range of topics that were bound to influence our writing: the history of African-American culture in the United States and its connections to the African diaspora. We examined the roots of poverty, crime, bad housing and chronic health problems in the black community; the then-raging Vietnam War and the resistance to it by thousands of Americans; the liberation struggles in Africa and the Far East; America's support of repressive regimes in San Salvador, Nicaragua, Venezuela and elsewhere in South America; the blockade of Cuba; the aftermath of the Cultural Revolution in China. We discussed how these events tied into the struggles of black Americans. And we discussed the ideological split that developed with the Black Panther Party on the one hand, and militant Black Nationalist organizations and groups on the other.[2]

Our discussions of politics were spirited and long lasting (and often long-winded), but Ed was a quiet and patient teacher. He listened politely and let us rant as much as we wanted to as long as he felt we knew what we were talking about. But he could cut a conversation short the minute someone went off on a tangent, spouting a lot of slogans and talking points with few facts to back them up. Ed was an original founder of the Black Panther party, its first minister of culture. He knew bombast and empty rhetoric when he heard it, and he was determined that we not fall prey to it. He wanted us to be critical thinkers and discerning artists. Above all, he wanted us to be able to speak the hard truth to power. And not just to white people, in power or not; he wanted us to speak the hard truth to the black community, specifically.

Ed was adamant that we not become propagandists. He told us we'd be useless to the revolution if we did. He pointed to what he saw as the failures of the Cultural Revolution in the People's Republic of China and most of Mao's Great Leap Forward campaigns there as prime examples of what could happen when idealism and ideology are allowed to prevail over practicality and the willingness to face the truth. We read from Mao's famous Little Red Book, filled with quotations from speeches that Mao had given on the need for art to be sublimated to the political will of the day, and then debated the pros and cons of that idea within the context of what the Black Arts Movement was supposed to mean to the black community in America.

We also read political literature from some of the leaders of liberation movements in Africa. *Not Yet Uhuru* by Oginga Odinga, long a political rival of Kenyan President Jomo Kenyatta; *The Wretched of the Earth*, Frantz Fanon's highly critical look at the ravages of colonialism and neocolonialism in the Third World; *Ujamaa: Essays on Socialism* by Julius Nyerere,

2. The Nation of Islam, or Black Muslims as they were sometimes known, occupied a space of their own in these ideological squabbles because of the policy of NOI's leader, the Honorable Elijah Muhammad, of keeping the Nation completely outside of and away from all overt political activity. The Nation did not picket, march, or hold rallies advocating any direct action against the "white government." The Nation would always "obey the law, and keep to itself." However, Malcolm X dictated that "if a Muslim is attacked or suffers to have hands put upon his person or members of his family or upon fellow Muslims in a manner that threatens bodily harm then that Muslim has the right, as does any citizen, to defend himself or his relatives to the fullest extent of his strength, by any means necessary." As a result, during this period and even to this day, although the Nation holds a place separate from the mainstream of black American life and politics, at the same time they are deeply respected if not universally admired.

the first democratically elected president of Tanzania; and *Dark Days in Ghana*, Kwame Nkrumah's critical look at the overthrow of Nkrumah's presidency in the then newly formed nation of Ghana.

These books and others like them gave us the background we needed to understand the prevailing ideologies and intellectual foundations of the political arguments then roiling the so-called Third World. But, as writers, we discerned something far more important: we began to see the leaders themselves. These books provided our first glimpses into their humanity. Through their anecdotal observations and sometimes pithy asides, we were able to glean how personality, ambition, education, and rage—sometimes repressed, other times freely expressed—could shape character, and thereby bring unexpected shadings to how events in history could be shaped, on a large scale and in intimate settings. Kwame Nkrumah was a man of enormous intellect and vision, but also victim to arrogance, overconfidence, and even pettiness. Did Mao's personal foibles lead to his political mistakes, or did his political failures exacerbate his personal character flaws?

Ed encouraged us to read these works not only to gain a clear understanding of the politics driving the world around us, but also to recognize as fully as possible that these ideologies were the creations of men and women with flaws like the rest of us. Nothing was perfect; success and triumph are not givens.

And was I not seeing examples in events unfolding around me? In too many instances, the same character flaws, the same internal politics (though on a smaller scale), the same petty arguments and rivalries, and the same proclivity for violent solutions to difficult problems were as evident within the Black Power movement as they were within the political bodies assuming leadership in newly emerging Third World nations. Sadly, the domestic leadership emulated its heroes too closely, too often.

Ed encouraged me to think of myself as a teacher as well as a writer. In this, he was not that much different from Owen Dodson and Ted Shine, who both had often said the same thing at Howard. "Think of playwriting as an avocation," Ed would say. "Recognize that our skills require us to be more than artists." In addition to thinking of ourselves as teachers, Ed wanted us to see ourselves as philosophers, folklorists, storytellers, mythologists, and theologians. *All* writers are, he'd say. Voltaire, Chekhov, Pirandello, O'Neill, Shepard, Mamet, or Hansberry—no matter who, the very best of us will find that our plays exist on one of those planes.

I felt strongly that being a writer meant being willing to become the antennae of my society. It meant being willing to be a literary Cassandra—

warning, beseeching, risking madness if need be, if only to change one mind in a thousand. Art is a direct appeal to the best that resides in our souls, and when we are confronted by the best that resides inside us, we have to respond to that vision. Anything less than our best becomes unacceptable, and should we look the other way and compromise, *we will always know it*. Is it any wonder, then, that in the aftermath of violent revolution, whether on the right or the left, no matter who is victor, it is always writers who are among the first to go to the wall?

An army without culture is a dull-witted army, and a dull-witted army cannot win the Revolution.

—Mao Zedong

A few years before I came to Harlem, Amiri Baraka had founded the Black Arts Repertory there. He quickly attracted a core group of talented young writers, actors, designers, and other artists, all of them eager to explore black culture and, in the process, further develop their own skills. Classes ·in acting and writing were quickly established, and in no time, small performances were being presented for public consumption.

The Black Arts Rep was just the latest incarnation of arts-oriented community institutions that had borne fruit in Harlem over the years. After many fits and starts by theater troupes starting in the early 1920s, the Rose McClendon Players, founded in the late '30s and named after a venerable black stage performer of the time, became the first Harlem-based theater company to attain any kind of permanency, offering a subscription series of plays during each season of its existence. Playwrights Abram Hill, author of a very popular all-black comedy called *Strivers Row*; George Nordford; Loften Mitchell; Warren Coleman; and actor, producer, and activist Ossie Davis all came out of this theater company. With the exception of Warren Coleman, I had the pleasure of conversing with and learning from all of them in the late '60s. Ossie Davis—who often visited Howard University with his wife, Ruby Dee—introduced me to George Nordford after my graduation. Nordford had, by that time, become an executive with Metromedia, a communications and television network corporation. Their advice and direction gave me my first real introductions into the entertainment business.

In 1942, in a space in a branch of the New York Public Library, Abram Hill brought together a group of actors, directors, and playwrights to form the American Negro Theater. The McClendon Players had, by this time, ceased to exist, and a number of talented people from that troupe—including the character actress Helen Martin, actor-writer Maxwell Glanville, and Frederick O'Neal, later to become the first black president of Actors Equity—joined the ANT, along with a troupe of younger performers that later included teenagers Sidney Poitier and Harry Belafonte. The ANT lasted until the late '40s, when many of its top talents were lured away to Hollywood and television. Small community-based talent groups tried to take up the slack, but none were able to duplicate the kind of successes the McClendon Players and the American Negro Theater enjoyed, and the idea of a center for the development of original work devoted to the life and culture of African Americans lay dormant for over fifteen years.

The Harlem Writers Guild came into its own during the 1950s. By the end of the decade, it had a membership that would include, among others, Maya Angelou, Alice Childress, Lonne Elder III, Rosa Guy, Lorraine Hansberry, Louise Merriweather, and Douglas Turner Ward. But the guild was primarily a writers' workshop and not a performance entity. Its membership was always in flux. Some members came regularly, others seldom, if at all. If you were not a member of the guild you barely knew of its existence. The Harlem Writers Guild, however, still exists to this day and is one of the longest-lasting writers' workshops of its kind in all of New York.

LeRoi Jones's decision to come to Harlem in 1965 to establish the Black Arts Repertory was, in and of itself, a major lightning bolt. Harlem was seen as being in decline, beset by a crumbling housing stock, crime, deteriorating schools, chronic unemployment—virtually every negative indicator of the quality of life one could imagine. Black professionals began moving away in droves, as restrictive housing covenants disappeared and opportunities to buy homes on Long Island and in the northern and western suburbs around New York City opened up. Though some black professionals and middle class workers chose to remain in Harlem, the area was now largely poor and working poor. This was not the population traditionally thought of as necessary to sustain an entity as expensive as a theater company. But the availability of government funding designed to improve living conditions in depressed areas like Harlem quickly changed perceptions of what was and was not possible.

Inspired by Malcolm and still reeling from his then-recent assassination, Jones decided to use the strength of his celebrity as a playwright (*The Dutchman*) and as a historian and social essayist (*Blues People*) to acquire the funding to establish the Black Arts Repertory Theater, reestablishing

Harlem's place as a center for the development of African-American art and culture. Black actors, dancers, musicians, philosophers, poets, playwrights, and sculptors would have a place to come to, with a mandate to develop new ideas for artistic expression throughout the African diaspora in the post-colonial and post–Civil Rights era.

The center was an immediate success, and word about it spread all across black America. I was in my junior year at Howard University and remember hearing one of my playwriting classmates, Gaston Neal (later to become a key figure in the arts and arts education in Washington, DC) speak highly of Black Arts Rep and of his desire to be instrumental in starting a similar center in the District of Columbia. Black Arts Rep was, for many, a dream come true. And then, overnight, it turned into a nightmare.

They began showing up at the poetry readings, in the salons and in the workshops: loud, abrasive "brothers" (and a few "sisters"), proclaiming their militancy and impatience with what they deemed inadequate measures to redress the ills afflicting the black community. They never wrote any plays; they never designed any sets or costumes; they were not interested in choreography, or graphics and sculpting. But they loved to pontificate. And they loved to point fingers and accuse, complain, and ultimately intimidate. They were often a self-righteous lot, certain of their points of view. They saw themselves as the true representatives of the *lumpenproletariat*, a Marxist term for the underclass romanticized by Eldridge Cleaver in his book *Soul on Ice*. They would say they spoke for the urban underclass—the street hustlers, the addicted and afflicted, the dispossessed, the unemployed—black men and women who existed on the margins of society. These were the people, they'd say, who were forgotten even by the Civil Rights movement dedicated to helping them. The lumpen, the "splibs on the block," didn't need plays and poetry. They needed action. They didn't need to raise their consciousness; they needed to raise Hell!

In the year before his death, Malcolm had given a number of speeches in which he alluded to revolution and the violent overthrow of oppression. He spoke of seizing freedom "by any means necessary." But he uttered these words within a specific context. He was speaking about a long-suffering people—often marginalized and historically discriminated against in their own country—recapturing their sense of self-worth and dignity, and once having attained this new sense of self, demanding their rights and being prepared to fight aggressively for them if denied. One could easily recall nineteenth-century abolitionist Frederick Douglass's famous adage that "Power concedes nothing without a demand. It never has, and never will." Nothing Malcolm was saying a century later was that different.

However, what happened at the Black Arts Rep was a literal siege by individuals who had completely misinterpreted and misapplied Malcolm's assertiveness. They had decided that anything less than aggression in the face of resistance to "black freedom" was "cowardice" or "backsliding." They had long since grown impatient with the nonviolent protests championed by the Reverend Martin Luther King Jr.

They argued that Black Arts Rep had to become a center of activism focused on preparing the black community to engage in aggressive "revolutionary acts," and to concentrate on being more "political." Jones and the artists at the center replied that it was indeed political and revolutionary to be engaged in creating work that reflected the idea that art capable of repairing and nurturing the battered soul could be as important as hurling a stone. The writers and poets insisted that Black Arts Rep already had a sense of where it was going and what it needed to be. In reply, the "politicals" pulled guns. Soon after, the Black Arts Repertory ceased to be.

LeRoi Jones headed west to the Bay Area, where a group of young people, including Eldridge Cleaver and Ed Bullins, founded an institution known as Black Arts West. In addition to Jones, Sonia Sanchez was among the regulars in attendance. As the Black Arts West began to grow in acceptance and popularity, it was not long before the militants with guns showed up demanding the artists sublimate their needs to the realities of politics. Cleaver, a cofounder, was in the forefront of those demanding this change in tactics, which put him on a collision course with Bullins. Jones soon returned to his hometown of Newark to establish the Spirit House Movers and Players. Ed Bullins, by that time having been driven out of several theaters at gunpoint, as he often would say later, received an offer from Robert Macbeth to come to New York City, where Macbeth was forming the New Lafayette Theater. He'd read some of Ed's work and was interested in having Ed become his resident playwright, an offer Ed eagerly accepted.

Later, as I read more of Mao Zedong's writings and speeches, there were two quotations that defined for me the tension that existed within the Black Power movement. The first quote, "Political power grows out of the barrel of a gun," certainly seemed to apply to those who wanted to pick up weapons, and the second quote, "An army without culture is a dull-witted army, and a dull-witted army cannot win the Revolution," was certainly something every artist could relate to. Ultimately, this tension between those who wanted to emphasize armed revolution and those who wanted to concentrate on efforts to build the black community from within boiled down to a philosophical distinction that pitted "revolutionaries" on one side against "nationalists" on the other. Few realized it at the time, but this philosophical debate would soon take on tragic proportions.

In January of 1969, tensions had boiled over between the Los Angeles chapter of the Black Panther Party and the Black Nationalist organization known as US, also based in LA. Desperate to cool things down, the leaders of both groups sent emissaries to a meeting that was held in a cafeteria, on the campus of the University of California at Los Angeles, in the Brentwood section. At some point in the meeting, an altercation occurred—the reasons for it have long been obscured—and guns were drawn. Two well-known Panther leaders, John Huggins and Alprentice "Bunchy" Carter, were shot dead. The US organization remained marginalized for years, as a result, and is largely forgotten today.

A few months later, Alex Rackley, a member of the New Haven, Connecticut, branch of the Black Panther Party, came under suspicion of being an informant for the FBI, whose harassment of the party had increasingly raised members' fear and rage to unprecedented levels. Rackley was kidnapped, brought to a secret location, and tortured into confessing that he had indeed provided information to the FBI. Rackley was then driven to a secluded location and shot through the head. His body was dumped into a river, where its discovery ultimately led to the arrest of several Panthers. The similarity of Rackley's death—torture, death, and then having his body dumped into a river—to the deaths in Mississippi of Emmit Till at the hands of a white vigilante mob and the civil rights workers Chaney, Goodman, and Schwerner at the hands of the KKK did not escape many in the black community. The idea that an organization that was supposed to be dedicated to lifting up the African-American community was now killing black people in the same cruel and ugly manner as the white mobs that been lynching and murdering blacks since the end of the Civil War began destroying the credibility of the Black Panther Party in some circles, wounding it in ways that never completely healed.

These events and other less violent confrontations roiled all of us in the movement every day. Those of us who were far away from the small rooms and meeting places where the "big decisions" were being made hardly knew what to think. We were angry and confused by the constant arguing, dismayed at the deaths, simultaneously fearful of the continued harassment by the police and yet accepting of its inevitability. Some openly sought martyrdom. And as more and more evidence of the involvement of the FBI's COINTELPRO began to manifest itself—deliberately spreading false rumors, distributing bogus communications, and planting informants—others began to recognize that the idea of "revolution" in the United States was going to have to take on a form radically different from the liberation movements overseas.

I wanted to write. I wanted neither a prison sentence nor martyrdom. What value would I be to the movement, to African people *at all*, if I were dead or locked away? That may be a counterrevolutionary notion, or exceedingly self-serving, but there it is. Ed's warnings to us to understand the difference between being artists *driven* by ideology and artists *understanding* ideology became ever clearer to me in those violent days, and I determined that I would follow my own path and would not become the prisoner of dogma.

LeRoi Jones and Larry Neal, who together wrote the seminal anthology *Black Fire*, were at the forefront of codifying the characteristics of the Black Arts Movement. In 1968 *The Drama Review*, Richard Schechner's influential periodical covering the latest developments in the American theater, invited Ed Bullins to edit an entire issue devoted to the then-emerging Black Theater/Black Arts Movement. Among the essays and plays that Bullins included was an essay written by Larry Neal entitled *The Black Arts Movement*, which in its very first paragraph describes the movement as "radically opposed to any concept of the artist that alienates him from his community." Neal continues:

> Black Art is the aesthetic and spiritual sister of the Black Power concept. As such, it envisions an art that speaks directly to the needs and aspirations of Black America. In order to perform this task, the Black Arts Movement proposes a radical reordering of the western cultural aesthetic. It proposes a separate symbolism, mythology, critique and iconology. The Black Arts and the Black Power concept both relate broadly to the Afro-American's desire for self-determination and nationhood. Both concepts are nationalistic. One is concerned with the relationship between art and politics; the other with the art of politics.

The ideas and concepts Neal put forth in his essay had been written about and talked about earlier, in different forums across the country. But this essay, which was widely read and disseminated at the time, was the first time the Black Arts Movement was codified in print, with all of the ideas, opinions, and parameters brought together in the coherent form of a manifesto. The politics owed something to the writings on art, literature, and politics by Mao, as well as a more than passing nod to earlier African-American thinkers like Alain Locke (*The New Negro*) and Langston Hughes (*The Negro and the Racial Mountain*).

In 1971, the scholar Addison Gayle Jr. edited *The Black Aesthetic*, an anthology containing lectures by black scholars, artists, educators, and philosophers from DuBois (1903) to Sarah Fabio Webster (1971)—sixty-eight years of discussion on the development of a uniquely African-American cultural point of view in the arts across the twentieth century. The ideas and definitions refined themselves or expanded in each decade. But one idea remained consistent: the need for black people to define themselves, to take control of their own narrative and benefit and grow from it as a people.

African Americans needed to explain themselves to themselves for themselves. It was more than our physical appearance that separated us from white people. Why did we speak English the way we did? The drum, and the pulsating rhythms we created from it, were important to black people. Why? Why did we change Western dress in ways that made it more palatable to our own sense of comfort and style? And where did this notion of "our own sense of comfort and style" come from? Weren't African Americans born in the United States like everyone else? Why were our dances so "physical," even sensual, even in the face of the most puritanical social pressures from outside (and often inside) the black community? Why was there such a strong oral tradition in the African-American community? Where did all of this come from? Africa? If so, how and why? All connection to Africa was supposed to have been broken through generations of enslavement. Mention of Africa barely existed in most American school textbooks. The number of African Americans alive in 1968 able to cite one word of any African language could probably have been totaled in single digits.

I came to recognize that the more we knew about ourselves, the more we understood about ourselves, the better we'd be able to cope in and with the world around us. And so the violence in the revolution, the violence toward the revolution, the manifestoes and philosophies that *drove* the revolution in 1967 and 1968 coursed through me like the blood flowing in my veins. And every Saturday in the Black Theater Workshop represented another dose of artistic and political amphetamines injected directly into my nervous system. I was a playwriting time bomb waiting to explode, and the weekly meetings in the Black Theater Workshop were the detonators.

I wasn't the only one. All of my fellow writers in the workshop were similarly moved, as were emerging black playwrights all over the country. That was something else that encouraged and sustained us: we were not alone. There were young writers like us all over the country. We were part of a national—even international—movement. Everywhere, everyone was writing: plays, novels, poetry, and short stories. In others areas—cinema, dance, graphic arts—the same kind of explosion in new creativity was expressing itself. New music was emanating from composers in jazz and rhythm and blues: Miles Davis, James Brown, Ornette Coleman, John Coltrane, Fela (the Nigerian artist whose music mixed heavy beats with incendiary political and socially relevant lyrics), Curtis Mayfield, Holland-Dozier-Holland, Smokey Robinson, Wayne Shorter, and Sun Ra, among so many others. At any given time, one could expect to see these and other musicians in the audiences of black theaters across the country, particularly in New York, Chicago, or Los Angeles. The Black Power/ Black Arts era marked the first time since the Harlem Renaissance in the 1920s that an entire generation of black artists across art forms was actively engaged in a mass movement designed to reframe and reinterpret African-American cultural expression for a worldwide audience.

We were all borrowing from each other, learning from each other, conversing with each other. It was not unusual to go to a party in Harlem, or Chelsea, or the Village and find author Maya Angelou, jazz percussionist and composer Max Roach, and theater producer Woodie King Jr. huddled in a corner together in conversation. Years later, August Wilson would point out how he always wrote his plays to the strains of the blues; Amiri Baraka often discussed the impact the lyrics of songwriter Smokey Robinson were having on black social consciousness across the country; choreographer Dianne McIntyre was already experimenting with dances based on African and African-American musical styles as well as the influences of black literature and anthropology.

Black artists across the nation, and throughout the African Diaspora, were engaged in the same kinds of conversations and attempts to define a black aesthetic. They linked themselves to both to the Harlem Renaissance and the Negritude Movement (during the 1930s) of those blacks in colonized Africa and the Caribbean.

Eubie Blake, Duke Ellington, Owen Dodson, and Osceola Archer (founder of the American Negro Theater) were still alive in the late 1960s, as were many followers of Marcus Garvey. It was possible to sit down with them, and use their experience and wisdom to inform the art of the contemporary era. For those of us willing to pay attention, Black Arts was rapidly moving beyond its political constraints.

In the winter of 1970, Ed decided that just over two years of discussion, study, and theory were enough. It was time for the workshop to present itself to the public. Ed wanted us to put on a show. Well...no pressure there.

It was important to our training that we learn something about management and production as well as writing, so Ed put all of us in charge of organizing the box office, developing the marketing, and maintaining the house. Certainly we had plenty of models to emulate, beginning with our "parent," New Lafayette Theater.

Our first presentation was not an evening of drama. The most accomplished writers in the workshop did not feel they had plays worthy of public viewing, at least not yet. I had an idea for a one-act, but an idea is not necessarily a story. We decided, instead, to present an evening of poetry. This would allow us to introduce ourselves to the Harlem community, perhaps develop the beginnings of an audience, and finally prove to ourselves that we could indeed mount a successful presentation for the public.

We had seating for about one hundred and fifty people. We charged a one-dollar admission (wildly inexpensive even by 1970 standards). We placed a notebook at the entrance and asked each patron to leave his or her name and an address, and after two nights of readings, we had a mailing list of close to three hundred names.

Ed immediately set us to planning our next production. We announced an evening of one-acts, scheduled for two months hence. We immediately began sending out flyers to the names on our mailing list, posting other flyers around Harlem. Kris Keiser, an actor with the New Lafayette and a director of one of the plays, went to a local bank and withdrew one hundred single dollars from his account. He then folded each dollar into a flyer, went to a housing project across from our theater on Lenox Avenue, and slipped each dollar-filled flyer under the door of the first hundred apartments he came to.

Kris's amazing and unexpected gesture certainly brought the workshop notoriety in the neighborhoods around our theater. We took a little survey, and it was safe to say that less than ten of those dollars ever made it back to our theater. But word on the street was that sooner or later people were going to have to come and see what "these actor people are up to," because people who are just giving money away in these hard times have got to be "out of their minds."

On opening night and every night thereafter during our two-week run, every seat in the theater was filled. All of the writers attended each performance, and members of the New Lafayette Theater company, which was running its own show farther uptown in the main theater, came to see the plays when their performances were over.

We'd learned how to organize our box office and raise money on our own. Kris's experience showed us that we could use unusual tactics to market ourselves and have some success. In this we were no different than other black institutions, starved for capital and struggling to survive. We'd used our creativity and scored a success, however small it might have been in the broad scheme of things. (We were not in a position to compete with the New Lafayette Theater, The National Black Theater or the Negro Ensemble Company, for instance, and never would be.). It was expected that the Black Theater Workshop's example would inspire other small groups of artists to create their own theater companies, write plays, develop actors, directors, and designers, and grow a national network of functioning African-American theaters in every community in America where there was a black audience. Contrary to what the revolutionaries with the guns might have thought, the creation of a national network of arts institutions had very specific economic implications, and that in turn had political implications. Change images, change minds. Change minds, and you can transform a nation.

Our job is to show black people who they are, where they are and what condition they are in.

—the motto of the New Lafayette Theater

The New Lafayette Theater does not exist anymore. It ended all operation in late spring of 1973. It enjoyed a six-year run and was the artistic home of Ed Bullins. It employed fourteen actors, fourteen musicians, a design staff who came to the theater through its affiliation with the Weusi Gallery, a Harlem-based graphic artists collective located only a few blocks from the theater, a technical staff, office staff, maintenance crew, and two persons who comprised the editorial staff that composed and printed the *Black Theatre Magazine*, an in-house publication that was mailed out to subscribers across the country and around the world. Yet today it is largely forgotten. The story of the New Lafayette Theater—its strengths and failings—contains elements of the history of the Black Arts Movement and the reasons why it may even have succeeded when so many thought it had failed.

The New Lafayette Theater was the brainchild of Robert Macbeth, an Air Force veteran and struggling young actor who was working in the HARYOU-ACT anti-poverty program in Harlem when, at the height of Lyndon Johnson's Great Society initiatives, he developed the idea of bringing professional theater back to Harlem. Charming, well-read, and physically imposing at nearly 6 feet, four inches, with a rich speaking voice and possessing the charisma of a natural leader, Macbeth had the ability not only to make his concepts and ideas palatable to the average listener, but also to draw to his side those with the talent necessary to make his ambitions reality. Macbeth presented a proposal for a professional theater to W. McNeil Lowery of the Ford Foundation. His theater would serve the Harlem community, though its audiences could include people from all backgrounds and walks of life. However, the primary thrust of the New Lafayette Theater would be to serve the black community.

In 1967, when the New Lafayette opened, there were as many black people living in Harlem as the entire population of the city of Newark, New Jersey. Yet it was a community that seemed isolated from the rest of New York City. Within its borders were people who had never seen a live theater presentation beyond the weekly revues in the Apollo Theater. Except for school trips, few had ever been to a museum or to the main library at Fifth Avenue and 42nd Street. Off-Broadway theater would have barely resonated. But Harlem was also a community that had produced Sammy Davis Jr., Diahann Carroll, Glynn Turman, and Leslie Uggams, among others. Harlem had a rich cultural history, and Macbeth was convinced that a professional theater company—well-run, with plays of the highest quality that celebrated and reflected the black community in all of its complexities and possessed an uncompromising commitment to artistic excellence—was a theater that could succeed. The New Lafayette had chosen to locate itself in the heart of an area that had come to see itself as abandoned. Robert Macbeth saw his theater as a means of saying no to that idea and yes to the notion that Harlem did matter, and would continue to matter long into the future.

There at 132nd Street and Seventh Avenue, Macbeth strung a huge banner some two stories tall, adorning the façade of one of the buildings. It announced the opening of the New Lafayette Theater.[3] Right out front, in the median that ran down the center of the wide, six-lane boulevard, was an old tree stump, referred to for years as the "Tree of Hope." Young

---

3. The original Lafayette Theater company was located in another section of the same building. Rex Ingram, who later had a successful career as a character actor in Hollywood, had starred in several productions there, including a famous *Macbeth* produced by John Houseman and directed by Orson Wells. The New Lafayette Theater was located in the rehearsal hall of the old Lafayette Theater. The original Lafayette Theater building was now a church. (Years later, the film director, Francis Ford Coppola, would come to Harlem to shoot his film, "Cotton Club." He would place a facsimile of the original marquee on the church and construct a false entrance to the Cotton Club just next door. It all worked very well because the exterior of the church was virtually unchanged.)

participants in the weekly Amateur Night at the Apollo Theater had, for decades, stopped by to rub the stump in hopes of attaining good fortune in their efforts before one of the world's most critical audiences. Ella Fitzgerald and Sarah Vaughn were said to have done so the night before they took to the Apollo stage on Amateur Night, and the rest is history. Members of the New Lafayette were confident of success. They knew they had hope sitting right at their front door.

Their first two productions—*The Blood Knot* by Athol Fugard and *Who's Got His Own* by Ron Milner—proved to be great successes and established the New Lafayette with its target demographic. Meanwhile, Macbeth was pursuing another idea he had for his theater: the addition of a writer in residence, a playwright who would have the New Lafayette as a home base. Macbeth read the work of a number of playwrights, and the writer whose work struck the strongest chord within him was Ed Bullins.

Robert Macbeth identified a new location[4] for the theater some five blocks north in the abandoned Renaissance movie house, and the architect Hugh Hardy was brought in to redesign the interior space. At 250 seats, the theater had more than twice the capacity of the original space, a larger performance area, and a state-of-the-art light and sound system—everything bigger and better than ever before. There was a marquee that stretched out over the broad sidewalk out front, large enough to rival the marquee of the original Lafayette Theater of the Harlem Renaissance era. An abandoned barbershop next door was also acquired, gutted, and refitted to serve as a combination box office and administrative office. The wall separating the space from the theater was hacked into so the two areas could be joined into a contiguous whole.

In September of 1968, a space in an office building on West 135th Street that had served as the original administrative offices became the new location of *Black Theatre Magazine*, which the New Lafayette intended to publish quarterly. The magazine was intended to feature articles on theater and politics by writers and actors in black communities all over the United States and, whenever possible, from throughout the African Diaspora. Ed Bullins became its editor. *Black Theatre Magazine* was the

---

4. Toward the end of the first season, a fire, later determined by the New York City Fire Department to have been arson, completely destroyed the theater. The perpetrator or perpetrators remain unknown to this day, though it has long been suspected that the act was in retaliation for the site having been used to host a political forum that featured individuals and political ideology that was opposed by certain factions in the Harlem community and beyond. Afterwards, Bob Macbeth refused to ever again allow the New Lafayette Theater to be the site of any political or cultural gatherings that were not produced or organized directly by the New Lafayette Theater.

major form of communication for the New Lafayette Theater. Ed Bullins used its circulation to develop contacts with artistic directors and playwrights in arts institutions all over the world. Ultimately, the contacts expanded beyond the arts. At the height of the liberation struggles in Mozambique and Angola, information and news was being exchanged between the theater's office on 135th Street and the information office of FRELIMO, the then-rebel organization in Mozambique, and the PAIGC, the primary rebel group struggling to free Guinea-Bissau and Cape Verde from the grip of the colonial power of Portugal. In time, the magazine also received pamphlets and press information from the MPLA, the primary rebel group in Angola, also seeking to free itself from Portuguese rule. Bullins's growing international reputation as a playwright soon brought him into contact with exiled members of the African National Congress (which was banned in apartheid South Africa), who were living in the United States.

Over the next three and a half years, the New Lafayette Theater mounted fourteen productions, including the premieres of Bullins's Twentieth Century Cycle dramas: *In the Wine Time, Goin' A Buffalo, The Duplex,* and *The Fabulous Miss Marie.* In these dramas, Bullins covered twenty years of black social history, from the end of World War II to the middle of the 1960s. (The National Center for Afro-American Artists in Boston performed another play from the cycle, In *New England Winter,* in 1970.) The New Lafayette also developed and performed a new ensemble piece each season: *A Ritual to Bind Together and Strengthen Black People So That They Can Survive the Long Struggle That Is to Come* (1969), *To Raise the Dead and Foretell the Future* (1970), *A Black Time for Black Folk* (1970), *The Devil Catchers* (1971), and *Psychic Pretenders* (1971). Bullins's dramas were among the most dynamic plays by a black dramatist of the era.[5]

The ensemble pieces established the New Lafayette Theater as a black theater company unafraid to approach nonlinear, nontraditional structures in order to communicate different ideas to the black community, and to establish new parameters for artistic expression beyond some of the limitations being proscribed by political thinkers and writers in the Black Power/Black Arts Movement.

---

5. Charles Fuller, inspired by Bullins, wrote a series of plays chronicling the mid-century, multigenerational history of a black family, entitled In *My Many Names and Places.* Woodie King Jr. produced Fuller's series over several seasons at his New Federal Theater in Lower Manhattan Years later, August Wilson, who often cited Bullins as one of his major early influences, wrote the most famous cycle of plays ever by an African-American playwright, with one play set in each decade of the twentieth century.

The National Black Theater, under Dr. Barbara Ann Teer, moved in a similar direction, developing ritual dramas, and ultimately making such work the cornerstone of their presentations for many years. Other theater companies, such as the venerable H.A.D.L.E.Y Players in upper Manhattan, specialized in traditional musicals. The Olatunji African Cultural Center on East 125th Street specialized in traditional African music and dance forms and their incorporation into allegorical plays. Similar forms of presentation were being tried by black theaters all across the country: among them the Free Southern Theater in New Orleans, the Black Arts Theater in South Bend, and the Ujamaa Theater Workshop in Pontiac, Michigan. The years 1967–71 were a creative caldron, with theaters and artists competing, collaborating, and continuously learning from each other.[6]

The Black Theater Workshop ultimately developed a backlog of fifty-four production-ready plays, including several new works by Bullins. This led to the development of the New Lafayette Theater Play Service, which was formed by Whitman Mayo, one of the actors in the company. The play service used its database and its contacts across the country and internationally as an attempt to develop production possibilities for the writers, while hoping to further enhance its own reputation as a major force within the Black Theater Movement.

The international contacts with political groups were important for us in the New Lafayette—particularly for me, as I was not only a member of the Black Theater Workshop but by this time had become managing editor of the magazine. I worked closely with Bullins, overseeing the operation of the magazine and communicating with many of the artists and political

---

6. However, if there was one periodical during this era that occupied a paramount position of importance for the Black Arts Movement, it could be argued that it was *Black World*, based in Chicago and published from 1966 to 1976 by the Johnson Publication Company. The editor was Hoyt W. Fuller, a Detroit-based artist/activist/scholar who was instrumental, along with Woodie King Jr., in founding the seminal Concept East Theater in Detroit.

Black World had been published under the title *Negro Digest* from 1946 through 1951. But with the explosion of black consciousness in late 1965, publisher John H. Johnson decided to resurrect the periodical. And in Fuller Johnson, he hired the perfect man to edit his magazine. Fuller not only attracted the best poets, essayists, and scholars in black America, but he also published the works of outstanding artists in the diaspora—from the Caribbean, from black communities in Canada and South America, and of course, from the continent of Africa.

We were doing the same thing in *Black Theatre Magazine*, but we were only publishing four magazines in a year and far fewer articles. *Black World* appeared monthly, with a much larger subscription base, and in some markets it was also on the newsstands. It was in circulation at least two years before *Black Theatre Magazine*, and it ultimately became the most important black literary magazine in the country, holding that position right up until its demise in 1976.

people who dropped by our office: among them the actor William Marshall, the jazz artist/composer Max Roach, poet-activist Keorapetse Kgositsile, playwright Adrienne Kennedy, South African actor and playwright Duma Ndlovu, and the novelist Ishmael Reed.

The magazine helped give the theater an international footprint quite apart from that of other companies such as the Negro Ensemble Company, which was known, quite deservedly, for the quality of its productions and the introduction of new voices in the American theater (including Lonnie Elder III and Derek Walcott). The New Lafayette was different: it placed itself in the heart of the "capital of Black America." Our theater was insular, an artists' collective, with a tendency toward aloofness. We made ourselves mysterious, seemingly impenetrable.

Macbeth kept our repertory eclectic. He wanted us to be unpredictable. The Harlem public never knew, from one production to the next, what to expect or become comfortable with. We were a theater that did not seek to make its audiences *comfortable* as much as *informed*. The motto "Our job is to tell black people who they are, where they are and what condition they are in" delineated our purpose very clearly. This might be seen as arrogance. Every black theater in the country sought to deliver a similar message. But very few could deliver that message with the kind of punch we could. Our funding, and Macbeth's efficient use of it, allowed us to make art unmatched in Harlem or any other black community. Well funded, we were free to let our imaginations run wild; we could create rituals based on those of the ancient Sufis, infusing our stage with special effects, live music provided by some of the finest jazz studio musicians in the country, and sound delivered by a state-of-the-art sound system. And we weren't downtown. We were in Harlem, far outside New York's theatrical mainstream.

Critics like Edith Oliver of *The New Yorker* and the playwright and theater scholar Eric Bentley made their ways uptown to see our presentations and comment on them—positively or negatively, it was immaterial. We were playing to audiences who didn't read *The New Yorker* or the *New York Times* theater section. We had the freedom of depending on word of mouth inside the community. Each member of the theater received a silver medallion to wear around his or her neck, with the theater's logo on one side and his or her name on the other. We all wore them all the time. They were like badges that identified us to the world outside, and they set us apart. We loved it.

During the summers, members of the company and a few of the artists from the nearby Weusi Gallery would go up on the roof of the theater to play drums and wind instruments, their music wafting out over Seventh Avenue. No one could see them, but everyone knew the music was coming from the theater. Local children would stop by and dance; adults kept walking but smiled.

The Harlem Democratic Club was just across the street from our location. We could see Congressman Adam Clayton Powell; David Dinkins, the future mayor of New York City; Denny Farrell, a power in the State Assembly; Basil Paterson, father of a future governor of New York; and Percy Sutton, the former president of the Borough of Manhattan—sometimes together, sometimes separately, almost any day of the week.

Filmmakers from Sweden and television reporters from Germany and Italy found their ways to Harlem to visit us and learn as much about us as they could. We had acquired for ourselves an undeniable position of leadership in the eyes of foreign media, and the quality of our work, Bullins's expanding reputation, the growth of the magazine, and the success of the Black Theater Workshop all served to make the theater a recognized leader in the Black Arts Movement. It was easy to believe that the success of the New Lafayette Theater was a dream come true.

Well…it was.

In 1970, the Ford Foundation, the sole source of funding for the New Lafayette Theater, advised Bob Macbeth that it would soon discontinue its support. The New Lafayette was not the only theater company in New York to receive this news. The same word was delivered to Joseph Papp at the Public Theater and to Douglas Turner Ward and Robert Hooks at the Negro Ensemble Company. (Each of these theaters was receiving an equal amount of several hundred thousand dollars per year.) There were other theaters in other parts of the country that received similarly bad news. It was clear that the New Lafayette Theater was going to have to develop alternative means of funding if we were going to stay afloat.

The New Lafayette was not equipped to pursue a "plan B." Bob Macbeth had never developed a strong marketing campaign for the New Lafayette beyond posters, flyers, and a mailing list. The company did not attend community rallies or meetings. We took no sides in any of the political debates among the activists in Harlem. The memory of the fire that destroyed the first building, and of the political dispute that precipitated it, was burned deep into the memory of every member of the company.

Our aloofness and insularity grew, in large part, out of Macbeth's determination not to allow people outside the theater to gain access to it ever again. We did not have community meetings or symposiums sponsored by outside groups in the new theater—*ever*. When Amiri Baraka's play *Slaveship* ended its Off-Broadway run and Baraka sought to make a deal with Macbeth to run the play in the New Lafayette, Macbeth declined. No matter how much Baraka entreated him, he would not change his mind. When the play was forced to vacate its downtown theater and Baraka was unable to find another one, his relationship with Macbeth pretty much ended. These two men had known each other ever since the mid-1950s in the Village. They'd shared a friendship, laughter, and drinks. They virtually never spoke to each other again.

Macbeth never applied for funding from the National Endowment for the Arts or the New York State Council on the Arts, because they were government programs and he did not want the federal government to have any involvement with the theater. Bullins, a former minister of culture for the Black Panther Party and someone who had seen firsthand the kind of damage the FBI had done, concurred. So in spite of the fact that the NEA had offered to provide the theater with funds matching the Ford Foundation grant, Macbeth turned them down flat.

He also resisted the idea of community outreach to build a strong base of private donors. He did not have much faith in the idea that a strong cadre of black professionals could be developed to support the theater. For one thing, there weren't that many of them to go around. Macbeth felt strongly that only the kind of large funding provided by the Ford Foundation could allow the New Lafayette to do the art it did, and once that funding dried up, the New Lafayette Theater would cease to exist.

Macbeth's position met resistance from inside the theater, but he was the artistic director and he signed all of our checks. The New Lafayette received funding for two more years, and in June of 1973, it closed its doors for good. The end was that abrupt.

The members scattered. Some of us continued our professional careers elsewhere; others slipped quietly into private lives away from the theater. The Black Theater Workshop morphed briefly into a group known as the Black Troop, but after a few years its members moved on. There was talk of resurrecting the New Lafayette and starting over. But nothing like that happened in the years immediately following its demise.

As time went on, the New Lafayette receded into memory, but as more and more new artists came along, even memory would not suffice. The theater left no trace of itself— no copies of the scripts that were written for the ensemble pieces, no detailed diaries or records. The artwork that decorated its walls has disappeared. There was film footage of moments from rehearsals or scenes from one of the rituals, but they have not seen the light of day in years, and it is even possible that the footage no longer exists. Four members of the company—well-known actor Roscoe Orman, events promoter Jesse Boseman, filmmaker Karma Stanley, and William Lathan, a retired physician and former ring physician for the New York Boxing Commission—each have an extensive private collection of photographs that chronicle the years of the New Lafayette. New generations have come of age that were not even born either when the theater was functioning or when it closed. Unless someone who was there mentions the theater in conversation or at a symposium, the New Lafayette Theater remains obscure.

All these black militants talking about going back to Africa...
I ain't going back...
I can't drive my Cadillac in the jungle.

—Redd Foxx

It was sometime in 1973 or 1974. The Temptations were headlining a show at the Apollo Theater in Harlem. Redd Foxx was the emcee for the evening. The theater was packed. It had been several years since the Tempts, as they were often called, had played the Apollo. Times had changed. They were international stars by this time, playing in arenas and on the Strip in Las Vegas, so their coming to the Apollo, a small house of only about fifteen hundred seats, was a major event. It was quite possible that this would be the last time the group ever performed on 125th Street.

And having Redd Foxx as emcee was also quite a treat. He had been a force in black entertainment at least since the 1950s. Every black household had several of his risqué "party" albums, filled with bawdy jokes and double-entendres. Young people in my generation often joked about how, growing up, one of the best ways to get in trouble with parents and grandparents was to be caught trying to play one of those albums on the record player. A sure sign of being grown was when you were no longer ushered from the room when people wanted to listen to a Redd Foxx album. The Temptations may have been the headliners, but Redd Foxx's humor almost made you forget whom you were actually at the Apollo to see.

And then Redd told the joke quoted above. I was having a grand time up until that moment and, frankly, not a care in the world. The preliminary acts were very entertaining, and Foxx was really on his game. When he told the joke, I did not laugh. I was not amused at the idea of having our connection to our ancestral homeland made the butt of a joke, certainly not at that point in time. Perhaps sometime in the future when we'd completed the psychological rebuilding so many of us deemed necessary to the success of the Black Revolution, but not at that moment. No. The audience thought otherwise. As I was still sympathetic to activist social change and Black Nationalist thinking, the burst of laughter, applause, and cheering that followed Foxx's punch line was at first shocking to me, then, in the next instant, illuminating. I remember thinking, "The Revolution is over."

If a survey had been taken among all of the black people crammed into the Apollo that night, including Foxx, the Temptations, and the other entertainers, the vast majority would have had favorable opinions of Malcolm X, a majority would have supported the African liberation struggles, a plurality would have told you how much they liked African music (Olatunji and Manu Dibango were on the radio at the time), many would have told you of seeing pictures of various African people and immediately recognizing features that reminded them of family members, quite a few would have let you know about the dashikis or other forms of African dress they'd recently bought, fewer might have been able to speak of journeys to Liberia, Tanzania or Ghana. But in one way or another, all would have referenced some part of themselves that was inextricably American. All would have had to acknowledge on some level, whether they wanted to or not, the ties that held them to *this* land, this place called America. Foxx's joke went right to the core of how most black Americans interpreted the Black Power movement: the real battle was for peace, freedom, and respect in America, not on the continent of Africa.

By this time, LeRoi Jones had taken the name by which he would be known for the rest of his life: Amiri Baraka. He had become one of the leading proponents of Black Nationalist thinking in the United States. He promoted Kawaida, an Afrocentric philosophy developed by US leader Ron Karenga that attempted to lay down guidelines through which black Americans would rebuild not only their wounded psyches but also the physical conditions of the communities in which they lived.[7]

---

7. In Kawaida, Karenga posited that there were seven fundamental principles without which no society or civilization could survive, much less prosper: unity, self-determination, cooperative economics, collective work and responsibility, a clear sense of purpose, creativity (or innovative thinking and adaptability) and faith. The seven principles survive to this day as Kwanzaa, incorrectly seen either as some sort of black alternative to Christmas, or as a rediscovered ancient African ritual.

The term *Kwanzaa* is Swahili for "first fruits," certainly a reference to harvest time. There are many celebrations designed specifically for the harvest in nearly every society in

Amiri Baraka led the founding of a political coalition of black and Latino representatives, which ultimately led to the election of Kenneth Gibson as mayor of Baraka's hometown of Newark, New Jersey. Gibson became the first nonwhite mayor of Newark and the first black mayor of a major Northeastern city. Soon after, Baraka organized the Committee for a Unified Newark, which put Kawaida to practical use daily, developing community programs to help disadvantaged youth, and art and cultural programs to raise consciousness. There were seminars on community organizing, voting rights, and nutrition and health, and plays exhorting political activism. Amiri and his wife Amina Baraka turned their home into an arts and cultural salon, entertaining prominent figures in their living room and later using their basement for poetry readings. (A few years later, by 1977, these poetry readings morphed into one of the key hotbeds of hip hop creation in the city of Newark.)

And then Baraka, one of the leading Black Nationalist voices in the United States, changed course abruptly, declaring that he had evolved from nationalism into Marxism. The announcement caused dismay among his followers and nationally among those who had hewed very closely to the nationalist line. In their minds, Baraka was, in effect, saying he had come to believe that everything they stood for in the preceding decade was a lie. What Baraka was actually saying was that the Black Nationalist philosophy had been absolutely necessary *in its time*, but that time had passed, and it was necessary to move on to more progressive thinking. Nationalism was limiting because it also precluded the possibility of alliances with like-minded communities beyond African-American neighborhoods and organizations. Doctrinaire Nationalism did not adequately take into account that the struggle in the United States was not one of race but of class, as black sociologist William Julius Wilson had written in his book *The Declining Significance of Race*.

The denouncements of Baraka were pretty intense on the political side of things, but in some circles among those in the Black Arts, not as much. I was immediately reminded of what Bullins had been saying in *Black Theatre Magazine* only a few years before about an artist's need to stay above or outside of ideology. There were a lot of artists, playwrights, and poets who

sub-Saharan Africa. But each is specific to its location and tribal traditions. None, as far as is known, specifically refers to "Kwanzaa," "Nguzo Saba" (the seven principles) or to the time of year that Kwanzaa is celebrated in the United States. However, the lasting legacy for both Karenga and Baraka has been the impact that Kwanzaa has had on both the community and the country. It is celebrated and discussed in many African-American homes every year, and the seven principles have survived as a topic of discussion in African-American history courses on college campuses across the country.

understood and supported Baraka. All artists needed their independence— the right to change their minds.

Baraka went on to write more plays, such as the epic drama *The Motion of History*, and to publish books of essays, such as *RazoR*. He also moved into the classroom, teaching on the Stony Brook campus of the State University of New York. Karenga was teaching in the University of California system. A number of playwrights and poets, including Sonia Sanchez, Charles Fuller, and Aisha Rahman, also joined university faculties.

The waning of emotional energy, the physical exertion required to maintain the movement, the constant pressure placed on the political organizations by the US government and local law enforcement, the drying up of funding sources, the in-fighting, the relative peace that had come with the liberation victories in the Third World, the end of US involvement in the war in Vietnam, the election of Richard Nixon in 1968, the *deaths* of so many—all had combined to create massive exhaustion, both physical and psychological, within the movement. As with runners after a long marathon, activists were winded, doubled over, hands on knees and breathing heavily.

How would you have us, as we are?
Or sinking 'neath the load we bear,
Our eyes fixed forward on a star,
Or gazing empty at despair?
—James Weldon Johnson, "To America" (1917)

Huey Newton was in prison, as were David Hilliard, Geronimo Pratt, and Bobby Seale. Eldridge Cleaver had fled the country into exile—first to Cuba, later to Algeria, and finally to the south coast of France. Leadership in the national headquarters of the Black Panther Party soon fell to women like Elaine Brown. And it was then that the party may have enjoyed its greatest success in the community in terms of actually delivering services to the people: the Free Breakfast Program, an initiative aimed directly at the poor in Oakland. Under the leadership of the women, the party engaged in programs designed to increase access to health and set up independent schools and arts programs, the very initiatives many in the Black Arts community had long advocated.

Black history, though still hotly debated, was beginning to find places for itself in the curricula of increasing numbers of institutions across the country. African-American culture and literature were being taught on the high school level. In areas of business, entertainment, and politics, the African-American presence not only increased but also saw African Americans moving into positions of leadership and influence.

The Black Power movement was absorbed into the American mainstream, with remnants turning up here and there—in high school and college classrooms, in plots for "B" movies in Hollywood, in political campaigns for black politicians. This may not have been what was expected back in 1966, but it was what was happening by the end of 1976.

A few weeks after the New Lafayette Theater shut its doors, graffiti appeared on one of its front walls. It read, "Nothing Lasts Forever." A bitter epitaph for the New Lafayette, perhaps, but not so for black theater—either in Harlem or across the United States. While it is true that many of the 250 theaters that existed during the Black Power era have folded, a large number have not.

In Harlem, The National Black Theater and the New Heritage Theater, born the same year as the New Lafayette, survive and offer seasons to this day. In Brooklyn, the Billie Holiday Theater has opened a full season in what is now its fourth decade. The Karamu Theater in Cleveland is nearly sixty years old. The Ebony Showcase in Los Angeles is nearly the same age, and the Center Stage in Baltimore is at least thirty-five.

Al Simpkins of the Bushfire Theater in Philadelphia founded his company during the conservative administration of George H. W. Bush. The conservative swing in the country's politics caused a drying up of many funding sources, particularly the National Endowment for the Arts, which many theaters, white as well as black, depended upon. Though there was some private support in black communities, the numbers were simply not there. The belief in the seven principles may remain, but an increasing number of business-savvy artistic directors, less driven by political dogma than by sound economic principles, have worked to see that their theater companies remain viable.

In late 1969, or early 1970, in a moment of pique, Stokeley Carmichael, in answer to a reporter's question about the role of women in the activist movements then sweeping the nation, said, "The only position for women in the Movement is prone." Carmichael had a well-known record of supporting women activists—from Ella Baker, who helped found the Student Nonviolent Coordinating Committee; to Diane Nash, who was major organizer of the Freedom Rides of 1964 and other Civil Rights demonstrations; to Ruby Robinson who was a key leader of SNCC—so it was assumed he was being sarcastic. Whatever his intentions, however, the statement followed him everywhere. It ultimately prompted questions both inside the movement and among many women on the left, critiques that would later gain strong voice in the women's liberation movement of the late '60s and early '70s.

In the Black Power movement, questions about the role of women were quickly dismissed as not being "relevant to the struggle." Women had long assumed leadership roles in the black community, from the days of enslavement forward. As Sojourner Truth famously pointed out, enslaved women worked out in the fields and stables right alongside the men. They did heavy lifting, wilted in the sun, and suffered injuries just like the men. But inside the movement, men, by and large, held most of the leadership positions, and in the Black Arts/Black Theater Movement the situation was similar. Men wrote most of the plays, and the plots and storylines reflected a male point of view. Lorraine Hansberry may have kicked off what has been described as the modern era of black theater, but in the first fifteen years after the premier of *Raisin in the Sun*, Adrienne Kennedy with *Funnyhouse of a Negro* and J. E. Franklin with *Black Girl* were perhaps the only female dramatists of note in an era that was otherwise dominated by males—Amiri Baraka, Ed Bullins, Lonne Elder III, Charles Fuller, Charles Gordone, Leslie Lee, Charles Russell, Derek Walcott, and Joseph Walker being among the most prominent. However, things were about to change.

For Colored Girls Who Have Considered Suicide When the Rainbow Is Enuf, a new play by Ntozake Shange, premiered at Joseph Papp's Public Theater Off-Broadway and later moved to the Booth Theater on Broadway, where it would run for over seven hundred performances. The play touched on the issues of abandonment, empowerment, self-esteem, and domestic violence. Seldom had a woman's voice been so direct, and in its directness so powerful. And that "female power" was both exhilarating and, for many black men at least, unnerving.

For Colored Girls was often seen as a direct "attack" on the image of black males in the media and the country. The most memorable of the monologues that make up the play is "A Nite with Beau Willie Brown," in which a violent boyfriend, angry that the mother of his two children has broken off the relationship, bursts into their apartment, assaults her, and then grabs the children, both toddlers, and holds them out of a window several stories above the street. He threatens to drop them if the mother does not return to him. She is overcome with fear and pain, and can barely speak. A garbled whisper barely leaves her throat. Beau Willie drops the children to their deaths.

For Colored Girls arrived at a time when publishing houses were releasing new novels by black women that also talked about domestic violence, ruined relationships, and misogyny in the black community. Stories abounded, in public media and in private conversations, about moral turpitude on the part of prominent black male politicians and media and sports stars. In real life, one only had to remember the Black Panther Party or the numbers of black males in the streets during the long, hot summers of urban unrest in the 1960s.

And now, here was a young black woman, Ntozake Shange, speaking from the "inside," with a voice as new and uncompromising as any anyone had seen up to that point, with stage images that were emotionally gripping, searing and perhaps revealing behavior that many had long believed only too common in the Harlems and South Sides of America.

The black male reaction to *Colored Girls* could have been divided according to generations: pre–Civil Rights Movement, movement activists, and Post–Civil Rights Movement. Black men over thirty-five in 1975 fit into the first two categories. They were, in the main, very unhappy with *Colored Girls*. The older men argued that while the play certainly had artistic merit, it was ultimately hurtful because it painted all black men as potential Beau Willies. The fact that Shange was lauded in the white press and received major awards for her work only served to raise more questions. The same cultural and ideological barriers that had been used for years in an attempt to control and corral black artists during the Harlem Renaissance and Black Power eras were soon being employed against Ms. Shange. She might have spent years fighting back, but rather than doing so, she largely ignored them.

The younger black men of the post–Civil Rights era, born in the 1950s and just coming into adulthood in the '70s, had a different point of view. They grew up in an era when the number of black children growing up in single-parent households increased from one fourth of all black children to more than half (today, the figure is even higher). Unlike their male elders, the majority had also grown up in the urban North as opposed to the rural South. There were no extended families to help out with child rearing, no grandmas and grandpas living in the home. These younger black men were the beginning of the "latchkey" generations soon to follow. These were the young men who had grown up feeling the loneliness of abandonment, had seen fathers who had become estranged from their families. These were the young men who could point to half brothers and half sisters who were fathered by the men who had left them behind when they went to live with another woman and start their lives over with her. For them, "Beau Willie" may have been painful, but it was also "truth."

Ntozake Shange's success as an artist made room for black women playwrights to speak their hearts and minds in a bold new way. *For Colored Girls* kicked away the constraints of ideology and cultural "propriety" that had limited many black women playwrights, and within a very short period of time, Pearl Cleague, Elain Jackson, Cassandra Medley, and P. J. Gibson were among those who stormed through the opening Ntozake Shange created.

The Black Theater Movement was no longer a cultural and intellectual conversation dominated by the opinions and ideas of learned men. Ntozake Shange's success helped greatly to place women playwrights directly in the center of the circle. From then on it would be impossible for a black theater company anywhere in America to consider producing a season of plays that did not include the work of black women writers.

Moving into the 1980s, it was clear that the new generation of African-American playwrights—the post–Black Power/Black Arts generation—were ready to come to the fore. Among the first of these playwrights was a young man who actually straddled the Black Arts era and its aftermath.

August Wilson first began perfecting his writing in his hometown of Pittsburgh in a workshop headed by the writer Rob Penny, a contemporary and friend of Ed Bullins. Later, Wilson was invited to the O'Neill Playwrights Center in Waterford, Connecticut. Here, he began a long and fruitful relationship with the director Lloyd Richards, the man who had brought Lorraine Hansberry's *Raisin in the Sun* to life on the Broadway stage a little over twenty years earlier.

Wilson ultimately became the most produced and perhaps the most widely recognized black playwright in the history of the American theater. He must be included in any conversation that involves assessing the most influential American playwrights of the last fifty years. He was successful in turning images and stereotypes of black people and their behavior into revelatory commentaries, not only on the social histories of twentieth century African Americans, but ultimately on the social and racial history of America itself.

Meanwhile, his contemporary, George C. Wolfe, a few years younger with both feet firmly planted in the post–Black Arts consciousness, represented the push for still newer directions. Wolfe's play *The Colored Museum* declared the arrival of a new generation of black writers and thinkers no longer constrained by the anger, pain, or rage of the past. His play acknowledged that history, but the new youth no longer wanted to define themselves or to be defined by it. I felt I was seeing a new set of aesthetic parameters or, at the very least, witnessing a representation of an American reality seen through the eyes of youth who had missed the Civil Rights era and the anti-war movement, but were determined to have their voices heard in the shaping of a new black consciousness in the 1980s and 1990s. George C. Wolfe had, in essence, declared that the black revolutionary playwrights of the 1960s and 1970s, of which I was a part, were no longer the vanguard. We were the "establishment" and the gates George and his generation were storming were ours.

The fiery young writers of the 1960s have become elders now. Sadly, some are infirm and no longer active; others are dead. Even the first post-Black Arts artists are now late middle-aged. They now find themselves facing a new generation that is looking to supplant them.

Interestingly, there is a hip-hop generation of poets and playwrights emerging, who are looking back at the work of Baraka, Bullins, Sonia Sanchez, and others from that bygone era. They also continue to explore the plays of August Wilson and Jeff Stetson, while allowing musical influences ranging from Miles Davis to Tupac Shakur to Prince to act as inspirations in an effort to try to develop new forms of theatrical presentation. Some of these new voices include Shaun Neblett in Harlem, Nicole Salter in New Jersey, and Radha Blank in Los Angeles.

Meanwhile, Suzi-Lori Parks, Lynne Nottage, Kia Corthron and Katori Hall are paramount among those voices that most define playwriting in black theater today. The number of times Ntozake Shange must have smiled at that realization is unknown.

Each One, Teach One
—Popular Harlem political slogan, 1968

I was the product of years of shaping by men and women at Howard, in the Black Theater Workshop and New Lafayette Theater, in the professional world of the arts, who passed on to me the idea that the stage should be seen as a laboratory where the belief systems, the mores, the myths, the histories and strivings of a people may be presented in full dimension, so that audiences might judge for themselves what is right, what is wrong, what needs to be changed and what need be left alone.

Bob Herbert of the *New York Times*, in lamenting the death of one of America's finest playwrights, Arthur Miller, talked of the "loss of a great public thinker." He wrote:

A...public thinker believe[s] strongly that the essence of America—its greatness—[is] in its promises. Mr. Miller knew what ignorance and fear and the madness of crowds, especially when exploited by sinister leadership, could do to those promises.... [Miller's] greatest concerns were, as Christopher Isherwood wrote, "...with the moral corruption brought on by bending one's ideals to society's dictates, buying into the values of a group when they conflict with the voice of personal conscience."...The individual, in Mr. Miller's view, has an abiding moral responsibility for his or her own behavior, and for the society as a whole. He said that, while writing *The Crucible*, "The longer I worked the more certain I felt that as improbable as it might seem, there were moments when an individual conscience was all that could keep the world from falling."

Each one of the plays included in this anthology was born out of the idea of the public thinker, and also that each generation must give back, must inform and inspire the generation that follows. No people—and certainly not the African Americans still striving and struggling in the twenty-first century—can thrive if they fail to adhere to that simple idea.

The Black Terror, set in an imagined unsettled future; *The Sirens*, moored in a recent past; *The Mighty Gents*, mired in an emotional and social wasteland; *The Talented Tenth*, marooned in middle-class, middle-aged angst; and *Autumn*, sequestered in a quagmire of empty promises—each of these plays, in its own way, addresses the notion of how our generations have always been tied to each other. In these early days of the new century, we see the consequences of allowing the ties between our generations—the connectedness of our families, traditions, beliefs, and faith—to be broken. What we shall do in response is something I hope my plays inspire.

—Richard Wesley
April 30, 2015

Notes on *The Black Terror*

I began thinking about writing a play about the "revolutionary phase" of the post–Civil Rights struggle after a series of national incidents made me question the efficacy of armed resistance as a means of protest and an engine of change.

In 1967, the Spanish film director Guillermo Pontecorvo directed a landmark film entitled *The Battle of Algiers*. The film takes place during the 1950s and is set in the Kasbah, the segregated Arab quarter of Algiers, the capital of French-occupied Algeria. Mr. Pontecorvo's picture presented a fictionalized account of the first insurrection against French colonial rule and showed how, though ultimately unsuccessful, that insurrection led directly to the struggle for Algerian independence. The French were overwhelmed by the end of the decade, and this led to a newly independent Algeria in the early '60s. Shot in a semi-documentary style, in grainy black and white, the film had a major influence on young liberation militants the world over, not the least in the United States, where youthful black men and women compared life in the Kasbah with life in the inner cities of their own country. Ultimately, many young people began to wonder if the "lessons" of *The Battle of Algiers* could not be applied to the armed struggle at home. Such conversations were held among young people in private parties, across tables in smoky cafés, on street corners, and even in college classrooms on campuses across the United States. And not just black kids, but white and Latino and Native American as well—everywhere the film was shown, oppressed and suppressed people were sure to begin drawing parallels.

However, my own response to the film, while very much appreciating its sentiments, was muted because of one particular memory. Not too long before seeing Pontecorvo's film, I was called into the Homicide Division of the Newark Police Department to answer questions. It turned out that a friend I had worked with in a program sponsored by HARYOU-ACT, an anti-poverty agency based in Harlem, had been found shot to death in a rooming house. My name was among his belongings, and the police were seeking out everyone who knew him to determine any leads.

As I sat there speaking to a detective, my eye couldn't help but take in my surroundings. What stood out for me were the street maps on the walls and their level of detail: alleys, dead ends, the locations of police boxes—they were all there. The memory of those maps came back to me as I noticed the way the French Commander depicted in *Battle of Algiers* used similar maps to track down and defeat the Algerian militants. It would also come back to me two years later, as I read about the police raid on the Black Panther Party headquarters in Los Angeles.

Fred Hampton was a young, charismatic leader of the Chicago branch of the Black Panther Party. He was twenty-one years old, handsome, athletic, intelligent, and erudite. If ever there was an heir apparent to Huey Newton, the party's by-then-imprisoned national leader, it was Fred Hampton—even more so than the party's internationally known minister of defense, Eldridge Cleaver. Hampton was assassinated in his bed by members of the Chicago and Illinois police. The world would later learn that he had been betrayed by an informant who was in the employ of the FBI, and that the operation was just one more offshoot of their COINTELPRO (or counterintelligence program), designed to delay, disrupt, and ultimately destroy any and all "militant" movements or operations within the African-American community.

A group of young white sympathizers of the then-nascent Weather Underground were sharing an apartment in a Greenwich Village brownstone in New York City. They had become radicalized by what they saw happening to the Black Panther Party, the slow but steady dismantling of the war on poverty by the Nixon Administration, efforts by the CIA to undermine or destroy leftist liberation movements across the Third World, and foremost, their deeply felt opposition to the United States' expansion of the war in Vietnam. These young people were secretly making bombs in their apartment when, inexplicably, one of the bombs blew up. It destroyed virtually the entire building and killed all of the young people, save one, Bernadette Dorhn, who was seen, bloodied, naked, and in shock, fleeing the rubble. She would remain on the FBI's Most Wanted List for nearly thirty years before voluntarily turning herself in during the Clinton administration.

Out on the West Coast, political tensions had arisen between the Black Panther Party—Marxist influenced and politically aligned with a loose and racially mixed amalgam of domestic and foreign leftist political movements—and US, a Black Nationalist organization that eschewed such political alliances in favor of total commitment to, and concentration within, the African-American community. Those political differences—coupled with an ever-growing dependence on guns as a means of both defense and imposing the political will of members of the Los Angeles chapter of the Black Panther Party and the Los Angeles chapter of US—ultimately led to violent confrontations between members of these organizations, escalating to such intensity that the leadership on both sides attempted to arrange a meeting to effect a truce and dial down the temperature. One such meeting was supposed to occur in a cafeteria on the campus of UCLA. Instead, gunfire erupted and two Panthers were killed. A pall was cast over the entire Black Liberation movement and remained for years to come; some might say it never lifted.

The LAPD attempted a raid on the Los Angeles headquarters of the Black Panther Party during the summer of 1970. A sixteen-square-block area around the building was cordoned off; residents were ordered to remain in their homes and off the streets. The police used an armored car (similar to the one featured in the original *Die Hard* movie), and all of the officers were armed with AR-15s, the civilian version of the M-15s US troops were using in the bush and marshes of Vietnam. It turned out, however, that the Panthers had fortified their headquarters, and they resisted the superior firepower of the police for a number of hours before surrendering when their ammo ran out. There were fewer than ten Panthers inside, some of them young women. When I heard the news, I thought again about those street maps in the Newark Police Headquarters building.

And then Huey Newton, in an article in the Black Panther Party newspaper, introduced and advocated the idea of "the urban kamikaze"—revolutionary guerrillas, on suicide missions, prepared to sacrifice all for the movement. It was a notion that was quickly abandoned, but for me it was a clear declaration that the armed faction of the black liberation movement had finally run out of ideas.

I was determined to say something. I decided, finally, to put "the Revolution" onstage, to write a play that would take place "in the very near future, given the nature of American society." I wanted a play in which all of the ideas about armed struggle, and the unquestioning fealty to nationalist as well as leftist ideals, would be presented not as possibilities but as fact; my characters would exemplify and live out these ideals before our eyes, and they would execute the armed struggle.

The stage would serve as a laboratory, allowing the audience to determine, through the dramatic presentation of ideas in action, whether the revolution that was being waged in their name needed to be changed, improved, executed exactly as it was, or abandoned.

I began work on the play almost immediately after the raid on the Los Angeles Black Panther Party headquarters. I collected newspaper articles and photographs of the raid and studied them daily. Ed Bullins, one of the finest playwrights in the country at the time, loaned me a book he'd bought on a trip to London: *Zero*, about the Nihilist movement in nineteenth-century Europe. I learned how the Czar of Russia had ordered his secret police to wage a counterintelligence operation that not only infiltrated the various Nihilist cells in Russia, but also fomented dissent, ran smear campaigns against the leadership, took over cells and ran them, and functioned as informants. The resemblance to the FBI's COINTELPRO was unmistakable.

I attended symposia on art and politics in Harlem, Brooklyn's Bedford-Stuyvesant, and Newark, New Jersey, and every day, every spare minute I had, I was writing—a sentence here, a scene there—all by hand, on a yellow legal pad that I carried in a military map bag slung over my shoulder. I wrote at home, on the bus to visit my then-girlfriend, on the subway to work, at parties, and backstage at the New Lafayette Theatre where I was managing editor of *Black Theatre Magazine*, until finally, some six months after I began, the play was completed. I settled on the title *The Black Terror* because I knew it was provocative and people would come to see it. I intended to write a play that could be performed in gymnasiums, on portable stages in open parks, in the quadrangles of housing developments—plays for the people, where the largest number of people were most likely to be. I also knew that designing a play that could be performed in the community, particularly a play that carried the message this one did, meant that the primary audience for *Terror* would be those who would most suffer the consequences of an armed struggle in the streets of America.

Terror's first public exposure was a reading in the Black Theatre Workshop, headed by Ed Bullins. Later, a former Howard University classmate, Rafique Bey, presented *Terror* as his thesis play. The FBI, which had already been on campus to observe student activism protesting the Vietnam War and support of Black Nationalist leaders on campus, attended in large numbers. At the same time, Ed Bullins showed the play to producer Joseph Papp, artistic director of the New York Shakespeare Festival/Public Theatre. Papp—himself an old-school activist from the '30s and '40s—immediately took a liking to *The Black Terror*, reached out to me, and made a commitment to producing the play in his theater, where it opened in October 1971.

The Black Terror

A Revolutionary Adventure Story

Brothers and Sisters Involved in the Struggle

ANTAR: *Late twenties or early thirties. College education. Strong, well-muscled, and stern. Relatively quiet. Speaks in soft tones. Not given to boisterousness.*

AHMED: *Somewhat younger. Full of fire. Could be a good leader if he would calm down and check things out.*

KEUSI: *Full name, Keusi Kifo ("Black Death"). He is in his mid- to late twenties and is a war vet. He is always a man who knows whereof he speaks.*

M'BALIA: *Named for M'Balia Camara, a Black woman who is known in Africa as a woman whose death was one of the sparks of the Guinean drive for independence from France. The sister is strong, determined, and a devoted revolutionary. She is not unfeminine, but displays her womanness only when she feels it suits her.*

GERONIMO: *A fiery revolutionary. Leader of the local chapter of the American Liberation Front. Quick-tempered; a flair for the dramatic. At times he seems almost unreal.*

CHAUNCEY RADCLIFFE: *Middle-aged. A moderate Black man who thinks he is doing the right thing.*

OTHERS: *Three Brothers, a Sister, other members of the Black Terrorists, and white-sounding voices coming in over the radio.*

The setting will alternate between the Terrorist headquarters, a tenement apartment, and the home of Dr. Chauncey Radcliffe.

Time

The very near future, given the nature of American society.

The New York production of *The Black Terror* opened at the Public Theater in the fall of 1972. The production was directed by Nathan George. Lighting by Buddy Butler; sets by Marjorie Kellogg.

The Cast

KEUSI: Gylan Kain
M'BALIA: Susan Batson
ANTAR: Paul Benjamin
AHMED: Kirk Young
GERONIMO: Don Blakely
RADCLIFFE: Earl Sydnor
DANCER: Dolores Vanison
PRIESTESS: Freda Vanderpool
BROTHERS AND SISTERS INVOLVED IN THE STRUGGLE: Preston Bradley, Niger Akoni, James Buckley, Sylvia Soares

Musicians

Babafemi Akinlana, Ralph Dorsey, Ladji Camara

Scene One

Blood-red lights on a dark chamber. A number of young, Black revolutionaries are gathered to perform a ceremony. Drums are playing. The women sing in eerie, high-pitched voices; the men make grunting and moaning sounds that blend in with the voices of the women. Bodies are swaying. Dancing. The smell of incense is in the air. A fire burns at an altar, ANTAR *stands in front of the altar. The music, singing, and dances build to a frenzy until* ANTAR *bids silence.* AHMED, *standing nearby, steps forward, raises clenched fist.*

AHMED: We are the Black Terrorists, sworn to the liberation of our people.

ALL: May we never lose sight of our duty.

AHMED: We seek the death of those who oppress us.

ALL: May our vengeance be as swift as lightning.

AHMED: We are the Black Terrorists, sworn to uphold the dignity of our African bloodline.

ALL: May we suffer death before disgrace to our ancestors.

AHMED: We live by the will of the Supreme Black Spirit to create a world of peace and beauty after the revolution.

ALL: May the blood of our oppressors never cease to flow until that world is realized.

AHMED: We are the Black Terrorists, sworn to die for the liberation of our people.

ALL: The oppressor of our people must die! We shall kill him where he works, we shall kill him as he sleeps, we shall kill him wherever he is. He must know of the wrath that befalls those who consider themselves above the laws of God and humanity. His death will free our nation! His death will free the world! AAAAAAAAAAAAIIIIIIIIIIIEEEEEEEEEEEE!!!!!!!!!

(*Drums. Wild dancing. Women dancing. Men shuffling in place. Shouting and screaming. Chants are heard. Silence as* ANTAR *raises his hands.*)

ANTAR: Bring in the candidate.

(*Two young Terrorists escort* KEUSI *to the altar. Drum is heard softly in the background.* KEUSI *kneels before* ANTAR *and altar.*)

Ndugu Keusi Kifo, you kneel before me having been chosen by vote to carry out a mission of assassination against the most vicious and ruthless enemy of the people in this area.

Your target is Police Commissioner Charles Savage, organizer of the mad-dog Night Rangers of the police department. He is an avowed enemy of the revolution and he is therefore an oppressor. He must die.

ALL: (*Chant.*)
Lasima Tuchinde Mbilishaka!
Lasima Tuchinde Mbilishaka!
Lasima Tuchinde Mbilishaka!

(M'BALIA *will come forward from the assembly and kneel at the altar before* KEUSI *Sing.*)

Spirits of our forefathers
Come forth
Reach into our hearts
And remove the fear
Reach into our minds
And remove the doubt
Release the anger in our souls
And give us strength
To do
What must
Be done.

(*Chant.*)

Sifa Ote Mtu Weusi
Sifa Ote Mtu Weusi
Sifa Ote Mtu Weusi

ANTAR: Dada M'Balia, you kneel before me, having volunteered to team with Ndugu Keusi in the execution of this mission. Your past performances in action have proven you to be an outstanding revolutionary and an expert terrorist. Your knowledge and experience will prove to be the perfect complement to Ndugu Keusi's own revolutionary talents.

(*The others will sing the lines below as* ANTAR *is given a large knife by* AHMED. *He places the knife in a fire on the altar to purify it.* ANTAR *holds the knife aloft. Drums grow louder, then subside.* ANTAR *takes* KEUSI'*s arm and makes an incision, then does the same with* M'BALIA. *Meanwhile, the others are singing.*)

ALL: (*Sing.*)

Spirits of the Black Nation
Come.
Take hold of your servants
Guide our lives
Make us strong
Place steel in the marrow of our bones
Grant us inner peace
To fulfill our terrible missions.

(*Chant.*)

Lasima Tuchinde Mbilishaka
Lasima Tuchinde Mbilishaka
Lasima Tuchinde Mbilishaka

ANTAR: Ndugu Keusi and Dada M'Balia, the two of you have been joined together by blood. Until this mission is complete or until I terminate this mission, you will guard each other with your lives.

(AHMED *steps forward with an array of weapons on a dark red pillow.*)

You will assume secret identities and live within the community and await the opportune moment to carry out your orders.

(*Hands weapons to* KEUSI.)

These are your weapons. You will use them well, my brother. What say you both?

KEUSI and **M'BALIA:** (*In an incantation.*)
Spirit Guardians of the dark regions
Hear my cry
Let not my will falter
Let not my desire fall
With all my strength

Let me defeat my enemy
With all my soul
Let me defeat my enemy
Let me see to the will of
The Black Nation
Show me
No mercy
Should I fail my
Sacred oath.

AHMED: (*Steps forward, raises clenched fist.*) We are the Black Terrorists, sworn to the liberation of our people.

ALL: May we never lose sight of our duty.

AHMED: We seek the death of those who oppress us.

ALL: May our vengeance be as swift as lightning. AAAAAAAAAAAAIIIIIII IIIIIEEEEEEEEEEEEEE!!!!!!!!!!

(*Drum, music, dancing as* KEUSI *and* M'BALIA *exit. Lights go down.*)

Scene Two

Lights up on a room in a tenement apartment. Very little furniture. Large rug on the floor. KEUSI, M'BALIA, *and* AHMED *sit on large cushions.*

AHMED: All right, listen up. Ndugu Keusi, your target has a set pattern of behavior. He plays golf at the Golden Triangle every weekend from 11 a.m. to 5 p.m. He showers, then leaves the golf course promptly at 6:45 p.m. He always takes the parkway back to the city.

KEUSI: He travel alone?

AHMED: Always. Now, about twenty-five miles south of the city, the parkway has this big curve in it that goes through this valley. There are a lot of trees, high grass, and shrubbery. He usually hits that curve around 7:15. And he drives in the left lane.

KEUSI: What kinda car do he drive?

AHMED: (*Piqued.*) Man, didn't you study the briefing notes on the target?

KEUSI: Yeah, well, I don't remember seeing anything in it about the kinda car he got.

AHMED: It was in there, man. Dammit, man. Get yourself together. You blow this mission—

Keusi: (*Annoyed.*) Just tell me what kinda car he drive. I don't need no lecture.

Ahmed: You better watch your mouth, man. You still only an initiate. One word from me and your ass'll be crawling in the dirt.

Keusi: I'm sorry, man. Nervous, I guess.

Ahmed: Don't be sorry, just keep in mind your position when you talk to someone who got rank over you. Now, in view of the fact that you ain't studied, I gotta take time out to get up off a whole lotta insignificant information. The target drives a 1965 Buick LeSabre; four door; blue. License plate number NPD-911.

(Keusi *writes info down.*)

Keusi: Got it. Thanks, man.

Ahmed: (*Ignoring him.*) It's important that you be on the right-hand slope of the valley at 7:15 to get the best shot at the target. The high grass will hide you. We figure once the oppressor is hit his car will veer out of control and crash. In the confusion, you can make a sure getaway. Be sure you can find the ejected shell and take it with you. We don't want no clues left behind, at all.

Keusi: Aw, man, now how the hell am I gonna find an ejected shell in all that grass?

Ahmed: Look, stop questioning your orders and do like you're told. All the FBI gotta do is find a shell, or some other seemingly insignificant shit, and the next thing you know they'll be banging on our door.

Keusi: They ain't gonna find us behind no goddamn shell.

Ahmed: Stop questioning your orders and do like you told.

Keusi: Yeah. Okay, I'm sorry. You got anything else to tell me?

Ahmed: No. That's it. The rest is in your notes.

Keusi: Yeah, okay, I got a question. This shit sound too risky. Have y'all got an alternate plan?

Ahmed: Yeah, but it's more difficult 'cause you got to eliminate your target in front of his home. The target is pretty much of a loner. He's a bachelor, so he lives alone in his house. He got very few real close friends and seldom gets visitors. His house is at 631 Peachtree Drive, near Talmadge Avenue. He works a sixteen-hour day and usually gets home about 9:30 at night. Usually all the lights in his house go out around 11:30, so we figure that must be about the time he goes to bed.

Observation shows that he usually gets outa his house by 7:30 a.m. The best time, then, to eliminate him is between 9:30 at night and 7:30 in the morning. There's a park across the street from where he lives. Lotsa trees and good cover. Ideal for a mission like yours.

Keusi: Yeah, I like that. A park. Nighttime. Good cover. Hell, yeah, I like that idea. I'll probably do the job at Savage's house rather than on that stupid highway. Shit, why not?

Ahmed: Where you eliminate your target doesn't matter. The idea is to execute your mission clearly, efficiently, and without the possibility of detection. Complete your assignment by the end of the week.

Keusi: It'll be done.

Ahmed: (*To* M'Balia.) Have you any suggestions or amendments, my sister?

M'Balia: No. Y'all the men. I trust your ideas.

Ahmed: Okay, then it's all set. Good. I've got to leave, 'cause Antar and I got things to discuss.

(*All rise, they move to door.*)

A word of caution, Ndugu Keusi Kifo. Your mouth is too big, man. You got the makings of a damn good revolutionary, but you try to think too much. You know? Don't think. Let your leaders do the thinking. That's their job. Your job is to do or die. Remember that. Okay?

(Keusi *smiles and nods.* Ahmed *and* Keusi *shake hands. Then* Ahmed *embraces and kisses* M'Balia *on both cheeks.*)

Good luck to you both.

Keusi: Yeah, man, thanks.

M'Balia: Asante, Ndugu Ahmed.

Ahmed: Kwaheri.

Keusi: Later.

M'Balia: Kwaheri, Ndugu Ahmed.

(Ahmed *exits.*)

Keusi: Jive-ass motherfucker. I wouldn't follow him across the goddamn street.

(M'Balia *looks at him very hard.*)

Well, it's all set. That's good.

M'Balia: I'd better go and clean your weapon.

KEUSI: Hold it a minute. I'm not so sure I wanna use that rifle.

M'BALIA: (*Harshly.*) What do you propose to use then? A knife? Your hands? You could fail if you try those methods. The revolution can't afford any failures, Ndugu Kifo.

KEUSI: I'm hip to that, M'Balia, but look at it from this angle. Out on the parkway, if I got to take aim and fire in all that high grass, how the hell am I gonna know where the spent shell falls? I could be up there for days looking for some goddamn shell just so the FBI don't have too many clues. I could get caught up there looking for that shell. And that park across from where Savage lives. It's in a white neighborhood. I'm gonna have a helluva time even gettin' into that area. Then fire a high-powered rifle. The sound of the shot is gonna bring people. Someone's bound to see me running. Of course, I could put cushioning and wire mesh around the barrel and chamber of the gun to muffle the sound of the shot, but then there's the problem of the gun flash. Suppose I need more than one shot—highly unlikely as good as I am, but possible anyway— suppose I need more than one shot, people are bound to see the gun flash. It's warm out, there gonna be people all over the place. Then, 'cause I shouldn't question orders, I gotta crawl around in the dark lookin' for some stupid-ass shell. After I do that, I gotta worry about gettin' my Black behind outa there with cops crawlin' all over the place lookin' for the sniper who offed the pig. Naw, there got to be an easier way. I don't wanna wind up a martyr on my first mission.

M'BALIA: We know it is risky, Ndugu Keusi, but you should realize that the success of your mission overrides any consideration of the success of your escape. You should not expect to survive the revolution. As an initiate to the Black Terrorists that realization will be some time in coming. But as you become more of a part of us, you will accept that point of view as a reality.

KEUSI: I don't accept the inevitability of a revolutionary death. Understand? He who assassinates and gets away shall live to assassinate another day—if he's clever. And I intend to be clever. I ain't hardly suicidal.

M'BALIA: No one asked you to be. You have an assignment to carry out. You will not shirk your duty.

KEUSI: I ain't shirkin' no duty. I'm just tellin' you that to kill this man there must be a simpler way just as efficient as a gun that won't give me the problems I mentioned before. I know I'll think of something. Just give me some time. Commissioner Savage will not see the weekend. Imagine, he's walkin' around thinking about his golf game this weekend not knowing that there's a nigger right now thinking of offing him before he even gets one stroke in. Life is funny like that. One minute everything is cool, the next minute, CRASH!!!! Just like that it's all over. Too bad. I almost feel sorry for that old bastard.

(M'BALIA *looks at him incredulously.*)

Yeah, I kinda feel sorry for his ass, you know.

M'BALIA: (*Firmly.*) Don't. Your target is the oppressor. He is not a man, he is the enemy. He is the devil. The beast. Your target is zero. Compassion is an emotion that is wasted on him. When you eliminate your target, you are destroying a non-man. You are killing a no-thing. The oppressor's life is zero. The death of your target will mean life for the revolution. You should remember that. Reduce your enemy from humanity to zero. Once you have done that in your mind, such emotions as compassion cease to have relevancy, and pulling the trigger becomes easier and easier. Ultimately you can kill with the same nonchalance as brushing your hair.

KEUSI: You really believe that?

M'BALIA: Of course. I'm a revolutionary. The total extermination of the enemy is my goal. After you've been with us awhile, you'll come to adopt this point of view as well.

KEUSI: Yeah, uh-huh, well, I recognize my duty to fight and maybe die for the revolution, but I ain't never been able to see killin' in a machinelike fashion. I'm a man, not a machine.

M'BALIA: You refuse to understand. Compassion is beyond the emotional range of the true terrorist. We say that the only true emotion in the revolution is revolutionary fervor.

KEUSI: I can see that my education is going to be a long and hard one.

(M'BALIA *looks at him but says nothing.*)

Hey, I'll tell you one thing, though: That info that Ahmed had on Savage was very meticulous. Whoever was assigned to check him out sure did a good job. Looks like they got his shit down pat.

M'BALIA: I watched the target. I worked as a maid in his house for a coupla months. I got to know him pretty well. He tried to get me to sleep with him a couple of times, but I kept refusing, so he fired me and got someone else. But by that time we had most of the information we needed. When I think about it, though, I should have slept with him. It would have been so easy to execute him then. One of the other sisters did it. I understand it works very well.

KEUSI: I don't see why y'all need a female assassin's unit in the first place.

M'BALIA: Manpower needs dictated it. There just weren't enough brothers to do all that needed doing.

KEUSI: Yeah, but could you as a woman, a giver of life, teach a doctrine of terror and death to your children?

M'BALIA: I'll never know. I'm an assassin and we're not among those women who're allowed to have a husband and children. Our tasks are too dangerous and they require our full allegiance and dedication to what we do. Besides, our duty overshadows any considerations of love and/or motherhood.

KEUSI: But you will have a man and kids someday, won't you?

M'BALIA: I've devoted my life to the revolution. A man and children are luxuries a woman can afford when there's peace. We're at war and I haven't the time to even think of such things. And don't be getting any ideas. Just because I have a womb, don't think I'm that eager to put something in it. I won't be judged by my sex. I'm a revolutionary before I'm a woman.

(KEUSI *and* M'BALIA *look at each other.* KEUSI *is bemused and* M'BALIA *is dead serious. She starts out. A sly smile comes over* KEUSI'*s face.*)

KEUSI: M'Balia?

(*She turns.*)

Are you for real? Y'all really can take sex or leave it?

M'BALIA: (*Trying to deal with* KEUSI'*s insolence.*) Well...every now and then some of us still have the need, Keusi. After all, it is a natural human function, you know.

KEUSI: (*Smiling.*) Yes, I know.

M'BALIA: (*Insulted.*) Don't be vulgar.

KEUSI: M'Balia, you got a man?

M'BALIA: (*Bitingly.*) No. I haven't found one who interests me.

KEUSI: You sure?

(KEUSI *looks at her.* M'BALIA *avoids his eyes and the question.*)

M'BALIA: I'll go clean your weapon. You should rest. You have important work to do.

KEUSI: Yeah, okay,

(*Sarcastically.*)

"Mommy."

(*Angry,* M'BALIA *exits in a huff.*)

Ain't this a bitch?

(KEUSI *laughs to himself and lights up a joint. Lights go down.*)

Scene Three

Lights up on ANTAR *and* AHMED *seated in the headquarters of the Black Terrorists.*

ANTAR: You know, once we eliminate the oppressor Savage, we will have to be prepared for some very hectic times. Many of us will probably be killed.

AHMED: Yeah, I know. Well, we all have to die sometime. I guess going out with the blood of the oppressor on our hands is the best way for the true revolutionary to die.

ANTAR: Once Savage has been eliminated, we must prepare ourselves for full-scale reprisals. The oppressors will scour the entire Black community until they find us, and when they do, I guess it'll be a fight to the death.

AHMED: I know it'll be a fight to the death, 'cause I ain't hardly gonna go to jail behind destroying some oppressor.

ANTAR: Assassinating the oppressor will probably mean that another, more beastly oppressor will take his place. He will unleash the Night Rangers and that could signal the beginning of the next phase of the revolution: open all-out warfare between the Black community and the local forces of the oppressor. I just hope we are prepared

AHMED: We're ready as ever. The Night Rangers will have one helluva time gettin' in here and if they do, they'll have less than half the men they started with, no matter how many men they send at us. The revolutionary example we set will inspire revolutionaries all over the world.

ANTAR: That's the greatest honor any revolutionary can have. The death cries of the enemy can serve as our dirge.

AHMED: Dig it.

ANTAR: It's good to know that, as a leader, I am surrounded by brothers of such courage. I know that none of you will let me down when the time comes.

AHMED: All of us except maybe that new brother.

ANTAR: Which one?

AHMED: Keusi Kifo.

ANTAR: What's the matter? Don't you trust him?

AHMED: I wouldn't go so far as to say that. But I am kinda worried about where his head is at.

ANTAR: You don't think he's the man, do you?

AHMED: No, we've had him followed and we've checked as thoroughly as we could on his background. He's clean as far as we can tell. Our spies in police headquarters said that they couldn't find nothin' on him, but they still keepin' they ears open. Kifo's a veteran of the Vietnam War and he's a weapons expert and was also a sniper. Much decorated and alla that shit. The brother who recommended him is one of our most trusted revolutionaries. No, I don't think he's the man. That's not the kind of vibration I get from him.

ANTAR: Well, then what's the trouble?

AHMED: I was with him a little while ago. He's a very incorrect brother. No discipline, no revolutionary fervor; just a very uncool nigger who acts as though what we're involved in is just an advanced stage of gang-banging.

ANTAR: I guess it's a carryover from his war experiences. You should remember that, unlike most of us, Kifo has fought and killed for a number of years while in Vietnam. This is all old hat to him. I think we should be patient and try to coax him along gently.

AHMED: Yeah, well, I went to check on his efficiency report an' that report ain't that good. I told you before that I didn't think he shoulda been selected for this mission. Just 'cause he got a good military record that don't mean that that's enough. Hey, man, listen to this report: "Too compassionate… given to feeling sorry for his targets… hangs on to such emotions as pity and mercy… doesn't realize that such emotions are beyond the range of the true revolutionary." Antar, any brother who got any kind of political knowledge knows that our situation in this country is the result of inhuman treatment that has in turn dehumanized us. We are outside humanity because inhuman beasts have forced us there. Now they threaten us because we seek to return to humanity. But the beast blocks our path. We got to use inhuman means to defeat inhumanity. See, Keusi Kifo won't acknowledge that fact and I feel that in the long run he gonna be a detriment to the organization.

ANTAR: I see. Ahmed, I think your suspicions have some validity, but on the other hand, the War Council decided unanimously on Ndugu Keusi, with you, of course, abstaining. It's too late to call everything off, now. The wheels of death for the oppressor are rolling and no one can stop them.

My own opinion is that you exaggerate just a little. Kifo is certainly no troublemaker. Recognize that you've already decided that he is not the man and you've determined that he is a good killer. His loyalty, at this point, is not in doubt. So what you should understand, then, is that his lack of discipline and fervor are but the characteristics of a great many new members of this cadre. His fire is much like yours when you first came to us.

AHMED: But I understood the seriousness of what we did and what we had to do. Therefore I took the revolution seriously. I don't think Ndugu Keusi does and that's the shit that's botherin' me.

(*A young* TERRORIST *bursts in, salutes, and addresses* ANTAR.)

YOUNG BROTHER: Excuse me, Mkuu Antar, but Geronimo of the American Liberation Front is outside. He's been shot in the shoulder and he's all beat-up lookin'.

ANTAR: How the hell…

(*To the* YOUNG BROTHER.)

Bring him in here soon as you can.

YOUNG BROTHER: (*Saluting.*) Ndio, Mkuu Antar.

(*Exits in a hurry.*)

AHMED: Great, now Geronimo's ass is lit up. Who's gonna be next? We gonna have to put an end to this shit, man. Kifo better not fuck up. I'll put fire to his ass if he do.

ANTAR: (*Softly.*) Take it easy, man.

(*Two* BROTHERS *bring in* GERONIMO. *He is wearing a brightly colored headband, Apache-style moccasins laced up to his knees, and wears an army fatigue jacket. A* SISTER, *who remains silent and in the "background," enters and begins to dress* GERONIMO's *wound.*)

SISTER: Please try to relax, my brother. This is going to hurt a bit.

GERONIMO: (*Ignoring the* SISTER; *to no one in particular.*) Those white motherfuckers!! Goddamn spirtless, devil-eyed dogs! Aw, man! Oh man!! Goddamn!!!

ANTAR: (*Calmly.*) Geronimo, be cool. Calm down.

GERONIMO: The pigs, man, the pigs!!! They put all my best shit to sleep!

AHMED: Geronimo, damn, man, make some sense.

GERONIMO: The Night Rangers destroyed my headquarters, man. They took weapons, records, smoke, everything. Three of my men are dead, more of my warriors are wounded or in hiding, and I'm here all shot up.

SISTER: Geronimo, I'll have to ask you not to move so much. I can't fix your bandages right if you keep movin' like you do.

GERONIMO: (*Ignoring the request.*) The bullet went clean through my shoulder, man. I ain't never been shot before. It hurt like hell, but it was wild. Ow! Goddamn, watch it, sister!

SISTER: I'm sorry, my brother, but I told you before it was gonna hurt.

GERONIMO: Yeah, well, okay, sister. But don't let it hurt too much.

AHMED: You gonna tell us what happened, man?

GERONIMO: Yeah, okay. This was extremely well planned and coordinated. They killed Ramon, my Chief of Security, Victor, my Chief of Culture, and Juney-bugs, my Chief of Propaganda. I think the Night Rangers probably got all my records. If they do then they got the who's who of every chapter in the country. They got a list of all my known contacts and a list of the white boys who was payin' my expenses when I gave speeches at colleges and shit like that. Man, the pigs got the American Liberation Front by the balls.

AHMED: I guess y'all have had it, brother. You better make preparations to go underground and split.

GERONIMO: Hell no! That punk Commissioner Savage pulled off this shit and I want his ass! He's responsible for the deaths of three of the baddest brothers who ever lived. I shaped and molded those cats myself. Victor, Ramon, and Juney-bugs was smokers, man; very righteous revolutionaries. Good sharp minds. They learned well and followed orders to the letter. Damn, man, they was *revolutionaries*! Man, I shudda died with them. They were the best, man. You know?

ANTAR: You still haven't told us what's happened.

GERONIMO: (*Angry; excited.*) Hey, man! Goddamn! I told you, the pigs vamped on us!

AHMED: How? I thought y'all had some security.

GERONIMO: We figured we did. We had these five Marxist white boys covering for us.

AHMED: White boys?! Aw, *man*!! Geronimo, was you crazy?!

GERONIMO: Well, hey, man, we thought they was different.

AHMED: See, man, we told you about that alliance shit in the first place.

GERONIMO: We thought they was bad, man. You know, these cats been blowin' up the Bank of America, draft offices, Dupont Chemical property, goin' on days of rage and shit, and quotin' Marx better than the Russians. You know, these cats was those crazy motherfuckers who called themselves "The Narodnikis." Hey, man, we thought we had some dynamite dudes with us…and the pink pussies punked out!!! The pigs musta moved fast 'cause the first thing we knew Finkel and Schmidt came bustin' thru the door headin' for the escape tunnel shouting, "Pigs outside! Pigs outside! Let's get the hell outa here!" They hit the tunnel shaft and we didn't see them no more.

ANTAR: We told you a long time ago about alliances with those white radicals. They are either suicidal in outlook or thrill-seekers who have no real stomach for true revolution. I thought that a lesson had been learned by all of you alliance-prone brothers after the way Bobby got used in Chicago a couple of years ago.

AHMED: The only place for white boys in the struggle is *outside* the struggle.

GERONIMO: Yeah, I realize that, now. They all the same, all those white radicals. All they can do is sell woof tickets and hide behind Black revolutionaries' coattails, waitin' for us to tell them what to do next. They stand around wavin' Viet Cong flags and shit, and spittin' at pigs. But soon as they start gettin' they heads cracked by some pigs, they start cryin' and shouting.

(*Very effeminate.*)

"Oh my God, what's happening. But we're the kids! We're the kids!" They got no heart, man. No heart, at all. They don't understand revolution. Not really. So fuck 'em! They all pussies! The faggots, they oughta drop they pants and spread they "cheeks." That's all they good for, anyway.

(*Calms down a bit. Tries to pull himself together.*)

SISTER: Brother, you gonna have to try to control yourself. I can't do nothin' for your shoulder if you remain in your overexcited state.

GERONIMO: (*Breathing hard; looks at the* SISTER *a moment. Face grows hard.*) Aw, later for my shoulder. My men lyin' dead, wounded and scattered all over the fuckin' city. And you botherin' me about a stupid-ass flesh wound! Fuck my shoulder. Woman, get away from me, I ain't asked you for your advice!!

(*Hurt, the* SISTER *quietly bows her head and starts to leave.* AHMED *looks hard at* GERONIMO, *who does not notice him. He seems almost in another world. Realizing he has been rash,* GERONIMO *takes the* SISTER*'s arm.*)

Wait, hold it, sister. Please stay. I'm sorry. You doin' a good job. Please… I'm sorry.

(GERONIMO *kisses the* SISTER *on the cheek.*)

Finish what you were doin'. I'll try to be cool.

(*The* SISTER *looks at* ANTAR, *who nods approvingly; she smiles slightly at* GERONIMO *and resumes dressing his wound. It takes only a few seconds and she has finished. Having done that, she moves to a quiet corner of the room, where she remains.*)

That's a good job, my sister. You do your work well.

SISTER: Asante, Ndugu Geronimo.

GERONIMO: (*Smiles.*) Hey, man, that's a beautiful sister. I almost forget what I been through when I look at her. You know?

(*The* SISTER *smiles.*)

But I can't forget. Nothin' can ever make me forget. Nothin'll make me forget what went when those pigs staged they massacre. But we made them pay. We made them pay!

(GERONIMO *becomes exhilarated as he relates the following details.*)

Me, Ramon, and three other brothers was on the windows. Juney-bugs was downstairs guardin' the door. Everybody else scattered at every other available position. We put the steel shutters up. Then I put a sister on the phone callin' up the Black radio station, so she could tell the shit as it was happenin'. I didn't want the pigs floodin' the airwaves with their version of battle. We had to be ready for those motherfuckers on every level. These pigs was the Night Rangers an' we knew they was better armed than the 101st Airborne, so we wasn't takin' no chances. Then these two pigs tried to dynamite the door open. Ramon leaned out the window an' fired twice: Bam! Bam! Two pigs fell for the revolution! AAAAAAAAIIIIIIIEEEEEEE!!!!!! Then, I heard a loud crunch an' I saw Ramon's face turn into a charred lump of blood. Ramon! Ramon! Oh man, goddamn… But we held 'em, man. The chumps threw everything they could at us an' we held 'em off. Then there was an explosion an' screams an' the place was fillin' up with smoke. They finally managed to dynamite the door open. The explosion busted Juney-bugs all up. He couldn't move, man. The brother didn't have a chance. But that didn't stop Juney-bugs. He had a piece in each hand. The first four pigs thru the door died. Juney was settin' a beautiful revolutionary example: four pigs lyin' dead at his feet, two more lyin' wounded in the doorway cryin' for they mamas an' they gods. Juney-bugs just kept on firin' into that cloud of smoke an' not one pig dared to move from behind the cars an' shit they was hidin' behind.

An', man, there was bullets zingin' all past my head, people screamin', guns an' shit, an' I was feelin'…I was feelin'…damn about nothin'. I could feel the spirits of all the great revolutionaries with me. Man, it was like I was feelin' mystical an' shit. An' then, with everything blowin' up all around me, I saw the spirit of death laughin' at me. He raised a clenched fist. An' I raised a clenched fist an' shouted, "Right on, motherfucker!!!" an' laughed back. I swear to God, man, an' I'm ashamed to admit it, but I loved it! I LOVED IT! We was heavin' the righteous wrath of the people on the pigs.

(*Hysterical laugher.*)

HAHAHAHAHAHAHAHAHAHAHAHAHAHAHAHAHA!!!!! Another explosion an' there was only seven of us left alive by this time. I could hear the pigs comin' up the stairs an' I knew that Juney-bugs musta been killed. It was time to get outa there. We got the sistuhs out first…Then, man, the craziest thing: Victor knelt down beside Ramon's body an' he put his hand in his blood, an' he started tremblin' an' screamin' an' actin' wild an' shit. He charged the pigs, firin' as he went. No! No! Nooooooo!!!…It was just me, now. I ran inside the main room an' bolted the door shut. I could hear the pigs tryin' to bust it down. I set the room on fire. Couldn't afford to let the pigs get nothin'. Then someone shot thru the door an' I got hit. I started to fall, but I held on. I knew if the pigs found me alive, they'd kill me on the spot. I stated to crawl to the tunnel. The room was burnin' when I left, but I'm sure the devils musta been able to put the fire out an' get those files.

AHMED: You shudda had summa those sisters destroyin' those files the minute the first shot was fired.

GERONIMO: They was all upstairs on the third floor when the shit started. An' they was asleep. When the shit started, it was started. Either you shot or got shot. There was not time to worry about files.

ANTAR: You should have taken time, Geronimo. Now, the whole Front's gotta go underground or maybe even disband. The FBI's gonna be bustin' ass right and left.

GERONIMO: My only hope is that the fire I set took care of business. That's all I got to say on the matter, so don't be bustin' my ass about no goddamn files.

(*Mood changes. Body sags a bit.*)

Oh, man, those three brothers. Oh, man, they was so beautiful. Blazin' away even as they fell. Ramon, with his face blown off, lay on the floor still holdin' his piece. Even in death he was settin' a perfect revolutionary example. Man, why do dynamite brothers like those three cats always have to be the ones to get offed?

ANTAR: They have attained the ultimate freedom in this oppressive condition Black people live in, Geronimo. Those brothers chose to die rather than live in squalor and deprivation. Their concern for their plight and the plight of their Black brothers and sisters all over the world led them to sacrifice the ultimate for a remedy to their situation. Those of us who are left can only be inspired by their revolutionary deaths.

AHMED: That's right, my brother. Even in death the brothers have provided impetus for the revolution.

(*During the last exchange the* SISTER *has moved to* GERONIMO*'s side to inspect his bandages.*)

SISTER: Mkuu Geronimo, you movin' so much you startin' to bleed again.

GERONIMO: (*Looking at the wound.*) Wow. Dig that.

(*He touches the wound then pulls his hand away, marveling at the sight of the blood. Then, he clenches his fist and closes his eyes.*)

Oh man, oh man! I can feel it, my brothers! The revolution, Victor, Juney-bugs, and Ramon. I can feel it all. Oh, my God!

(*The* SISTER *tries to redress his wound, but he pushes her hand away.*)

No don't!! Not yet.

(*He places his hand over the wound once more.*)

Yeah…yeah…Now, I know what Victor felt when he touched Ramon's blood. My wrist! Alla y'all grab aholda my wrist.

(*He clenches his fist. All grab his wrist.*)

Can you feel it? You feel the spirits? You feel 'em? Oh God, it's beautiful. Can you feel it, brothers? Can you feel it, sister? It's the spirit of the revolution. Can't nothin' hurt me, now; I know it!! Oh, wow, man! The blood! The feeling! It's really taking me out.

SISTER: Geronimo, you're trembling all over.

AHMED: He must be getting' the fever.

GERONIMO: (*Angry.*) It ain't no goddamn fever!! It's the revolution. It's my only reason for being alive from this moment on! To fight and die for the revolution. I won't live beyond it! I don't want to. I don't care what goes down after we win. I only want to live to destroy my enemy. Once that has been, my usefulness to the revolution will be done. From now on, I'm a revolutionary warrior. I live for the battle. Peace would kill me. I only want to live to destroy my enemy. That's my goal. Death and destruction will be my weapons of war.

(*Clenching his fist tighter.*)

Oh God, can ya'll feel it? The blood is burning in my fist.

ANTAR: (*Looks warily at the others.*) Geronimo, maybe you'd better try and rest. You keep up like this and you'll lose a lot of blood and that could lead to you dyin'.

GERONIMO: No, man, not! Not Geronimo! Geronimo ain't gonna die on no hummer. I seen my death. I'm gonna die like a revolutionary with the blood of the enemy on my hands. To die for the revolution is a glorious thing. It is, man, it is. Make no mistake. I'll meet my moment in a true revolutionary manner.

My brothers, I ain't splittin' into no goddamn exile. I'm stayin' here to fight and die in the revolution. Let me join you. I need to hook up with some revolutionary freedom fighters. Let me work with you. Please. Y'all are revolutionaries, an' I'm one, too. Don't deny me the chance to get even for Victor, Ramon, and Juney-bugs.

ANTAR: (*Smiling.*) Geronimo, you were always one of us, my brother. We would be honored to have you serve with us.

(*They embrace.*)

AHMED: Death to the oppressors!!

ANTAR: Long life to the revolution!!!

GERONIMO: Death and destruction! Pain and agony! Let the blood of the enemy flow in the streets purifying the revolutionary cause. Let nothing remain standing before the power for the revolution!!!

ALL: AAAAAAIIIIIIIIEEEEEEE!!!!!!!!!!!!!!

(*Blackness.*)

Scene Four

A few days later in the apartment occupied by KEUSI *and* M'BALIA. *He and* M'BALIA *are eating. The radio blares in the background.*

RADIO NEWSMAN: …And now the top news story of the week: Some eighty-five policemen, members of the elite Night Rangers, earlier this week raided the headquarters of the American Liberation Front at 221 Chapel Street in the Penny Lane District. Twenty-two persons, including thirteen policemen, were killed in the blazing twenty-minute gun battle that ensued when police reported that they were met with gunfire when they sought entrance to the headquarters to ask the ownership of a Volkswagen double-parked illegally outside. Police eventually had to use a special cannon and dynamite to gain entrance to the building, which was destroyed by fire in a successful attempt to destroy certain records and files that the ALF members apparently did not want the police to obtain. The bodies of nine members of the ALF, seven males and two females, were found in the rubble. Police have also had to deal with increasing sniping incidents in the surrounding neighborhood, as well as with rampaging bands of Black youths who have been attacking foot patrolmen from rooftops.

Now, as we had promised earlier, here is a tape of the telephone call the WORL newsroom received from the ALF headquarters during the height of the gun battle that has been declared the bloodiest in the annals of modern American law enforcement:

(*We hear the sound of a* WOMAN'S VOICE *amid the reports of gunfire and explosions, shouts and screams.*)

REVOLUTIONARY SISTER: …The revolutionary headquarters of the American Liberation Front are now under siege from the racist, fascist, reactionary army of the pig power structure. They are attacking us with everything but we are holding firm. Already, at least three pigs have been barbecued, with minimal losses to ourselves.

(*Explosion. Screams.* VOICE *more excited.*)

Now the pigs look like they usin' cannon, but we still holdin' on. The revolution is moving to a higher level. Right on! Death to the fascist dogs and the imperialist criminals who control them! Death to the enemies of the lumpenproletariat! Long live the revolution!!

(*More shots, screams, more explosions.*)

They throwin' everything at us, yet we will persevere because we must!...

(*Tape is abruptly cut. The* NEWSMAN *takes over.*)

RADIO NEWSMAN: That was the voice of one of the members of the American Liberation Front speaking to this office in the midst of the shoot-out with the Night Rangers that took the lives...

(M'BALIA *rises from the table and cuts off the radio.*)

M'BALIA: Yessir! The American Liberation Front stone took care of business.

KEUSI: (*Nonchalantly.*) Yeah.

M'BALIA: They really did the job, man. I bet the oppressors never expected to be met with such revolutionary fervor. Thirteen oppressors revolutionized to death.

KEUSI: At the cost of the lives of nine ALF warriors. Alla that death and gun play was unnecessary, if you can dig it.

M'BALIA: Unnecessary? Their deaths had meaning. They died in order that the revolution might carry on. In that respect, their deaths were necessary.

KEUSI: You know you got too much idealism. That's your problem. You gotta recognize that at this stage, the death of *any* revolutionary is needless. We haven't the strength to face the honky on a large scale, yet. We can't even keep pushers outa our neighborhood with any real success, so how can we run down a program of armed struggle against the beast? Hit-and-run tactics, at best, are all we can do. The ALF had an out and didn't use it.

M'BALIA: They had no out. They had to fight. They had no choice other than to fight and die like men, or surrender and be herded to the electric chair in shackles. Those brothers and sisters chose to commit revolutionary suicide and in doing so advanced the revolution even farther. There is no tragedy in their deaths; only glory.

KEUSI: Hey, baby, how you gonna talk about glorious death, when to get killed now is really not necessary?

M'BALIA: In our daily struggles against the oppressor, the possibility of death is always present, no matter what level the revolution is being waged on. We acknowledge death and do not fear it.

KEUSI: But the revolution is about life—I thought. Our first duties as revolutionaries is to live.

M'BALIA: Is it? The first duty of the true revolutionary is to kill the oppressor and destroy his works.

KEUSI: But don't that come when the revolutionaries have got strength? Until that time he got to live, and he can't do that practicing revolutionary suicide.

M'BALIA: (*Angry.*) And when the tables are turned against him, when every avenue is blocked, every alternative closed to him, what then must the revolutionary do?

(*Without waiting for answer.*)

He must fight! He must fight or die. He has no choice. When his back is to the wall, he can't die like a lamb waiting the slaughter. No, let him have his gun and his manhood.

KEUSI: (*Silent a moment.*) Yeah, okay, my sister. But I still think Geronimo was crazy to pursue a gun battle with the police. See, like, his back wasn't totally to the wall. What he did was cause his headquarters to get burned down, nine brothers and sisters to lose their lives, and for the revolution to suffer another bad day.

M'BALIA: How can you say that?

KEUSI: 'Cause from listening to the reports and from having known some brothers who belonged to that chapter of the ALF, I know that the gunfight wasn't necessary.

M'BALIA: Are you accusing him of being a traitor?

KEUSI: No. I'm accusin' him of piss-poor leadership.

M'BALIA: What the hell do you know about it?! Who are you to say something like that?

KEUSI: I can't say what I want?

M'BALIA: Not when you go around disparaging one of the baddest brothers walkin'. I think you should watch your mouth. Ahmed is right. One of these days you're gonna be stepped on.

KEUSI: I guess I'll have to worry about that when the time comes, 'cause when I see things I feel are goin' wrong I gotta speak out. I've seen some things in the past week that have got me wonderin' what's happenin'. Suddenly, you know, I'm like, questioning which way the revolution is going.

M'BALIA: You're just afraid of revolution. That's what it is. You're afraid of a real revolution.

KEUSI: Damn right, if people like Geronimo are gonna be leadin' it. All the revolutionaries I've seen ever since I came outa the indoctrination classes got a colossal death wish. We all bein' oriented toward death. Once you get hooked goin' that way, everything you do is geared toward destruction and finally you can't think positively or constructively.

M'BALIA: Oh, I can think positive, alright. The most positive thing I can think of is the death of the oppressor. Ahmed once said that we shall bathe in the oppressor's blood on the day of our victory.

KEUSI: Suppose I was to say that we could build the Black nation without even firing a shot, if we really wanted to do that?

M'BALIA: I'd call you an insufferable romantic fool and a threat to the revolutionary fervor we are trying to promote in the people.

KEUSI: Yeah, M'Balia, I can see why Antar has placed you with me. I'm sure gonna learn a lot from you.

M'BALIA: You need to. You lack all kinds of revolutionary zeal.

KEUSI: Baby, I'm a trained killer. I've seen shit that would have you vomitin' all over this place and I seen buddies of mine die right in my arms. So what the hell're you talkin' about? Zeal? What the hell is some goddamn zeal? Zeal don't mean shit when it comes down to it. What counts then is quick thinking, discipline, holdin' up under pressure, and common sense. Zeal will get you killed if you don't watch out.

M'BALIA: Your incorrect mouth may get *you* killed.

(M'BALIA *rises without further comment and begins moving about the apartment straightening up. Her movements are graceful and very feminine. This is brought about by the lapa she wears.* KEUSI *lights a cigarette and watches her awhile, a wry and gentle smile coming over his face.*)

KEUSI: Hey, baby, tell me somethin'. When's the last time you been treated like a woman.

M'BALIA: I don't know what you're talking about. I'm always treated like a woman.

KEUSI: Well, Antar said that you was to be my wife and do everything a man expects of a woman.

M'BALIA: Provided I'm in the mood. Now look, I told you about this once before. Don't be disrespectful.

KEUSI: I'm not being disrespectful. I'm being a man.

M'BALIA: Well, I don't think I want you to make love to me.

KEUSI: A fine-lookin' sister like you? I'm sure you must need *some* lovin' *some*time.

M'BALIA: I'm—a Black Terrorist. Sex isn't a thing with me any more.

(KEUSI *bursts into a great laugh.*)

Well, what's so funny?

KEUSI: (*Laughing.*) Yeah, okay, baby, we all must make sacrifices for the revolution.

(*Laughs harder.*)

M'BALIA: You stop laughing at me! There's nothing funny. It's the truth. A true revolutionary has no time for such emotions. I'm a Black Terrorist…

KEUSI: (*Interrupting.*) You're a woman…

M'BALIA: I'm an expert assassin…

KEUSI: You're supposed to get fucked and have babies. Let the men fight.

M'BALIA: That's not true. The Black Terrorist Women's Organization said that my main function was that of a revolutionary, not those mundane feminine things. I'm a free woman, not a whore.

KEUSI: Aw, woman, ain't nobody said you wasn't a revolutionary. Now, c'mere and shut up!!

(*Moves toward her.*)

M'BALIA: (*Backing away.*) Keep away from me.

(*She strikes a karate stance.*)

You keep away from me, you hear!

(KEUSI *moves on her, whereupon she tosses his behind on the floor.* KEUSI *looks up at her in angered bewilderment. He rises slowly and faces her. Gradually he begins to relax, then smiles. Eventually,* M'BALIA, *feeling she has made her point, lets her guard down. At that instant* KEUSI *smacks the shit outa her. She hits the ground hard on her behind. She fights back a few tears.* KEUSI *kneels beside her.*)

KEUSI: Awww, what's these? Revolutionary tears? I thought you was beyond such emotion.

(*Laughs, reaches into pocket, and wipes her tears away with a handkerchief.*)

You're a woman before anything else. When I get through with you, you'll never want to forget that. Now, come here and don't hand me nunna that "I'm a revolutionary" bullshit.

(*Pulls her close.*)

Hey, baby, you lookin' g-o-o-o-o-d.

(KEUSI *begins to undress her as the lights go down.*)

(*Lights up on* KEUSI *and* M'BALIA *lying together.*)

Hey, baby, I'm sorry I hit you.

M'BALIA: You could have broken my jaw.

KEUSI: Aw, the only thing hurt was your pride. I half pushed you, anyway. I'm sorry, though, honest.

(*She does not answer him.*)

Hey, baby, I really mean it.

(*Leans over and kisses* M'BALIA *long and hard.*)

See?

M'BALIA: Yes. I believe you, but…well, Keusi, you know this can't lead to anything. I can't get involved with you in any deep way because I'm an assassin and because of what I do. I won't always be able to see you. Let's end it, now. We had a good little time, but—

KEUSI: Uh-uh. We ain't endin' nothin'. I dug you the first time I laid eyes on you an' I ain't gonna lose you now.

M'BALIA: Keusi, my life belongs to the revolution. I live it and breathe it. Anything beyond that just isn't real for me. To become your woman, I'd have to leave the Female Assassins unit, and I could never do that. I've been with them for two and a half years; I've lived with them, and laughed and cried with them. They're my family, my sisters in the revolution. I just can't up and leave them.

KEUSI: Yes, you can.

M'BALIA: No. It's impossible.

(*Hoping to change the subject.*)

Hey, you'd better get some sleep. Tomorrow's the day you eliminate the oppressor.

KEUSI: (*Smiling.*) Sleep is somethin' I don't wanna do, right now.

(*Half whisper.*)

Now, c'mere.

(*He kisses* M'BALIA *as the lights go down.*)

Scene Five

Lights up. The next day—very late...evening. M'BALIA *worriedly paces the floor,* KEUSI *appears in the doorway. He carries a duffle bag with him, his appearance grim.* M'BALIA *stands in frozen expectation, watching him.* KEUSI *slowly nods his head. Excitedly,* M'BALIA *approaches him.*

M'BALIA: There's no doubt? He's dead?

KEUSI: (*Quietly.*) They should find his body in his driveway a coupla hours from now. Maybe sooner.

(M'BALIA *embraces him.* KEUSI *gently pushes her away. Reaches into his pocket and takes out a slip of paper and pencil. He writes a telephone number down.*)

Here, call this number. Let the phone ring three times. Then hang up. That'll signal success.

(M'BALIA *does as she is told.* KEUSI *moves into room and sits wearily. He removes his shoes and begins to unwind.* M'BALIA *finishes the telephone call, then approaches* KEUSI.)

M'BALIA: (*Looking at duffle bag with curiosity.*) How...how did you do it? I got worried when I looked into the room and saw you didn't take any of your weapons.

(*As she rummages thru the bag she comes up with the crossbow and takes it out of the bag.* KEUSI *sits quietly, not really paying any attention.* M'BALIA *eyes it, both repulsed and fascinated at the same time.*)

Keusi, did you use this?

KEUSI: (*Remembering every detail of the assassination.*) Yeah...it was simple.

(*Laughs sardonically, then becomes silent again. Noticing* M'BALIA *with the crossbow,* KEUSI *takes it from her and puts it back in duffle bag. Tired and drawn.*)

Yeah...so simple.

M'BALIA: Did anyone spot you?

KEUSI: No.

M'BALIA: But a crossbow? I don't understand.

KEUSI: Quick, silent, and very accurate.

M'BALIA: That's all you got to say?

KEUSI: What else is there to say?

M'BALIA: I suppose you're right. Um...are you hungry?

(KEUSI *looks at her, then looks away.*)

Is there…is there anything I can do?

(KEUSI *lies down.* M'BALIA *gets some oils, moves to him, and begins massaging* KEUSI*'s back.*)

KEUSI: Oh, baby…I'm tired. So goddamn tired.

M'BALIA: (*Massaging.*) This will help you relax.

KEUSI: He looked right at me…right at me…I saw him get out of his car. I took aim an' I fired. The arrow hit him in the back of the neck. He turned around and he had this weird, twisted, and frightened look on his face. He saw me…he reached out, and started staggering toward me, bleedin' and coughin' blood…Then he fell dead. But his eyes was open, lookin' right at me.…Right at me.

(*With suddenness* KEUSI *takes* M'BALIA *in his arms.*)

Baby…baby…baby. Lemme just hold you.

(*Holds her tight.*)

God, it's so good to be alive. Living, breathing, loving. Never aware it can end on a hummer in a minute. Baby, lemme just hold you an' be glad I'm alive…

(*They embrace and kiss as lights go down.*)

Scene Six

The headquarters of the Black Terrorists. ANTAR, AHMED, *and* GERONIMO *are seated together. Laid out before them is what appears to be a large diagram. Also, an assortment of maps are strewn about.*

GERONIMO: There, that's it. Whatchall think? We can plant bombs under the sewers

(*Pointing to diagram.*)

along here. And here. You see? When they blow, those streets will be rendered useless. Also, looka here.

(*Reaches for another diagram.*)

This one's of the police station itself and shows that we can plant another bomb here and disrupt their whole communications thing. We can drop charges in other places. Look, me, Juney-bugs, Ramon, and Victor went over these plans backwards and forwards, in and out, day and night.

ANTAR: I don't know, Geronimo. I'm hesitant to try something like that.

GERONIMO: Me and my three chiefs went over this thing for months, man. It can work. Why you against it?

ANTAR: It's risky, man. It doesn't sound all that foolproof. I'm not all that sure it can work.

GERONIMO: You tryin' to say somethin'?

ANTAR: No, Geronimo—

GERONIMO: Don't be disparaging the memory of those three young brothers. They had good minds, man. They don't put together no shoddy shit.

ANTAR: I'm well aware of that. But I still feel that it's too risky. How do we know that the oppressors won't be guarding against just such a maneuver?

GERONIMO: (*Annoyed.*) The whole goddamn revolution is risky, Antar. Any revolutionary move you make involves the element of risk. What the hell you rappin' about?

AHMED: (*To* ANTAR.) I think it's a good idea, Antar. Psychologically, it'll blow the Man's mind.

ANTAR: I don't know. That kind of terrorism involves high risk. We've usually operated against lesser targets and much closer to home. I think more planning is needed. We have to look into every angle.

GERONIMO: What's there to look at? We have a target, we destroy it. No bullshit, no questions; destroy the target. Hey, man, you brother terrorists or not?

ANTAR: (*Calmly.*) We're terrorists.

GERONIMO: Then what the fuck's the problem?

ANTAR: That kind of guerrilla tactic is the problem. It may be beyond our particular training. I think we should be more cautious.

GERONIMO: Motherfuck, caution!!

(AHMED *looks angrily at* GERONIMO, *but* ANTAR *restrains him with a silent gesture.*)

Hey, man, look! All you do is get in the goddamn sewers, crawl through 'em, plant the bombs, and split. The men be underground. Who the fuck's gonna spot them?!

ANTAR: (*Calmly.*) Listen. Your idea is a good one. But I'm only trying to say that the nature of the venture requires more careful planning. Yes, I could give you some of my men, but they will run the risk of being detected in an action against a target all the way across town from the nearest Black neighborhood. If they are discovered, they can be trapped in those sewers and slaughtered like animals. All you've done is show me some diagrams, blueprints. Juney-bugs was the only one of the three of you who had ever been in that jail before, and that was only for a brief stay. He couldn't have possibly gotten the most precise information needed for an operation of this sort. Add to that the possibility of those diagrams y'all stole being old as anything and we could really have problems. Suppose the oppressors have renovated those buildings? We wouldn't even know it. And tell me, have you been in those sewers out there? Have you studied the logistics of getting men—*Black* men and bombs undetected into a white neighborhood that is already cringing in fear because of our activities? You know as well as I do that that area is heavily patrolled by the police. Have you taken that into account. My brother—

GERONIMO: (*Hurt; interrupting.*) Man, why you trying to stop this plan?

ANTAR: I'm not trying to stop the plan. I actually tend to agree with Ahmed. It would be a major psychological blow to the oppressor. But I want a more carefully laid out plan. I'd like to see all my people get back safely.

GERONIMO: Yeah, well, okay, Mkuu Antar. But you should recognize the inevitability of revolutionary death.

ANTAR: I do. But I don't want all my revolutionaries dying at once.

AHMED: I like the idea, Antar. If it's the implementation of it that worries you then I'd like to volunteer to work with Geronimo on a new plan that will meet with your approval.

(*To* GERONIMO.)

Provided that's all right with you, brother.

GERONIMO: I'd be very proud, Ahmed. I've always had the highest respect for you. So did Victor, Ramon, and Juney-bugs.

(*Just then, sounds of squeals of delight, shouts and pandemonium are heard. A* BROTHER *enters with a wide smile on his face. He snaps smartly to attention, salutes.*)

BROTHER: Antar! I am pleased to report to you that Ndugu Keusi Kifo has eliminated Commissioner Savage. The brother has offed the pig!! Keusi Kifo has offed the pig!!

AHMED: Wooooeeeeeee!!!

(*Joyous laughing.*)

GERONIMO: (*At first, unbelieving.*) The motherfucker's dead?! He's dead?!
(*The* BROTHER *nods.*)
AAAAIIIIEEEE!!!! He's dead! The beast is dead! His blood shall feed the revolution!!! Victor, Ramon, Juney-bugs! The motherfucker is dead! AAAIIIIEEEEE!!!!

ANTAR: (*As others enter; amid the shouts.*) This is the greatest moment in our brief history. The most brutal of all oppressors outside the federal government has been successfully eliminated. His death has opened the floodgates. The very foundations on which the oppressive law and order machine of this country is built is now quaking. But we can't stop here. The revolution must continue. More oppressors must die! There must be more victories! More life! More life for our parents, our brothers and sisters. More life for generations of Black people to come. Death to the oppressors! We shall be victorious.

(*Cheers.*)

AHMED: We are the Black Terrorists, sworn to the liberation of our people!

ALL: May we never lose sight of our duty!

AHMED: We seek the death of those who oppress us!

ALL: May our vengeance be as swift as lightning! AAAAIIIIEEEE!!!

(*More celebration. After awhile,* KEUSI *and* M'BALIA *enter amid cheers and congratulatory remarks. He moves to* ANTAR, *salutes him, and is embraced by* ANTAR, AHMED, *and* GERONIMO. M'BALIA *receives the same greeting, then is whisked off by the women. Cheering continues as lights dim to denote passage of time. Lights up on the aftermath of the celebration. Enter a* SISTER *with refreshments and places them before* KEUSI, AHMED, M'BALIA, ANTAR, *and* GERONIMO, *who are seated in that order. The* SISTER *exits.*)

ANTAR: A job well done, Ndugu Keusi. Zaidi ya asante.

(KEUSI *smiles.*)

But we gathered here not only to express our thanks. We have another assignment for you.

KEUSI: (*Surprised.*) Wow, I just…

ANTAR: We know, but this man is even more dangerous than Savage.

GERONIMO: (*Excited; interrupting.*) Whatchu use on the beast, man?

KEUSI: A crossbow.

GERONIMO: (*Laughing.*) Oh, wow! A crossbow? Check the cat out for gettin' into some Robin Hood.

(*All laugh except for* KEUSI.)

KEUSI: (*As if trying to provoke something.*) That's historically incorrect, Ndugu Geronimo.

GERONIMO: Huh?

KEUSI: I said you're wrong. Your reference is historically incorrect. The crossbow came after Robin Hood.

GERONIMO: Oh, I didn't know.

KEUSI: A lotta things you don't know, Geronimo.

(*The two men stare at each other.* M'BALIA *attempts to intercede.*)

M'BALIA: Antar, any new information on Radcliffe?

KEUSI: That's my new target?

(M'BALIA *nods and* KEUSI's *face grows solemn. He appears worried.*)

ANTAR: Nothing beyond the information you supplied us with some time ago, M'Balia.

AHMED: Keusi, when you gonna get started on Radcliffe? That nigger's gotta go.

KEUSI: (*Quietly.*) I guess I'll start first thing tomorrow. Anything special about him I oughta know?

M'BALIA: Nothing really. His son is dead, and his wife died of a heart attack years ago.

KEUSI: What happen, his son get killed in the Nam, or something?

GERONIMO: Hell no, he died fighting the enemy right here in the mother country.

M'BALIA: He died in a raid on a Panther headquarters two years ago. He was the only Panther to die. To show you what a lackey Radcliffe is, he refused to let any Panthers attend the funeral and swore to destroy Black militants because he said they had destroyed his son.

KEUSI: He must have loved his son a lot to be feelin' like that.

M'BALIA: That's beside the point. Radcliffe is an oppressor. He must die.

KEUSI: No doubt. But actually, to tell you the truth, I hate to be the one to set the precedent for killing our own people. Fratricide oughta always be avoided 'cause it's the one kinda killin' that always gets outa hand.

Look at Biafra and Nigeria. The death is appalling. Ain't there no other way to handle this misguided cat?

GERONIMO: No. He dies. Don't try to rationalize a way for this ass-licking scab to live. Off him!!

M'BALIA: He has sworn to destroy us, Keusi. It's almost an obsession with him. You heard him on that news broadcast when he turned three of our brothers in to the oppressors.

(*Lights go out. Stage black. Spot picks up on* CHAUNCEY RADCLIFFE *standing on a remote part of the stage.*)

RADCLIFFE: It's time the decent, law-abiding Negro citizens of this country stood up and shouted "Enough!" It's time for us to bring to an end this lunacy, this—this madness being perpetrated on our society today. We are fed up with being identified with these young fools. They are trying to tear down the greatest country in the world. America may have her faults, but there is no place on earth where the Negro has it this good. We're better off today than at any time in our history. We go to better schools, we have better jobs—better housing. Our middle class is growing stronger every day. What right do these disgruntled young thugs—for that's just what they are—thugs—what right have they to trample upon the rights and land for which so many Americans, colored and white, have died. These young disgruntles—spoiled brats and hooligans—are the creation of the television age. The sensationalist news media ignore the legitimate Negro leaders who are making positive contributions to Negro progress. They ignore those of us in my generation who've toiled for years, battling against mindless white racists on the one hand and Black fanatics on the other. Quiet but steady progress can't fit into the late news, so the media cover the misinformed Black power boys. Why? Because they make sensational news copy.

Well, I tell you, such madness has to stop. The responsible Negro element, the only true voice of the Negro since he first set foot on these shores; the responsible Negro element, which has survived the likes of Paul Cuffe, David Walker, Martin Delaney, Garvey, and the brilliant but misguided Malcolm X, now declares war on these young thugs. We will assist all local, state, and federal authorities in whatever way we can, in bringing to justice these criminals. They terrorize Negro communities and drive away our white friends who have suffered many humiliations while still standing at our sides. The three boys I have turned in today were only the beginning. By working with my good friend, Commissioner Charles Savage, I solemnly swear to you that all of the revolutionaries, Black or white, Jew or Gentile, will be brought to justice.

(*Lights down. Lights up on the headquarters.*)

KEUSI: Yeah, sister. I guess you're right.

GERONIMO: When the French people staged the French Revolution, a lotta French heads rolled. When the Anarchists tried to rip off Paris in the 1850s, more Frenchmen died. When the Bolsheviks changed the course of world history in Russia, they offed thousands of fellow Russians, and so on down the line, brother. When Mao took China, the blood of fellow Chinamen flowed like a mighty river. Before we can move on the enemy without, we gotta move on the enemy within. Killing the arch-traitor Radcliffe is necessary.

KEUSI: With you killing is always necessary.

AHMED: Look, man, we don't like the idea any more than you do, but the nigger's crimes can't be ignored. He cursed the name of the Panthers and assisted in the destruction of their headquarters, he turned in three of our men, and he drove his only daughter from his household when she refused to support his schemes. This lap dog seeks our deaths, man. What else we supposed to do?

M'BALIA: The faggot lackey is a scar on the face of the Black community. He must die.

GERONIMO: A pig is a pig is a pig, be he Black or white. When he oinks, his breath still stinks.

ANTAR: Ndugu Keusi, you must recognize that we have no other choice. To allow him to live is to invite our own deaths. Sooner or later the police may succeed in making one of those three prisoners talk and give away the location of this headquarters. A lot of blood's gonna flow. We have sworn it. And all of that will come about because of this man's treachery. Radcliffe is an oppressor—with the oppressor's values, the oppressor's way of life—

GERONIMO: (*Interrupting.*) And with the oppressor's dick up his ass.

(*All laugh except* KEUSI.)

M'BALIA: When you were in the army, Keusi, wasn't it true that a man who deserted in the face of the enemy was shot?

(KEUSI *nods.*)

Well, Radcliffe has not only deserted, he has *defected*. We are at war with the beast. Don't the rules count the same here?

KEUSI: Okay, okay, okay. Radcliffe will be taken care of. But I'm doin' it with reservations. Radcliffe looks and sounds like the kind of dude who's very active in the community. Is that true?

AHMED: Ndio. More or less.

KEUSI: So that means that he's into things like sending little kids to camp in the summer and young people to college in the fall. I'll betcha he's a member of a fraternity and he's probably a deacon in his church.

M'BALIA: Yeah, the society page of *Jet* magazine. That's him.

KEUSI: That means he's probably a hero in some segments of the Black community. A lotta Black mothers are grateful to him for helping to get their sons straightened out. You got any ideas of what that means to a lotta mothers? Working in the church automatically puts him in good with the older folks.

GERONIMO: So what?

KEUSI: So, even though he acts like a Tom to us, he could be regarded as a kind of hero to many of our people.

GERONIMO: Aw, bullshit. Radcliffe's an oppressor. He's got to go. And maybe those people who believe in him will have to go, too.

AHMED: When the target is eliminated, the people will understand.

KEUSI: I'm not so sure. Once you get a rep for killing your own people, popular support starts to dwindle.

GERONIMO: It depends on what Black people you kill, an' if the nigger is an oppressor, that's his ass.

KEUSI: Who are we to decide what Black people will live and what Black people will die? We got no mandate from the people.

GERONIMO: Fuck a mandate. We the vanguard of the righteous revolution. We don't need a mandate.

KEUSI: Y'all still don't understand.

M'BALIA: Chauncey Radcliffe is an oppressor. He oppresses the Black community and he oppresses the revolution.

AHMED: Hey, man, don't worry. The people will understand.

GERONIMO: It's not the revolutionary's job to take prisoners and rehabilitate. It's the revolutionary's job to eliminate.

AHMED: The people will understand.

KEUSI: The people will only understand that we are now killin' Black people. 'Cause, see, if we kill Radcliffe then we gonna haveta eventually do away with preachers 'cause a lotta them shuckin' and jivin', too. But if we do 'way with preachers we gonna haveta off teachers 'cause they teachin' in the oppressor's schools, an' if we off teachers we gonna haveta start on Black government officials 'cause they work in the oppressor's government administration an' they ain't gonna go for teachers getting' offed. We kill city and government officials, then we gonna haveta start on our families next 'cause we all got people who're teachers, preachers, civil servants an' alla that. See what I'm gettin' at? Chauncey Radcliffe is more than just one man. He's a whole heap of people. His death is gonna open up a whole floodgate of death and destruction for Black people at the hands of other Black people. Us.

M'BALIA: When we became revolutionaries we recognized the probabilities of having to kill our own people. Even members of our own families. That's why we accepted the credo of the revolutionary which states in part that the revolutionary can have no family outside his "family" of other revolutionaries.

AHMED: Don't forget, man. Seven Panthers are dead in this city, and three Black Terrorists are rotting in pig pens because of this one man.

GERONIMO: He's not a man. He's an oppressor. A beast. A no-thing, a non-man. His death will be of little consequence.

AHMED: His blood's gonna feed the revolution.

ANTAR: Ndugu Keusi, there is no way this man can be allowed to live. Your considerations are wise ones, but these are revolutionary times. We have to take into account the survival of the revolution. I hate to say it, but there are times when the survival of the revolution must come before the desires of the people.

GERONIMO: That's right, Keusi. The people don't always know what they want.

KEUSI: But the people *are* the revolution.

AHMED: Precisely, my brother. We articulate the desires of the people.

KEUSI: But how are we gonna do that if as revolutionaries we live only among ourselves. How we know what the people want if we don't deal with their wishes?

ANTAR: We always deal with the wishes of the people. The people wished the oppressor Savage dead and we fulfilled that wish. Deep down they want Radcliffe dead. We will fulfill that wish, too.

KEUSI: But suppose the people don't want a revolution? Suppose they ain't really ready?

AHMED: That's what we mean when we say that the people don't always know what's good for them.

KEUSI: But if we represent the people, we gotta always be responsible to them. Revolutionaries are responsible to the people. If they say stop, we have to stop. We should never try to operate independent from the people. I don't know, man, but somewhere along the line I think we got a fucked-up set of values.

ANTAR: We have a correct value system, Ndugu Keusi. You shouldn't get into disparaging the revolution. Such a habit is counterrevolutionary.

AHMED: It's the same thing I was tellin' you about before, Antar. His personality and his makeup, man. Hey, Keusi, man, you gotta overcome that. You a good killer an' you got the makin's of a good revolutionary. But watch it, man. Your shit's raggedy.

KEUSI: (*Piqued.*) Yeah, yeah, yeah. Yeah, man, okay.

GERONIMO: You should recognize that the revolutionary is responsible to the people only as long as they move forward to a revolutionary position. When the people falter the revolutionary must move on ahead as a righteous vanguard, smoothing the path for the people, so that when they catch up to the revolutionary in consciousness they will see what a glorious thing it is for a revolution to put into high gear. You gotta recognize that, my brother.

KEUSI: Bullshit. A revolutionary vanguard is impossible in this country 'cause without the people the revolution is lost. Can't no revolution be successfully carried out without the support of the people. If the people don't want a revolution there ain't gonna be none. And when you get into offin' Black people as though you were some omnipotent agents from heaven or someplace then, hey, man, you sealin' your own doom. "The saviors of the people must not become their tormentors as well."

GERONIMO: (*Very angry.*) We ain't no tormentors!! Goddamnit, we righteous revolutionaries!!! Just assassins!! Black Terrorists! We *are* the revolutionary vanguard. An' we gonna keep on vanguardin' 'cause too many brothers and sisters have died to get us to this point. We goin' forward all the time!! The oppressors will die! Alla them!! 'Cause it's only right and just that they do so!! And any deaf, dumb, blind, incorrect nigger that gets in our way, gets his ass *blown* away. You understand?! His blood flows! Motherfuck the nigger! He dies!!

KEUSI: Is that all you got to offer the people, man? Death? Black people been dyin' in the most vicious manners imaginable for the past four hundred years. Hey, man, all you got to offer people who seen too much death is more death? Why we gotta fight a revolution with a value system directed toward death? Why not wage a revolution directed toward life? Huh?

AHMED: Oh, will you listen to this romantic, idealistic motherfucker?

KEUSI: I mean it. Why y'all playin' up to death alla time? Don't nunna y'all wanna live?

GERONIMO: That ain't got nothin' to do with it! If we gotta live under the yoke of oppression then we choose death. At least in death we can have some measure of freedom!!

AHMED: If it's gonna take our deaths to secure life for Black people, then we say to our oppressors, "Take our lives, if you can!"

ANTAR: We don't glorify death. We just acknowledge its inevitability. To die for the revolution is the greatest thing in life.

KEUSI: To live for the revolution is even greater. To be alive to fight the next—

GERONIMO: Aw, nigger, you just scared of death!

ANTAR: (*Comfortingly.*) To be afraid of death is nothing to be ashamed of, Keusi. It's a fear we must all overcome.

KEUSI: I ain't afraid of death. I've risked my life countless times. It's the glorifying' of death I'm afraid of.

AHMED: To be unafraid of death is not to glorify it!

KEUSI: Aw, why the hell don't you niggers stop sloganeering an' come down to earth. Y'all runnin' around here talkin' about you ain't afraid to die, waitin' for a chance to die to show the world that you meant what you said. Hell, if I'm scared of death, then y'all just as scared of life.

GERONIMO: Life at the price of slavery is unacceptable! Like the motherfucker said, "Give me liberty or give me death."

KEUSI: Fucked-up references and fucked-up values.

GERONIMO: Ramon, Victor, and Juney-bugs was real revolutionaries. Brave cats who met their moment in true revolutionary fashion. They weren't cowards. Not like you. They died valiantly.

KEUSI: They died needlessly.

(*Shocked gasps from others.* GERONIMO *starts for* KEUSI.)

GERONIMO: (*Being restrained by others.*) You spittin' on they name?! You punk!! You punk motherfucker!!

KEUSI: I don't care what you call me. The facts are there for you to deal with. They died from an overdose of revolutionary fervor.

ANTAR: Don't be impudent!!

(M'BALIA *bows her head in silence from this point on. She seems hurt and dismayed. After a while she should move from the group to an area by herself near the door.*)

KEUSI: I'm not. I'm tellin' the truth. Hey, man, I'm sayin' that if cool heads had been in charge not a single member of the ALF would have died.

GERONIMO: The enemy was tryin' to kill us. We wasn't gonna cringe in front of them. Not in front of the beast!!! We wasn't about to give them that satisfaction.

KEUSI: You had an out, man, an' either you couldn't or you wouldn't use it. You let revolutionary zeal get in the way of effective, clear thinking and blew, man.

GERONIMO: What the hell you tryin' to say? We was attacked by the pigs. We had no choice *but* to fight.

KEUSI: You had a choice, man. You had the option to postpone that battle an' you refused.

GERONIMO: You sayin' we shoulda surrendered?! Huh?! Is that what you think we shoulda done?! Man, you must be crazy. We ain't scared of no pigs! You must be outa your mind!

KEUSI: You had a situation in which 'cause of the hour of the raid your station was undermanned. In fact, from everything I've learned about it, man, there was more sisters than brothers in the headquarters at the time. You were outarmed and outnumbered from jump street. You were in charge of the most crucial chapter of the ALF in the country because of the alliance you made with the Black Terrorists. Also, because you had built your headquarters into a fort valuable records from the chapters all over the country were stored there. Even though you had this fort everybody knew that no matter how strong the damn thing was history showed that when the Man wants to take it, he can. You can hold him off maybe six minutes, maybe six hours, maybe even six days, but eventually the Devil can mount a successful assault. Geronimo, you knew that, and that's why the out was built. An' you didn't use it, man.

GERONIMO: Man, I didn't have no out! We was attacked. We recognized that we had to deal with the Night Rangers on the spot. We knew we might die but we knew that even in death we would set a revolutionary example.

AHMED: They gave impetus to the revolution. Ndugu Keusi, you got no right to jump on Geronimo like this.

KEUSI: Aw, man, will y'all listen to reason?! Man, everything, all the records, weapons, and personnel were lost in that battle, when the truth of the matter is that it didn't even have to happen.

GERONIMO: It had to happen! The moment dictated it!

KEUSI: You had an out, man, and because you didn't use it, the whole movement has been set back.

GERONIMO: What "out"? Whatchu keep talkin' about? Our backs was to the wall.

KEUSI: Man, don't you see? I'm talkin' about the escape tunnel.

GERONIMO: We used it, dunce! How you think me and the survivors escaped?

KEUSI: Why didn't you use it from the git?

GERONIMO: Because we had to fight! We was under attack!

KEUSI: But you was outnumbered and outarmed. You had valuable records and documents. To engage in such a battle woulda been useless. You faced losing your men, your records and possibly capture. Hey, man, that escape tunnel was your out.

GERONIMO: We was supposed to run from some cowardly oppressors, is that it? You expect us to run like those five white boys did?

KEUSI: I expected you, as the leader, to have kept a cool head and to have looked past the emotionalism of the moment. You dig?

GERONIMO: I ain't a coward, man, an' neither was the brothers and sisters who was with me. We weren't gonna run like those white boys did.

KEUSI: In they fear, those crackers showed you just what you shoulda done.

Ahmed: (*Angry.*) You takin' the side of white boys against your brother?!

Keusi: No, man. They were even more wrong. In fact, we all know they shouldn't even have been there, in the first place. They coulda created panic and confusion runnin' like they did. But they got away, man. They alive walkin' around, totally useless to the revolution, while real revolutionaries are dead because their leader wasn't able to see the need to order an orderly retreat in the face of superior firepower.

Geronimo: Meaning what?

Keusi: Meaning you a piss-poor leader. You was so eager to fight the Man that you ignored the safety of your warriors and overlooked the need to protect those files.

Geronimo: Goddamnit, we was under attack by half an army. How you expect me to think of everything at once?

Keusi: 'Cause you was the leader. Your first duty was to the safety of your warriors and to keep those records and files from being lost. You gotta think of all the contingencies, man.

Geronimo: Look, motherfucker, I AM a leader, and a damn good one.

Keusi: You jeopardized a whole movement when you did what you did. Revolutionary zeal got its place, man, but it's outa place in a situation like the one you was in.

Geronimo: I'm a revolutionary. My job is to kill the enemy, foment revolution among the people, and lay my life on the line if necessary.

Keusi: You not a revolutionary. You just an angry nigger with a gun. You filled your head fulla a whole lotta slogans and you followin' an ideal that somebody lifted from the fucked-up minds of some nihilistic white boys who lived a hundred years ago.

Geronimo: Keep it up an' I'm gonna bust a cap in your ass.

Keusi: You had ample warnin' when those white boys did their thing. All you had to do was put the sisters in motion, carryin' the files out through the tunnel while the brothers fired to keep the police at bay. Then when the cops made their big push, y'all coulda gone underground, anything you wanted. Alla y'all woulda been alive to be *living* revolutionary examples, continuing to fight, instead of martyrs inspiring young impressionable kids to copy your suicidal deeds.

Geronimo: You sayin' we shoulda run?! You sayin' we shoulda imitated those cowardly white boys?!

KEUSI: Man, ain't you listened to nothin' I said? I'm only runnin' down to you what the V.C. did to us every day. This is how Frelimo is kickin' the Portuguese outa Africa. Hey, man, I ain't sayin' y'all gotta be cowards. I'm sayin' to calm down and use your heads.

GERONIMO: (*Still ignoring* KEUSI.) I'll die before I run!!

ANTAR: Hindsight is always easy, Ndugu Keusi. The brother described the situation to us himself. We too questioned his tactics, but he correctly, we felt, pointed out to us that there is little time to take all that you said into account.

KEUSI: It don't take no time to burn some files and split. Geronimo allowed all this revolutionary zeal to get him all jammed up. The nigger got the most colossal death wish I ever seen. So does the whole goddamn revolution. We walkin' around practically worshippin' death. We so eager to die that we forgot how to live. The revolution gonna fail if we keep this up.

GERONIMO: Bullshit! The revolution can't fail. We've seized the moment. Time is on our side. We can't fail!!!! The French Revolution, the Anarchists, the Bolsheviks—ain't nunna them gonna have nothin' on us!!

KEUSI: You should realize, Ndugu Geronimo, that ultimately the French Revolution has failed 'cause after all those people got their heads cut off, after the motherfuckin' Reign of Terror, after eight republics, France is still fucked up. If you gonna use the Anarchists as a reference, then study they *whole* history; didn't a single one of those cats survive the Battle of Paris in the 1850s. The French cops and the citizenry killed them by the hundreds down to the last man and stacked their bodies like logs in the streets, and the fuckin' Bolsheviks unleashed Stalin on the world. See what I mean about references! It don't seem right to me that the crazy ideology of some sick Europeans should be passed off as the revolutionary ideology of Black people. We got to offer our people life, y'all. Not more death.

AHMED: But we're talking about constructive death!!

(*Pause. All look at* AHMED.)

KEUSI: We are preparing ourselves to fight on the basis of a foreign ideology, brothers. We usin' the politics of the pig. And if we fight on that level then that fight's gonna be a futile, royal ass-kickin' with millions of our people dead, locked away in prisons or run out the country. I mean, if we gonna achieve some kinda change in this motherfucker we gonna haveta do it without usin' the politics of the pig. We got to use all the economic, political, and military know-how we got, but we gotta learn to use it wisely and cunningly. We got to wage our fight on a new level of thought and action. You dig? We gonna haveta run a master game down on this beast. Otherwise, Black people are gonna keep on getting' wasted on bullshit hummers. We stay on this path an' we gonna fail our people.

AHMED: He's lying!!

GERONIMO: (*Drawing a gun; angry as hell.*) Motherfucker, you standin' in the way of the revolution!!

(*Just as he is about to fire,* ANTAR *hits his arm and the gun misfires.* M'BALIA *screams.* ANTAR *and* AHMED *restrain* GERONIMO, *who breaks down and cries.*)

He's a traitor! Kill him! That nigger's blockin' the revolution! He's downin' everything we stand for. The motherfucker's destroyin' our beliefs!!

(*Two* TERRORISTS *rush in, guns drawn.*)

ANTAR: (To the two TERRORISTS.) Help this brother to his quarters.

(*The two* TERRORISTS *help* GERONIMO *out.*)

Ndugu Keusi Kifo, I will admit that some of what you say may have a ring of truth, but I cannot and I will not condone your conduct. You have behaved in a manner that, at best, can only be described as counterrevolutionary. You are a totally undisciplined individual and I, for one, found your little act here disgraceful. For all of your supposed knowledge you still have yet to learn that it is far wiser to be constructive in your criticism rather than insulting, arrogant, and vicious. Your powers of persuasion are virtually nil. I think you're one colossal ass. In view of your attitude, I cannot trust you to carry out your mission against your other target. I'm relieving you of your responsibility to that mission. I am also suspending you from all other revolutionary activities except attendance at our indoctrination classes. I should have listened to Ahmed when he first told me of your maladjustment. You are dangerous. Despite his eccentricities, Geronimo is a very capable revolutionary leader. Your attack on him was excessive, biased, and unforgivable. I only hope these indoctrination classes will help you. If not, I will expel you from this revolutionary cadre. You're dismissed, Kifo.

(KEUSI *starts out. He stops near* M'BALIA *who is by the door. They look at each other but say nothing. She turns from him and he exits.*)

AHMED: You should have let Geronimo kill him, Antar.

(M'BALIA *buries her face in her hands. Lights go down.*)

Scene Seven

Back at the apartment, KEUSI *is seen packing a knapsack. After a while,* M'BALIA *enters. She watches him a moment, then moves toward him.*

KEUSI: (*Noticing her.*) Hey, how ya doin'?

M'BALIA: Alright.

KEUSI: You come to jump in my ass, too?

M'BALIA: No.

KEUSI: Uh-huh. I'll tell you one thing. I was really surprised by them. I didn't think they were so reactionary.

M'BALIA: I didn't think you were so negative.

KEUSI: But I wasn't negative.

M'BALIA: Yes you were, Keusi. You tried to destroy Geronimo in front of the other men.

KEUSI: I tried to correct him.

M'BALIA: Insulting him and trying to undermine him is no way to get him to see your point of view.

KEUSI: I'm sorry, baby, but I got no patience with overzealous motherfuckers. I seen too much of that in the army an' I seen it get a lotta people wasted. Y'all act like the revolution is just one great big romantic gang war. It's serious business—

M'BALIA: (Interrupting.) Don't lecture me. I know what revolution is, and I know what death is, too.

KEUSI: Well, if you know what it's all about, then why you puttin' me down for comin' down on Geronimo?

M'BALIA: Oh, I don't know. I didn't feel you had to be as malicious as you were, but, Keusi, Ahmed wants you dead. He said as much to Antar after you left.

KEUSI: Fuck that nigger. Shit, it doesn't matter anyway. I'm gettin' out. I've had it. I would have thought that at least Antar would have seen where I was comin' from, but he's let the revolution blind him, too.

M'BALIA: You're going to run?

KEUSI: I'm not running. I don't believe in the Black Terrorists any more. So it's just better that I split. I'll never sit in any indoctrination and listen to revolutionary bullshit that came from the minds of crazy-ass Europeans.

M'BALIA: What will you do?

KEUSI: Keep on fighting. I don't know. I heard about these brothers who are into some new concepts and ideas. Maybe I'll join them.

M'BALIA: Can we really be that wrong?

KEUSI: Baby, times change. The whole world is different. You got to be flexible. An' the Black Terrorists just ain't flexible. They so dogmatic an' shit.

M'BALIA: I don't understand you. If you feel this way, why did you join us in the first place?

KEUSI: I don't know. Maybe then I was only beginning to see things. After meeting Geronimo and after listening to Antar take my ass over the coals an' shit, I began to realize that it was time for me to split.

M'BALIA: What if those other brothers don't meet with your approval? Will you leave them, too?

KEUSI: If they bullshittin', yeah, I'll leave them.

M'BALIA: Then, I guess you'll always be on the outside, Keusi. It just don't look like you can ever really find anything to believe in. As soon as something goes wrong for you, you leave. If what you say about us is true, don't you even think that maybe you should stay here and try to straighten things out?

KEUSI: With Ahmed and Geronimo both ready to kill me? You kiddin'? Naw, I'm splittin'. Maybe I'll just go into the Black community and educate the kids as to what I have learned in the world. Maybe that's the only thing I can do. But I can't stay here. Not another minute longer.

M'BALIA: Oh.

(*Pause.*)

Well, good-by.

KEUSI: M'Balia, I want you to come with me.

M'BALIA: No. You're asking me to be a traitor.

KEUSI: Please?

(*Moves to her.*)

M'BALIA: I can't. The revolution—

KEUSI: You can still fight the revolution, but as the mother of my children.

M'BALIA: (*As KEUSI takes her into his arms.*) I can't. Keusi, please, I'm an assassin. I've dedicated my life to what I do. Keusi, please don't. Please.

Keusi: M'Balia, baby, baby, baby…please.

(*He kisses her.* M'Balia *starts to melt, but gains control and pushes* Keusi *away from her.*)

M'Balia: I can't go with you, Keusi. Not now, not ever. I swore my life to the organization. I won't leave them.

Keusi: M'Balia, I love you. I want you with me.

M'Balia: No. My life is with my brothers and sisters. Anything beyond that is not real for me.

Keusi: Not even me.

M'Balia: Not even you. You don't seem to understand, Keusi. I told you before that the best you could ever be was my lover. I meant that. I could never let you get into my heart. I never have.

Keusi: I'm not leaving here without you.

M'Balia: And I'm not going anywhere with you.

Keusi: Then you don't know me very well.

M'Balia: I know you well enough. If you're going to, run, but don't expect me to run with you. I'll never run from the revolution.

Keusi: (*Exasperated.*) Goddamn!! Will you listen. Look, I'm not runnin' from the revolution. I'm runnin' from suicidal niggers who ain't got no idea of what they sayin' and doin'. Not really.

M'Balia: We know what we're doing.

Keusi: Is that so? When the revolution really begins and homes and neighborhoods get burned down, and blood really flows in the streets, and we face the full-scale cracker retaliation, you'll see what I was talkin' about. You'll see how far blind revolutionary zeal will get Black people living in white America.

M'Balia: You're a defeatist.

Keusi: I'm just tryin' to get y'all to see some truths, that's all.

M'Balia: The revolution will be victorious no matter what you say, Keusi.

Keusi: All we got is some semi-automatics, some carbines, some pistols, assorted rifles, knives, and a whole lotta revolutionary zeal. That little bit of near *nothing* against the baddest, most vicious war machine in the world. We have no means of stopping a police car, much less a tank. It took the local cops only twenty minutes to run Geronimo outa his headquarters. How long you think it's gonna take the U.S. government to TCB in a Black neighborhood. All the zeal in the world ain't gonna help us unless we learn to get our shit truly together.

M'BALIA: For every one of us who falls it will cost them ten oppressors.

KEUSI: So, it's gonna be that? With only forty million Black people in this country against at least one hundred million crackers we supposed to fight a fuckin' war of attrition. This ain't Asia, baby. We ain't got an endless supply of manpower.

M'BALIA: We can fight urban guerrilla warfare. *The Battle of Algiers* demonstrated how it could be done.

KEUSI: This is America, not Algiers. See what I mean about references? M'Balia, get it into your head that the revolution in America is gonna be the most unique in history. We can't imitate nobody. Not the Viet Cong, or Frelimo or even the Chinese Eighth Route Army. We got to make up a whole new revolution, 'cause unlike other revolutions we in a minority, and a highly visible one at that. All the beast gotta do is cage us in, surround us, and exterminate us, or, if he chooses, activate the McCarran Act.

M'BALIA: But we know the ghettos. They don't. We can hit and run through alleys an' all kinds of things. We could fight guerrilla war in the streets for months before the oppressor could do any real damage to us.

KEUSI: You ever walk into a police station and look on the walls in some of those offices. All over the place—maps. Maps of the city, maps of the neighborhoods, and maps of maps. The Man knows all there is to know about the Black communities of America. Don't forget, he built them.

M'BALIA: They wouldn't destroy their own property. We could always be able to fight and hold them off. Besides, if they did bomb us or try to kill the people off, world opinion would be very much against them, and they couldn't afford that.

KEUSI: World opinion didn't mean shit when America invaded the Dominican Republic. But that's beside the point. Look, as revolutionaries, we also the protectors of the people. So, how we gonna feed our people when the cracker stops sending food to the A&P? How we gonna get water to the people when the cracker turns off the water supply? How we gonna clothe the people when we take off John's Bargain Store? When we gonna get into educating the people as to how to take care of themselves in a revolutionary situation? We ain't been doin' this. All we been doin' is killin' cops, gangsters, and a few bullshit politicians, an' all that is doing is getting the cracker in the mood to make a big bust. That means our people are the ones who gonna suffer the most. An' that's all we can offer them, now, you know. Nothing but empty slogans, Pyrrhic victories, and more death. How we gonna sell them that kind of life? The kind of life we got off some dead Europeans?

M'BALIA: But we have to do *something*!! We can't just sit idly by and allow this oppression to continue. I don't know, your arguments are persuasive. You have a clever way with words. You can always make yourself sound so right, and I can't deal with that. But I know that unless we Black people take a stand and try to end this oppression, we'll never be free. We have to fight. We have to make war so that we can end this oppression and live as free men and women. How much longer are we supposed to put up with the terrible way so many of our people are forced to live?! What, are we insane or something? Are niggers a race of morons?! The Indians, the Africans, the Asians, all chose to fight. No people will submit forever to oppression. So, what's wrong with Black people? No, Keusi, no more generations of Black children will be born into a country that kills and oppresses us in the manner that this does. We must have our manhood and womanhood and we must have it now, or America will simply have to die. We're going to change this world, Keusi. We're going to place human values above market values, we're going to build governments that save lives rather than destroy them, and after the destruction we bring to the evil and wickedness on this planet, after we've cleansed the world of the beast and all his lackeys and all other counterrevolutionary elements, no one will dare pick up a gun in anger again. And we'll do all this because we must, or else we'll die trying. So go on and leave. What does it matter? You were never any good to the revolution, anyway. Geronimo was right. You *are* standing in the way of the revolution.

KEUSI: Then why don't you kill me?

M'BALIA: Because those weren't my orders.

KEUSI: And that's the only reason?

M'BALIA: Yes.

KEUSI: You could kill the man who loves you that simply?

M'BALIA: Without hesitation.

KEUSI: Nothing that's happened changed a thing, huh?

M'BALIA: No. I told you in the beginning that I was a revolutionary. I've pledged my life to what I do.

(*Mood changes.*)

Keusi, if you intend to leave, just leave. I really don't want to deal with you any more.

Keusi: I want you to come with me. There are more ways to fight a revolution than with a gun.

M'Balia: A gun is the only way. Keusi, tonight I'm going to have to prepare myself for a mission. I'd like to be alone. So…

Keusi: What's the mission?

M'Balia: Radcliffe. It'll be the ultimate test for me. If I succeed, it'll provide me with the ultimate freedom a true revolutionary can have. I'll be able to begin a whole new life after this mission. That is really something for me to think about. It'll even free me from doubts about being totally dedicated as a revolutionary.

Keusi: I don't understand what you talking about.

M'Balia: You don't need to.

Keusi: Wow, killin' Radcliffe is really gonna put y'all out there. I guess I'll have to read about it in the papers.

M'Balia: It'll be headline news.

Keusi: (*Trying to joke.*) Don't miss.

M'Balia: Oh, don't worry. I won't miss. I'm a very good assassin. I only miss when I want to.

Keusi: Well, good luck.

(*Pause.*)

So you won't change your mind, huh?

M'Balia: No.

Keusi: M'Balia, I know… I know you gotta feel somethin', baby. You gotta feel somethin'.

(M'BALIA *says nothing.*)

M'Balia?

(*She moves far from* KEUSI.)

M'Balia: You meant nothing to me, Keusi. I needed a man. You were available.

Keusi: You're lying.

M'Balia: Why should I lie? I have no time to be lying.

KEUSI: Am I so wrong to ask you to be my wife? Is it a crime for me to want to love you?

M'BALIA: (*Trying to remain emotionless.*) You want me to make a choice between you and the revolution, and you're conceited enough to think you should come out on top. If Antar had told me to I would have killed you the minute I walked through the door.

(*Voice starts to break.*)

You mean nothing to me, Keusi. You have no right to do this to me. These are not the days for trying to win a woman's love. The revolution takes preference over everything.

KEUSI: I'm not asking you to give up the revolution. Fight it at my side. Come with me, M'Balia. Hey, baby, I love you.

M'BALIA: Keusi, you're a fool. Leave me alone. Please. For me, there's no such thing as love. I'm a revolutionary. There's no love, or no male, no female; there's only the revolution...and victory. Do you understand?

KEUSI: M'Balia—

M'BALIA: (*Stifles a tear.*) Get out! I mean it! Just get out of here and leave me alone! You've hurt me enough already! Leave me alone!

(KEUSI *picks up the duffle bag and starts for the door. He looks at* M'BALIA *but she refuses to acknowledge him. As the door closes,* M'BALIA *turns toward the door, stands silently a moment, then buries face in hands.*)

Scene Eight

A lonely room in RADCLIFFE'*s house. We see him seated behind a desk; desk lamp burning. Busy reading, seems tired,* M'BALIA *enters unseen...watches him awhile. Inadvertently makes a sound...* RADCLIFFE *spies her.*

RADCLIFFE: (*Surprised.*) You!

M'BALIA: (*Speaks in subdued terms.*) Hello, Daddy.

RADCLIFFE: So, you've finally come home. You've been gone for a long time. No contact at all. I wanted to reach you to tell you how sorry I was...about...well, about everything.

M'BALIA: (*Quietly.*) Well, that's okay.

RADCLIFFE: Where have you been?

M'BALIA: In the city.

Radcliffe: All this time?

M'Balia: Yes.

Radcliffe: Rhea—

M'Balia: My name is M'Balia.

Radcliffe: What?

M'Balia: My name isn't Rhea any more. It's M'Balia.

Radcliffe: I see. What does it mean?

M'Balia: It's the name of a sister who became a martyr and served as an inspiration for the revolution in Guinea.

Radcliffe: When did you change your name?

M'Balia: I didn't change it. It was changed for me.

Radcliffe: When?

M'Balia: A few days after I left you.

Radcliffe: I suppose that now you're a revolutionary, too. Like David.

M'Balia: Yes.

Radcliffe: Rhea—I'm sorry, er—er—

M'Balia: M'Balia.

Radcliffe: Yes. M'Balia. It sounds nice. Has a pleasant ring to it.

(*Grins.*)

M'Balia...you know you're the only child I have left. David's dead...and your mother, too. I...I don't want to see you lying dead as well. If you die violently and senselessly, like David, then what'll be left for me? What'll be left for your father?

M'Balia: (*Unemotionally.*) Death.

Radcliffe: I suppose that's right.

(*Pause.*)

I'm sorry...I'm sorry that our lives have become so dismal.

M'Balia: Mine has been very fruitful, Daddy.

Radcliffe: It has?

M'Balia: I've found peace, contentment, and at the same time, great challenges.

Radcliffe: But you're a revolutionary...or better, I should say, a misguided young woman.

M'BALIA: I'm not the one who is misguided, Daddy. It's you.

RADCLIFFE: You young people amaze me. You all think you know so much. You all assume your ideas and opinions are fresh and spanking new. Well, they're not, you know. They're old hat. They've been hashed about for years and nothing has ever come of them.

M'BALIA: That's because they've always been betrayed by Negroes like you.

RADCLIFFE: (*Angry.*) I do what I must.

M'BALIA: And so do I.

RADCLIFFE: Why did you come back? We're enemies now. You know how I feel about your revolution.

M'BALIA: I came back to…to…to say, well, to say…hello.

RADCLIFFE: (*Nods.*) Yes. Whatever else, you're still my daughter, aren't you? Strange, this revolution you young people are trying to foment. It's pitting blood against blood. Whatever else, whatever new name you acquire, I can only see you as my only daughter. Just as I saw David as my only son.

M'BALIA: Daddy, please…believe me. I'm only doing what I think is right. I don't hate you. But my life is dedicated to the revolution. I have to do what's necessary to continue the revolution.

RADCLIFFE: I don't understand what you are talking about, Rhea. What you are doing and what David was doing are the things your mother and I have tried to keep you from—all our lives. Believe me, I understand your frustrations—your bitterness. But to lash out at this white man is to invite your death. I grew up in the South. I know what he's like. I know what he can do. Your mother and I had to swallow pride and dignity many times just to be sure you and David had enough to eat. When I was David's age—when I was a young man, I often thought of fighting— lashing out, but integration just seemed a better way to go. If we tommed a little, it was to feed you—to give you a chance for the good life—a life your mother and I never had. I'm fighting against your revolution because I don't want to see any of you dying in the streets at the hands of trigger-happy white policemen. At least, those boys I turned in will only get a prison sentence and that's better than getting your head blown off. I don't want to see any more Black women crying over the bodies of their men like I saw my mother crying over my father. I just don't want to see you kids dying needlessly and senselessly against such hopeless odds, and I'll fight anyone who tries to lead you down that path. I mean it. I'm not going to stand by and see an entire people exterminated, because of some disgruntled, misguided children who only half read their history books!

M'BALIA: Daddy, you're hopeless.

RADCLIFFE: I'm sorry you feel that way, Rhea, but I'm going to finish the job I started.

M'BALIA: Then I guess I'll never see you again.

RADCLIFFE: (*Sadly.*) Perhaps not.

M'BALIA: (*Almost pleading.*) Daddy...

RADCLIFFE: Yes?

M'BALIA: (*Thinks better of it.*) Nothing. Forget it.

RADCLIFFE: Oh.

(*Trying to make conversation.*)

So, tell me, are you still keeping a diary?

M'BALIA: Oh, no. I cut that kind of thing out. It's very childish, you know.

RADCLIFFE: I thought all young women kept a diary.

M'BALIA: (*Trying to make a joke.*) I wouldn't know. I'm not all young women.

(*Laughs uneasily.*)

RADCLIFFE: It's good to see you laugh again. I haven't seen that smile in a long time. I'd forgotten how much like your mother you really are.

(M'BALIA *bows her head.*)

M'BALIA: Mom was very...beautiful.

RADCLIFFE: She would have been proud to see you grow into such a fine-looking woman.

M'BALIA: Daddy, it's getting late. It's time...

RADCLIFFE: (Interrupting.) When you walk out of that door, part of me will die because I'll never see you again, Rhea.

M'BALIA: Yes...I...I know.

RADCLIFFE: Rhea, give up this madness and come back home. There is no life for any of you in the revolution. Leave there before you're killed or imprisoned. You can't cut yourself off from reality of the situation in this country. A revolution is suicide. You're a free woman. Don't be led into madness.

M'BALIA: (*Almost pleading.*) You refuse to understand. The revolution is already here. If it's madness we're into then it's a madness that will change the world! If we're so wrong to fight then you ought to recognize that we were driven to this point by your cowardice and the inhumanity of the enemy. Don't be so eager to put us down, especially since we're only doing now what Negroes of your generation have failed to do for years. Not another generation of Black children will have such an assortment of cowards and lackeys as...

(*Voice chokes.*)

...as...you...my father, Chauncey Radcliffe. They'll have brave men and women as their parents, who'll teach them to be true men and women. Free? I'm not totally free yet. I'll never be free until I free myself of this oppression that I have had to deal with all of my life.

(*Now looks directly at her father. Lips tighten with determination as she tries to muster up the words she must somehow bring herself to say.*)

And most of all, as a revolutionary, I can never be free until I'm free of you.

RADCLIFFE: What a well-rehearsed diatribe that was.

(*Angrily.*)

Don't you young people understand?! You're standing on our shoulders.

(M'BALIA *is unmoved and seeing this* RADCLIFFE *becomes dejected.*)

Well then, Rhea, what is it you want from your father? Money? My hatred? What do you want from me?

M'BALIA: (*Hesitant. Deep inside her voice tells her not to go through with her assignment. She forces this inner voice into silence, summons up a great inner strength, and, trembling, faces her father.*) Your death! Traitor!!

(M'BALIA *pulls gun, fires.* RADCLIFFE *grabs head, blood oozes. He falls. Gradually the realization of what she has done strikes* M'BALIA. *The stage turns red.* M'BALIA *screams. We hear the voice of a radio newsman as* M'BALIA *kneels at body of* RADCLIFFE.)

RADIO NEWSMAN: Acting on information obtained from three prisoners, local police and state troopers today raided the headquarters of a supersecret Black militant organization, the Black Terrorists. Reports are sketchy, but news reporters on the scene have said the picture here is one of horror and chaos. Scores of policemen lie dead or injured in the streets and in other sectors of the neighborhood policemen are being pelted with rocks, bottles, and other missiles thrown by roving bands of Negro youths. Reporters on the scene have said that some policemen have shot a number of these youths, otherwise killing or capturing them all, while the Night Rangers, anti-riot unit of the police department, is now involved in the process of occupying and clearing out a number of homes in the immediate vicinity. There are indications that the area may have to be cordoned off for the quote, "safety of innocent citizens," unquote. There are no indications as to whether or not this cordoning off will cease once the operation against the Black Terrorists is completed.

(*Sounds; the* REPORTER *being interrupted.*)

Uh, ladies and gentlemen, we take you to the scene of the action, live, where our local correspondent Neil Reiner has managed to get past security guards and is inside the headquarters to give us this exclusive report on the attack and probably capture of the Black Terrorists. Neil?

(*Sounds; gunfire, shouts, screams.*)

VOICE #2: Yeah?! Harry?

RADIO NEWSMAN: Yeah, Neil. You're coming through nicely. Can you tell us what's happening down there?

VOICE #2: (Anguish.) My God, it's awful. They're killing them all. The police are killing them all. Men, women, children—all *dead*!! All dead!! The police rampaged through the halls like madmen. They're covered with blood. They're like, like savages. Death is all around me. So far, I have not seen one Black alive. The police are killing them all. They're just shooting…it's unbelievable! I keep saying to myself, "This is America. It can't be happening! Not in America!"

(*In background, shots continue. We hear sounds of screams, death throughout until blackout.*)

The Blacks are fighting like crazed animals. They are shouting chants and somewhere someone is beating a drum. I don't understand all this. Why are they fighting so hard?! All of this death and destruction. It's all around me!!! I can hear gunshots coming from everywhere. Blacks are dying, police are dying! Harry, it's like the death knell of America! Believe me!! My God! My God! These militants are frighteningly unreal, Harry. They seem to laugh at death. Almost worship it!! Rather than surrender, they fight on until dead! There's an escape tunnel, yet no one seems to have used it. I don't understand these people! All of this death!! Why?! Why?! Harry, there's a group of revolutionaries at the top of a flight of stairs. They're identified as Antar, Ahmed, and M'Balia. They may be the only Blacks alive in this building. They've got to surrender! They must!

They *must!*

(*Lights on* M'BALIA *dim.*)

Only death can be the final victor in this battle. Harry, these Blacks are fools. Why do they fight so hard?! They can't win. We're white! This is America, the greatest country in the world. We've proved we can survive any inner turmoil. Why do these Blacks continue?! Why would they rather be dead than alive in America. I don't understand! This is America! They can't win! They're foolish to continue. All of this violence. Harry, I don't—

(*Gunshots, screams, shouts.*)

Oh no!! Oh, my God!! They've got DYNAMITE!!!!!!!!!!!!!!!!!!!!!!!!!!

(*Sound of explosion. Blackout.*)

(*BLACKNESS.*)

Peace   Power   Unity

THE
Sirens

Notes on *The Sirens*

Two African-American women find themselves fleeing into a darkened doorway on a derelict street somewhere in Newark, New Jersey. They cower in the shadows until the threat passes, and when it does, they reemerge, shaken but determined to carry on. Mavis and Pepper are working-class women, laid off once again from their low-paying jobs in a local factory, and have turned to prostitution in order to survive. However, mere physical survival is not the only issue. Each woman, in her way, is also struggling to maintain a sense of self-worth.

I came to this story after witnessing the everyday existence of a group of prostitutes who worked out of a pair of flea-bitten hotels on St. Nicholas Avenue in Harlem, near 125th Street. I had to pass them on my way to the subway station. It was impossible not to be propositioned or to overhear their conversations. I began to recognize pecking orders among them and soon began to see more deeply into them, or perhaps merely to sense that there was more to each of them than their existence in "the life." In Newark, which was my hometown, I'd heard stories of women who worked marginal, low-wage jobs in the few remaining factories, and found themselves laid off or otherwise unemployed. Rent was due, or children had to be clothed and fed, or boyfriends and husbands had run off with what little money they had, or there was some problem at the unemployment or welfare office. When these crises arose (as they often did), some of these women had taken to the streets, selling themselves. They abandoned the practice as soon as a job could be found. Some did this only once, others frequently.

I began to wonder about these women. At first, I simply wanted to understand why or how they could sell themselves. Certainly, I was aware of all of the social, political, and historical realities that surrounded their lives, and the lives of all the oppressed. But gradually, I came to see these women in a larger context, as part of a broader conversation that was going on among African-American women (and men) in the society. Dark skin, full lips, full figures, kinky hair, and almond-shaped eyes are not the standards of beauty in the United States or Europe—or in South America or the Far East. A woman like this seldom sees herself reflected in media, fantasies, or the histories of the land in which she is born. Too many of the men in her life, gripped by their own hang-ups, have failed to love her; or they have abandoned her, ignored her, or even worse, taken her presence in their lives for granted.

What happens, then, to young women who have come to view themselves through the eyes of others; who have abandoned hope, or who hope to find their salvation in dreams or expectations that may or may not come true?

The Sirens opened at the Manhattan Theater Club on May 15, 1974. It was produced by Ed Bullins and Richard Wesley, and directed by William Lathan. The cast included Veronica Redd, Loretta Greene, Debbie Morgan, Roger Hill, and Roscoe Orman.

The Sirens

Characters

MAVIS: *Age twenty-nine. Lonely; resigned to it.*
DUANE: *Age thirty-one. Ambitious.*
BETTY: *Age seventeen. High school girl with dreams of romance.*
BOBBY: *Age seventeen. Stone youngblood.*
PEPPER: *Age twenty-eight. A woman trying to survive the best way she can.*
JOHN 1
JOHN 2

Time

The present

Place

Newark, New Jersey

Production Note: This play is meant to be performed on a large bare stage with only a minimum of suggested sets to designate a given location. The intent here is that the actors bring the "reality" onstage with them so that the combination of acting, lights, and suggestive sets create the illusion of reality.

Property List (1) Onstage: couch; bed; rug; coffee table; lamp post; lamp; night stand; wine bottle and glass; magazine; dresser; telephones; cigarettes and matches. (2) Offstage: basketball; package containing dress; bottle of soda. (3) Personal: PEPPER—*purse containing cigarettes, knife, and straight razor;* BOBBY—*folding money;* MAVIS—*purse with brown case, matches;* JOHN 1—*folding money.*

A Play in Five Scenes

Scene One

Lights up on a street corner somewhere in Newark. It is very late at night. The smell of cooking food from a nearby "greasy spoon" permeates the air. Two men saunter across the stage, both fairly inebriated. One turns his back and urinates while the other stands humming a tune to himself. They continue walking and talking about nothing. R&B music blares from a distant speaker and the two men dance a few drunken steps as they move offstage. The stage is now empty except for the music and the smell. Suddenly, noises are heard. Shouts, footsteps. PEPPER *rushes onstage.*

PEPPER: Quick, Mavis, in here!

(MAVIS *comes rushing onstage and both duck inside a doorway. The headlights of a police car flash across the stage, then go away. The two women come out.*)

MAVIS: See, now? I thought them suckers was gettin' paid to be cool.

PEPPER: They must be new on this beat, or somethin'.

MAVIS: Yea. See, they still cruising. If they was the regular ones they woulda been inside the house gettin' their taste right now. The jive punks.

PEPPER: It's gettin' almost as bad over here as it was in New York. Well, no matter. I'm cuttin' alla this loose someday, anyway.

MAVIS: Yea, sure, honey. Tell Mavis anything.

PEPPER: It's the truth. I'm gettin' too old for this. Besides, these johns around here ain't hittin' on nothing'. Broke-ass nigguhs.

MAVIS: Hard times, you know?

PEPPER: Yea. There was a time when I could hit these dudes out here for twenty—twenty-five dollars. No more.

MAVIS: Wage and price controls, honey. Ain'tcha heard?

PEPPER: That don't break no ice with me. I need some big bucks, honey. (*Shivers.*)

Have mercy! It's cold as hell out here an' I ain't wore no drawers.

MAVIS: (*Smiling.*) Well, whose fault is that?

PEPPER: Shoot, later for you, whore.

(*Both laugh.*)

MAVIS: I hope there's some money to be made out here tonight. I don't wanna be out here freezin' my ass off for nothin'.

PEPPER: Maybe your truck driver friend will come by an' make it all worthwhile.

MAVIS: That man's gettin' to be a pain, chile. Wants me to marry him.

PEPPER: Shoot, why don't you?

MAVIS: Ain't nothin' he can do for me. 'Sides, I like my independence. Can't no man tell me what to do. But he is kinda nice, though. Nicer than most of the johns that come around here. Got a cigarette?

PEPPER: Yea.

(*Reaches into her purse and gives a cigarette to* MAVIS. MAVIS *takes it and lights up.*)

MAVIS: Thanks.

PEPPER: You hear from your job?

MAVIS: Not yet.

PEPPER: How long you been laid off, now?

MAVIS: Almost a month.

PEPPER: You gon' go back if they call you?

MAVIS: Prob'ly.

(*Both laugh.*)

PEPPER: You makin' more money out here than you ever did in that factory.

MAVIS: (*Begins to shiver.*) God, where the hell all the tricks at? It's way too cold out here.

PEPPER: You better believe it. It get too cold, I'm gon' go in. That's one of the advantages of bein' an outlaw. Over in New York, when I had a pimp, he used to make me stay out no matter how cold it got. There was a time with him that was so bad that I almost committed suicide.

MAVIS: Suicide? Pepper, you outa your mind?

PEPPER: (*Laughs uneasily.*) Yea, I know. But I was young and stupid, then. Today, a nigguh put his hand on me, I'll put a pot of hot grease in his face so fast he won't know what happened.

(*Looking offstage.*)

Hey.

MAVIS: (*Looking off also.*) Yea, I see him. You want him?

PEPPER: You can have him. I'm gon' see what's happening in the bar.

(*Enter* JOHN 1. *He looks at the two women.*)

MAVIS: Well, you like what you see?

JOHN 1: Maybe.

PEPPER: See you later, honey.

MAVIS: Okay.

(PEPPER *exits.*)

Well, mister?

John 1: What if she was the one I like?

Mavis: Well, hey, you got legs, go on after her.

John 1: No need. One box is just like any other. C'mon.

Mavis: That's fifteen dollars for me an' three for the room.

John 1: Fifteen?! I could buy a pair of kicks for that kinda money.

Mavis: Well, I ain't no shoes, motherfuckah.

John 1: Forget it.

Mavis: (*Conciliatory.*) Hey, wait a minute. Don't go away mad. Look, how much you got?

(*Moves close to him.*)

How's ten for me and three for the room?

John 1: (*Looks at* Mavis *as though he were inspecting a slab of meat.*) Yea, I can live with that.

Mavis: Solid. C'mon then.

(*They exit. Lights fade on the street corner and pick up on* Mavis's *apartment. A slow blues plays on a stereo in the living room, while offstage we hear soft moans. An alarm clock suddenly goes off. Then, we hear sounds of scurrying about. We hear offstage voices.*)

Betty: Oh shit, there goes the clock. Get dressed, Bobby.

Bobby: How soon 'fore your aunt get here?

Betty: About twenty minutes. C'mon, we got plenty of time. That's why I set the clock.

(Betty *and* Bobby *come rushing onstage adjusting their clothing and picking up wine bottles and food scattered on the table. Soon they are finished.*)

Bobby: I guess I'd better go. Your aunt would never understand if she caught me in here. She'd swear we was doin' somethin'.

Betty: (*Embracing* Bobby.) Oh, baby. You so good to me. I'm yours forever.

Bobby: (Pulling free.) Hey, baby, lighten up. I got to go.

(*Moves to the door as* Betty *follows him.*)

You gonna be at the game tomorrow?

Betty: Who y'all playin'?

Bobby: East Side.

Betty: Y'all gonna win?

BOBBY: 'Course. Watchu think?

BETTY: Bobby, do you love me?

BOBBY: Sure, baby. Ain't I your man?

BETTY: I ain't so sure.

BOBBY: Whatchu mean by that?

BETTY: All you ever want is whatchu can get.

BOBBY: Betty, is that what you think of me? Here I am, just got finished layin' up with you in your aunt's house all night an' her daughter sleep in the next room. I'm takin' a chance on gettin' *caught*, just to be with you an' you think I'm usin' you. Wow, what kinda jive is that?

BETTY: You don't never take me nowhere, like you ashamed to be seen with me.

BOBBY: I ain't got no money.

BETTY: Parks is free.

BOBBY: It's too cold to be walkin' through somebody's park. Besides, sweet thing, a park ain't good enough for a princess like you.

BETTY: It was good enough for Sheila.

BOBBY: What about Sheila?

BETTY: You took her to the park. You took her to the Continental Ballroom an' to the Five Kings, an' even to New York. Only place you ever take me is to the goddamn couch!

BOBBY: Where you hear lies like those?

BETTY: (*Angrily.*) They ain't hardly no lies!!

BOBBY: (*Grabbing* BETTY'*s arm.*) Bitch, I know you ain't been spyin' on me.

BETTY: Then you admit you been goin' out on me.

BOBBY: Hey, why I gotta answer any questions from you? You ain't got no claim on me.

BETTY: Solid. So, maybe tomorrow me an' Franklin Johnson will get a good thing goin'.

BOBBY: I catch you 'round that nigguh and I'll walk in both your asses. You my woman an' I don't play that.

BETTY: Oh, it's alright for you an' Sheila—

BOBBY: (*Interrupting.*) Ain't nothin' between me an' Sheila. I had to take her out see, me an' the fellas had this bet 'cause Sheila was playin' hard to get an' so we had this bet to see who could rap heaviest to her an' take her out an' I won. Hey, she don't mean nothin' to me. You the only mamma for me, baby.

BETTY: You ain't lyin', Bobby?

BOBBY: Baby, I'd never lie to you.

BETTY: Please don't, Bobby. You know I couldn't stand it.

BOBBY: You the only one for me, baby.

(*They kiss.*)

BETTY: It's always nice when I'm with you, Bobby.

BOBBY: It's nice when I'm with you, too, baby.

BETTY: Mama an' Daddy always be fightin' so much, it's like I don't even exist sometime. I like being held. I feel so safe.

BOBBY: (*Uneasy.*) Wow, baby. Uh…er…hey, look, I got to go.

BETTY: We still got a little time. You can stay a little longer.

BOBBY: No…uh…I'd better get goin'. My mother's already on my case about bein' out late so much.

BETTY: I'll see ya at the game tomorrow.

BOBBY: The first point I score'll be dedicated to you, Betty.

BETTY: Really?

BOBBY: I promise. Look, I gotta go. Take it easy. Hear.

(BOBBY *kisses her and rushes out as the music continues to play.* BETTY *goes back and sits on the couch as lights fade on her part of the stage to very low but not quite out. Lights come up full on another part of the stage where we see* BOBBY *in a phone booth somewhere. Lights also come up dimly on the street corner where* MAVIS *and* JOHN 1 *part company, and she stands alone shivering waiting for her next customer.* BOBBY *in the phone booth, laughing.*)

Yea, Eddie! Yea! I got her in the bed, man. A real bed. Huh? Oh, it was good, man. Damn right. You got more freedom than on a couch. Yeah. I bet I'm one of the first guys in our gang to get a girl in the bed. Yea, I'm a man, now. That's right.

(*Laughs.*)

Yea, man, we *nekked*. No clothes, at all. If I'm lyin', I'm flyin'. Oh man she was moanin' an' groanin' and all kinds of fantastic shit. Oooweee! Man, I musta got about seven nuts. Yea! I ain't lyin'. I couldn't help it. That was some good stuff.

(*Laughs.*)

You ain't foolin', man. Well, you know our names: "The Get Overs."

(*Laughs.*)

Aw, it was easy as hell. These broads go for anything you tell 'em. Sheila or Betty, they all the same. It ain't nothin' for me to rap my way into a broad's drawers, man.

(*Laughs.*)

If you were here, I'd slap you five, my man. Man, I got Betty's nose so wide open, I could drive a Mack truck through. Huh? Oh, yea, sure. You can rap to her when I get through. Just like with Sheila.

(*Lights fade to black on everyone and then come up on* Mavis's *apartment.* Betty *has just finished cleaning up the apartment and is now reading.*)

Mavis: Hi

Betty: Hi.

Mavis: Whatchu doin' up so late, honey?

Betty: Couldn't get to sleep.

Mavis: Uh-uh. Well, you have enough to eat?

Betty: Yea, but you shouldna fixed so much food, Aunt Mavis.

(*Smiling.*)

Can't nobody eat all the food you cook.

Mavis: I like to cook. It can be tiring sometimes, but most times it relaxes me. Keeps my mind off my troubles.

Betty: Will you teach me to cook like you, someday?

Mavis: What's wrong with your mama?

Betty: She ain't got no time. Too much mess goin' on in our house.

Mavis: My brother an' your mother. Don't seem like they ever gon' get it together. He still drivin' that cab?

Betty: Yeah, an' when he ain't drivin' for his boss, he schemin' on gettin' a coupla cabs of his own. He stay so busy tryin' to get money, he sometimes be out the house all week long. That's when him an' Mama get to fightin'.

Mavis: Yea, that's a familiar story, honey.

Betty: Daddy be scared there ain't gonna be enough money in the house, so he tryin' to get as much as he can. He scared we might have to go on welfare like the folks next door. Boy, when he found out about them it seemed like he just changed. Mama scared he gon' work himself to death.

MAVIS: That's 'cause she don't understand. Our family was on welfare for the longest time. Your grandfather couldn't get no jobs an' finally he left the house so Mama could get on the relief. He an' Mama used to have to meet in a friend's apartment or spend a night somewhere else in case the welfare inspectors came snoopin' around. Your father hated those days. He got his first job when he was thirteen an' ain't stopped since. The house changed when your father stopped laughin' like he used to.

BETTY: Maybe if I told Mama she'd understand more.

MAVIS: Don't you tell your mama nothin', you hear me? Your father find out I told you that story he'll beat the black off both of us.

BETTY: Okay.

MAVIS: My little girl sleep all right?

BETTY: Delores? Like a log. I swear, that child can "z" more than anybody I know.

MAVIS: Takes after her daddy. I remember he used to sleep so soundly 'til sometime you'd think he was dead.

BETTY: You ever hear from him?

MAVIS: No. Don't want to, neither.

BETTY: Yea, sure.

MAVIS: I mean it. Honey, the worst thing you can do is take a nigguh back after he has messed over you, 'cause then you've givin' him license to do the same thing over again and again.

BETTY: Don't you haveta start trustin' at some point? I mean, if you love a man—

MAVIS: (*Interrupting.*) Love? Is that in the dictionary?

(*Yawns.*)

Girl, if you don't get your buns in bed, you had better. You got to go to school tomorrow. I'm sorry I had to even ask you, but your grandmother just had to go down south so I had to find me another babysitter. I just hope your classes don't suffer tomorrow 'cause of this.

BETTY: Don't worry. Say, when you comin' off this night shift, anyway? You been on it the longest time.

MAVIS: Don't know an' I don't care, either. I'm makin' good money, girl. Go on to bed, now.

BETTY: (*Rising, yawning.*) Okay. See you, Aunt Mavis.

(*Exits.*)

(*Lights come up on* MAVIS *standing alone. The light should be a spot lighting an area large enough for her to move about in during her monologue.*)

MAVIS: I'm old. I feel old. I look old. Old before my time. Why? How did it happen? Can't say that I really care that much. I dunno. I feel so empty inside. Wasn't always like that. No. There was a time when I used to laugh and joke and play and just plain act wild like I ain't had no sense. They used to call me loud Mavis when I was in high school. Mama used to say wouldn't no man marry me 'cause my mouth was so big. But I loved life and I loved to party and wear bright dresses and just plain be myself. I felt beautiful. Beautiful. And every day was the summertime for me. I used to party for days, then. Knew all the latest steps and all the hit songs by heart. Couldn't nothin' get me down. Not this raggedy-ass town or summa the raggedy-ass people in it. I still don't know what happened. Why everything just suddenly dried up for me...me an' Duane used to be so happy. Just outa high school, both workin' an' makin' money. Doin' it to death.

(*Laughs.*)

Then I got pregnant an' we didn't party that much anymore. An' the money started goin' elsewhere an' suddenly me an' Duane had to grow up an' when we did Duane started actin' funny. Talked about nothin' but money. An' we didn't make love no more an' I started puttin' on weight an' Duane's face stared to change. An' suddenly Mama looked old, an' nothin' seemed to be the same. It was like I was caught in some kinda quicksand and the more I wiggled the deeper I plunged down. Lord have mercy. What's happened to me? That's all I wanna know? So now, I'm an old woman an' Duane is gone an' I don't laugh no more an' I don't care no more. I wish...

(MAVIS *does not finish the sentence.*)

Scene Two

The following day. BOBBY *and* BETTY *are on a street corner just after the basketball game against East Side High.*

BETTY: Sorry y'all lost.

BOBBY: Aw, those chumps got lucky as hell. That number forty musta traveled at least sixty times in the game and the ref didn't call it once. We gonna get 'em next time, just you watch.

BETTY: I was really proud of you. You did good. I was so happy when you scored your first basket 'cause of what you said last night.

BOBBY: (*His mind elsewhere.*) I just hope losin' to East Side don't hurt my chances of gettin' into the County Tournament. Scouts from summa the big-time colleges will be there. It'll be my big chance.

BETTY: Everybody was impressed with the way you played, Bobby. I betcha that East Side coach wished he had you.

BOBBY: Boy, if I can just make all-county, I got a chance. I'll get offers from all over.

BETTY: Did you hear me screamin' your name every time you got the ball?

BOBBY: I got to try to score at least twenty-five points a game. Can't nobody miss me then. I'll be able to cut this raggedy town loose.

BETTY: Bobby, I'm talkin' to you.

BOBBY: Yea, I hear ya, baby. That's nice.

BETTY: What?

BOBBY: What you said.

BETTY: What did I say?

BOBBY: Un...uh...er...c'mon, let's go.

BETTY: Bobby?

BOBBY: Yea.

BETTY: Why do you ignore me all the time?

BOBBY: I don't ignore you.

BETTY: Yes you do. I thought you said you loved me.

BOBBY: Of course I love you. Really.

BETTY: You tryin' to make a fool outa me?

BOBBY: Oh, wow.

BETTY: You know your friend Eddie tried to hit on me today.

BOBBY: Eddie? C'mon.

BETTY: In the cafeteria. Kept followin' me around. When I told him about you he talked like you didn't care if he rapped or not.

BOBBY: I'll talk to Eddie, okay?

BETTY: Did you say anything to him about me?

BOBBY: Betty, be serious.

BETTY: I *am* serious. Eddie ain't never even looked at me before today. He always kept his distance 'cause he knew I was your woman. Now, suddenly he's on me like white on rice.

BOBBY: Look, I said I'd talk to him.

BETTY: Same thing happened to Sheila when she was goin' with you. No one within a hundred miles of that broad. Then suddenly, every nigguh in the school was tryin' to pull her. What's your job? To break all the girls in?

(BOBBY *slaps her.*)

BOBBY: Fuck it. I don't' need to listen to this kinda bullshit comin' from a dizzy bitch like you. Later.

(*Exits in a huff.*)

BETTY: (*Crying.*) Bobby, wait. I'm sorry. I didn't mean it. I was mad. Bobby, don't do this to me. Bobby. Bobby.

(*Rushes off after* BOBBY *as the lights fade. Lights up on the street.*)

PEPPER: Yea, honey, someday I'm gon' cut alla this loose. Got to 'fore my looks are gone an' I'm shootin' up to keep from goin' crazy. Know what I mean?

MAVIS: Yea.

PEPPER: These men out here are freaks, Mavis. Gettin' so you take your life in your hands just to go in a room with 'em. If I could just save the money I make.

MAVIS: Hmpf. What would you do with it? Take a trip to the Bahamas, or somethin'?

PEPPER: Maybe. Look, I'm twenty-nine years old. I'm out here competin' with high school girls, so how much time I got left? You know these men. They go for young flesh.

MAVIS: That ain't no news.

PEPPER: You ain't no spring chicken, either, "granny." You five years older than me.

MAVIS: I'll make out. I been hustlin' one way or another all my life. If I got to do somethin' else, I'll do it. Later for it.

PEPPER: I hear the girls over in New York are holdin' johns up.

MAVIS: Them bitches is crazy. That's why I got my ass from over there.

PEPPER: Yea, I'm gonna get out. Just go away somewhere an' meet a man an' make some babies.

MAVIS: Pepper, be serious. You a whore. The kinda okey-doke you runnin' down only happens in the movies.

PEPPER: I'll make it happen.

MAVIS: How many men have you laid down with since you been on the block? You got any idea what your box must look like? Hell, ain't no man in his right mind gonna marry you.

PEPPER: (*Hurt.*) Oh, wow, Mavis. What's the matter with you?

MAVIS: Change of life. Okay?

PEPPER: No, it's not okay. Who you think you are talkin' to me like that? Just 'cause some man messed over your life don't be takin' it out on my dreams. Shit.

MAVIS: That ain't got nothin' to do with it. I just ain't got no time for people who refuse to deal with reality.

PEPPER: Reality is tellin' me to get my bootie off this corner. Times are changin', honey. These new broads and these johns ain't got nothin' to do with what we was about when we first came out here. Our day is past, Mavis.

MAVIS: Oh, broad, you don't even know what you talkin' about.

PEPPER: Don't I? Look up an' down these streets. Look at these people. They gettin' desperate. Nigguhs is broker now than ever before. I read that the suicide rate for Blacks is up and the life expectancy rate is down. More nigguhs is dyin' of cancer an' heart attacks an' high blood pressure than ever before.

MAVIS: You read all this?

PEPPER: You damn right. Our people are goin' crazy an' we gettin' old an' sick an' tired. So how much importance can a coupla whores on a street corner have?

MAVIS: (*Walking away from* PEPPER.) Don't tell me I ain't important. Don't take that away from me, too.

PEPPER: Huh?

MAVIS: Oh…uh…nothin'. I didn't say anything.

PEPPER: Oh.

(*Pause.*)

Tell you one thing, though. You lucky. You got that truck driver. I wish there was somebody who would come my way. Hell, Pepper'd be long gone. You a fool not to marry that dude.

Mavis: Maybe. But the man don't interest me. No man does.

Pepper: He still got your nose, huh?

Mavis: Who?

Pepper: Duane.

Mavis: Shit.

Pepper: What would you do if he came back?

Mavis: Duane ain't never comin' back.

(*Quietly.*)

Never.

Pepper: But what if he does? Would you take him back?

Mavis: Hell, no.

Pepper: Then you the one who's refusin' to deal with reality.

(JOHN 2 *enters.*)

Excuse me.

(*To* JOHN 2.)

Hey, baby, you goin' out tonight?

(PEPPER *walks toward him.*)

You ain't got much time, Mavis. This corner don't belong to us no more.

(*Lights dim as* PEPPER *and* JOHN 2 *go off together with* MAVIS *watching.*)

Scene Three

Betty: (*On the phone.*) Hello? Hi, it's me, Betty. Yea. Bobby, I'm sorry about what I said. I was mad…well, you act like you don't care no more and Bobby you mean so much to me…well, boys act so jive all the time, a girl takes a big chance lettin' herself feel like I do…I know you got your heart set on makin' all-county an' all-state an' gettin' to college, but you don't have to walk all over me to do it…yea, that's how I feel. What? Patience. It's hard to be patient with somebody like you, Bobby. No, wait; don't hang up. Please. Let's talk. No, we *don't* always talk. You're always tryin' to do it to me every chance you get. You seldom talk. An' usually when you do you talk about yourself. Bobby?…Of course I understand about gettin' the athletic scholarship, but that's not what I'm talkin' about. I'm talkin' about you an' me. What's so funny…yes, you *were* laughing. Bobby you ain't no damn good. You know that?…That's right. I love you an' I've given myself up to you. Don't that mean nothin' to you?…Oh, you're grateful. Thanks a lot…what?…Well, if you don't know what else you're supposed to say don't look to me to tell you…whatchu s'posed to *do*? Bobby, you can kiss my ass!

(*She slams the phone down and sits fighting back tears.*)

All I want is to be happy…and safe from bein' hurt alla time. Is that so much to ask? I want someone I can believe in. Someone who loves me. That's all. It's startin' already. I can feel myself gettin' tense an' angry all the time. Like Mommy an' Daddy. I don't wanna be like that, but sometimes it seem like there ain't gonna be any other way.

(*Lights come full up as* MAVIS *enters and sees* BETTY *near the phone.*)

MAVIS: Hi, Betty.

(BETTY *mumbles an answer.*)

How'd your day go? Oh, I picked you up somethin' at Bamberger's. Hope you like it. Here.

(*Hands* BETTY *a package.*)

BETTY: (*Opening package.*) A dress. Oh, wow, Aunt Mavis, this is very beautiful.

MAVIS: Yea, next time your boyfriend comes to take you out, you can have somethin' outa sight to dazzle him with.

BETTY: Yea…next time.

MAVIS: I get any calls?

BETTY: No. You work tonight?

MAVIS: No, I'm too tired. So, I took the night off. Called in sick.

BETTY: Yea, you need to stay home an' rest. You don't never seem to get no days off.

MAVIS: I need the money. Work as much as I can.

BETTY: You shoulda stuck to singin' in the clubs on weekends. You were very popular.

MAVIS: And very broke.

BETTY: You could work during the week and sing on the weekends. You'd be rich. You'd pull at least two hundred dollars a week from both gigs.

MAVIS: (*Chuckles.*) I don't mean to make fun of you, honey. But two hundred dollars a week.

(*The lights pick up* BOBBY *in another area of the stage as we see* BETTY *sitting.*)

BOBBY: (*On phone.*) Man, Eddie, I'm gonna put my foot up that broad's behind, I swear. What do hammers want from dudes? I told her from the giddyup that I didn't want no entanglements. Hey, what I look like tied down to one broad...no, well later for it, man. I'm gonna go on to college somewhere, then come out an' get me a job as an architect, just like I always planned. Make me some big bucks an' leave dizzy broads like her behind forever...yea, these chicks think their box is some kinda sacred ornament. Yea...hey, that's what I say, too. Look, a box is made to be opened, right? An' if I got the right key is that my fault?

(*Laughs.*)

No, man, I ain't takin' her back. I learned from my uncle that a woman hates a man who begs. He said any time a woman sees any signs of softness or weakness in a man she use him, 'cause she ain't got no respect for him. I ain't never gonna forget that...yea, that's right. Next time Betty sees me, I'll be hirin' her as a maid to clean up my apartment. Yea.

(*Laughs.*)

Look, man, I gotta split. I'm late for practice...Okay, later on, my man.

(BOBBY *hangs up then looks at the phone for a long time. On the other side of the stage we can still see* BETTY. BOBBY *picks up the phone and dials.* BETTY's *phone rings.*)

BETTY: Hello?

BOBBY: (*Starts to say something but gets cold feet. Instead, he disguises his voice.*) Uh...er...ah—sorry, wrong number.

(*Hangs up.*)

(*Lights fade on* BOBBY *as he moves slowly and sadly offstage.*)

MAVIS: Lord!

(*Laughs again.*)

Child, the things your old aunt could tell you. You hungry? I got some meat in the refrigerator.

BETTY: Naw, I ain't hungry. An' Aunt Mavis, you shouldn' eat so much anyway. One of these days you gonna lose your figure.

Mavis: It don't matter that much to me. What I got to look attractive for?

Betty: Why you say that?

Mavis: Oh, I don't know. Just the way I feel, I guess.

Betty: Oh.

(*Pause.*)

Aunt Mavis, why are boys so hard to get along with?

Mavis: 'Cause they can't be trusted.

Betty: There must be some.

Mavis: Nope. Nary one. Listen to the voice of experience, honey.

Betty: But—

Mavis: Men are born hustlers. Gettin', possessin', keepin', reachin'. That's all they're about. A woman is just another commodity. She goes good with penthouses and Cadillacs.

Betty: My father's not like that.

Mavis: Yea, maybe he ain't. Sorry.

Betty: There must be some way out.

Mavis: The trouble with young girls is they dream too much. Best you wake up and deal with the real world, Betty.

(*Lights change to pick up* PEPPER *and* JOHN 2 *sitting on a bed together after having conducted a "business transaction."*)

Relationships between men and women is mostly physical, 'cause that's the only way men been taught to deal. When you understand that, you can begin to learn how to handle nigguhs.

Pepper: Was I good to you, Daddy?

John 2: You was all right.

Pepper: Then that means every time you come 'round here you gonna look for me, is that right?

Betty: I don't believe you.

John 2: Pussy is pussy. If you be around, I'll look you up.

Mavis: All right, don't listen to me. But hard heads make soft behinds.

Pepper: Man, you can't be serious. Good as I am, you can't possibly be interested in summa these other broads around here.

Betty: I don't wanna spend my life bein' hurt.

JOHN 2: Any time I got the money, any one of you broads will do.

PEPPER: Damn, ain't you the cold one?

MAVIS: Yea, baby, yea.

JOHN 2: Not cold, just practical.

PEPPER: Okay, Mr. Practical Motherfuckah. I'll see you next time you come around.

JOHN 2: Solid, baby, later.

(*Lights out on* PEPPER *and* JOHN 2.)

MAVIS: A man will walk into your life, take everything you got to give, then split. Like it don't mean nothin'.

BETTY: Why?

MAVIS: Why do fish swim in the sea?

BETTY: Well, it ain't gonna be like that with me.

MAVIS: I used to be determined like that. Just like you. But that didn't stop Duane from splittin'. Woke up one mornin' and found a note an' some money. Nigguh said he had to find himself; had to get himself together before he could truly be righteous to me an' Delores. So, he split. Left me an' Delores by ourselves an' left some money on the night table like I was his whore, or somethin'. As if that money made his leavin' all right.

(*During the preceding speech by* MAVIS *lights pick up* DUANE *u., rising from a bed, dressing, and leaving as a woman sleeps.*)

Shit, this is gettin' depressin'. I'm gonna go lie down for a while. I'll see you later. Be sure an' lock the door when you go out.

BETTY: Uh-huh.

(MAVIS *goes off to another part of the stage and stands silently a moment. She reaches into her purse and removes the brown case and stares at it.* BETTY *sits alone on the couch, listening to soft blues as lights slowly fade on both women.*)

Scene Four

A spot comes up on BOBBY *alone, his foot propped up on a basketball and a fistful of dollars in his hand.*

BOBBY: Alla my life women have been tellin' me what to do. I been surrounded by women. My mama and my grandmamma raised me. In fact, *both* my grandmamas. They shared me on alternatin' weekends whenever Mama wanted to go out an' party. My aunts used to hug and kiss me and tell me how I was such a cute little boy an' how I was gonna break so many hearts when I got to be a man. They used to talk about it as though it was a badge of honor. They all used to spoil me an' cater to me an' everything. That is until they got into one of their sour moods about men. Then, they'd change. Mama stopped spankin' me when I was real young 'cause one day she found out she wasn't spankin' me so much 'cause I did somethin' bad as 'cause I looked so much like my father. Once, when I was nine, my aunt Alma was givin' me a bath an' my other aunt an' another woman was in the room an' they was talkin'. An' my aunt took me outa the tub to dry me off. An' for the briefest second, I could feel alla them women's eyes on me. I knew they was lookin' 'caused I was nekked, but I din't care 'cause it was mostly family and the neighbor knew me since I was a baby. But it was the look they gave me. It was different and then I knew. They was admirin' me. It was like I could hear them thinkin' that there was no doubt that I was gonna be a lover. I was developin' muscles…*everywhere.* It was the first time I ever felt a woman's eyes on me in that way. An' it scared me. It was like I was bein' sized up for the kill. They seemed to be more strict with me after that. Always bossin' me around. An' the teachers in school. More women. Seemed like from one end of the day to the other, all I could hear was women's voices. Got so I was able to tune them out whenever I wanted to. I got out onto the streets where there were men and I stayed there even though I knew it used to hurt Mama so. But I had to be there. I had to know who I was, what I was. Mama could teach me to be good, and she could teach me to have discipline an' she could teach me to love. But she couldn't teach me to be a man, an' the streets seemed to be the only place where I was gonna learn. Then, the girls in school started their clutchin' an' whinin'. Tryin' possess me before I could even possess myself. Ain't no woman gonna possess me…*ever.* I'm tired of women wantin' in on my life. I wish they'd just give me a chance to realize my own dreams. If they could just wait for me. Wait for me to do the things I got to do. Everything would be so cool, then.

(Bobby *continues counting the money as the lights go down on him and come up on* Mavis *and* Pepper *standing on the street corner.*)

Pepper: Your truck driver friend was by the other day.

Mavis: Yea, I heard.

Pepper: He was lookin' for you. Had a gift.

Mavis: No kiddin'? What was it?

Pepper: I dunno. He had it all wrapped up. 'Sides, it wasn't nunna my business.

Mavis: Well, well, well…gifts. Hmmmm. Guess I better stick around. I need some additions to my wardrobe.

Pepper: Thought you didn't wanna be bothered with him.

Mavis: This is business, baby.

Pepper: Girl, you'd better snatch that man.

Mavis: No, tell you what: You snatch him, if you can.

Pepper: What makes you think I can't?

Mavis: Nothin'. You the one with all the theories an' ideas about old whores on the block. Let's see if you can't pull this nigguh.

(*Laughs.*)

Fat chance, stale as your pussy is, girl.

Pepper: One of these days you gon' go too far in your teasin', Mavis.

Mavis: Look, don't you understand? That ol' truck driver see something' in us that ain't really there. All we really is is forbidden fruit. Once he's had his fill he'll go back to that old biddie he always been with.

Pepper: Ain't nothin' real far as you're concerned, but for me he's a way out an' a way for me to hold my life together. If you don't want him, then hey—

Mavis: Like I said, the nigguh's all yours.

Pepper: Don't be doin' me no favors.

Mavis: That truck driver ain't hardly no favor. He's prob'ly the best you can do…how long you think it's goin' be before that truck driver decides you ain't right for him? 'Specially when he start thinkin' about alla them men who've had you before him.

Pepper: I can be loved!!

Mavis: Loved! Pepper, be serious.

Pepper: I can be loved, Mavis. You ain't got no right to be talkin' to me like this. I had a beautiful relationship once!

Mavis: You a "ho"…

Pepper: Not forever…

Mavis: …just like me, Pepper…

PEPPER: ..I'm a woman...

MAVIS: ..you're a piece of flesh and you can be bought and sold every day of the week.

PEPPER: Just keep it up, hear?

MAVIS: "Meet a man and make some babies," ha! Your body's so scrambled inside you'll be lucky if you even manage to get pregnant, much less *have a baby.*

PEPPER: (*Slaps* MAVIS, *knocking her a few steps backward.*) No!!!

MAVIS: (*Angrily.*) Who the hell you think you slappin' on?

PEPPER: You keep away from me, you hear!

(MAVIS *angrily starts toward* PEPPER, *when* PEPPER *pulls a knife from her purse and swings wildly at* MAVIS, *causing* MAVIS *to back away.* PEPPER *cries uncontrollably.*)

Dontchu come near me, no more, Mavis. You keep away from me. I don't need to take this kinda shit from you. I hate you. I hate you. I hate...I...I...

(*Turns and runs off.*)

Goddammit! Goddammit!

MAVIS: (*Shouting after* PEPPER.) Your tears don't break no ice with me, Pepper! You still no better than me. So, later for you jive dreams, broad. You hear me?! You still just like the rest of the broads out here.

(MAVIS *is quiet for a moment. Speaking to herself.*)

PEPPER? PEPPER? PEPPER, come back. I didn't mean it. *Pepper.*

(*Lights fade as* MAVIS *stands alone looking off in direction* PEPPER *has run. Lights come up on* MAVIS*'s apartment as* BETTY *sits alone on couch reading, and* DUANE *comes to the door and knocks.* BETTY *answers.*)

DUANE: Hello, is Mavis here?

BETTY: No. She didn't get home from work yet.

DUANE: Oh, I see. Well, can I come in and wait?

BETTY: Sorry. She don't allow nobody in the house when she ain't home.

DUANE: Well, I ain't exactly nobody. Is Delores home?

BETTY: Yea, but she sleep.

DUANE: Let's see, she just had her tenth birthday three weeks ago, didn't she?

BETTY: Who are you, the police or somebody?

DUANE: No, no days like that. I'm Duane Carter.

BETTY: (*Stepping back.*) Oh, wow. Ain't this a blip?

(*Lights fade to blackness. In the darkness there is a loud scream, almost a wail. Light comes up on* PEPPER, *sitting alone with a bottle of cheap wine and a glass. A husky-voiced blues singer of the Etta James variety is heard on a nearby record player singing a baleful tune.* PEPPER *has been crying; screams again, then laughs.*)

PEPPER: Whew! Thanks, I needed that.

(*Laughs.*)

The girl gon' do it tonight. Yea!

(*Takes a straight razor from her purse.*)

I'm tired of these four walls an' this city an' this broke-down, twenty-eight-year-old, goin' on sixty-eight-year-old body that ain't never had a chance to be nothin' 'cept what it is. Yea, I'm gon' do it *tonight.* An' I won't be laughed at or ignored or hurt by blind nigguhs who don't love me or care about me...*no more!* That's right!

(*Starts to cry.*)

'Cause Pepper gon' die tonight. An' I'm gon' lock all the windows an' lock the door an' let the smell of my dead carcass funk this place up. Yea, that's right. An' when men come to get my body, it'll be one of the few times since I been on this earth that any man has touched my body for free!!!

(*Laughs. Then grows silent and sits thinking. She reaches for the bottle of wine and unsteadily pours herself another drink.*)

Pepper, girl, you better leave this stuff alone 'fore you wet your drawers.

(*Chuckles.*)

Yea, just as the last bit of life oozes outa me all my muscles relax an' I pee on myself. An' that's how they find me. I wonder if they would laugh. They probably would. That's all I need. Be just my luck. Yea, be just my luck!

(*Starts to cry again.*)

You a wrong broad, Mavis. I thought you was my friend. I thought you understood me. I can be loved. Yea. Somebody loved me once. That's right! Someone touched me once. For free. Yea, an' I felt good inside like 'Retha and Etta James be talkin' about on they records. Frankie was good to me, real good. Our times together were wonderful. I felt like I was alive, an' all the people who called me ugly an' all the men who walked all over me on they way to pretty women and fancy dreams just disappeared outa my life forever! An' I didn't care about what Frankie was or what anybody said about us, or how my mama cried an' carried on. Frankie loved me an' cared for me and treated me right. And when I was with Frankie I didn't never have to be out on that block. I loved Frankie…and she loved me. She wasn't afraid to touch me. She treated me like I was worthwhile. Somethin' no one else ever did. I didn't wanna fall in love with her, but I couldn't help it. It ain't that easy for me to be alone that much. But man, she split, too. That jive butch walked out on me. Left me for some high school broad in New York. What's wrong with me? I'm just a helpless, stupid "ho." I couldn't even keep a butch. Now, you know *that's* helpless. So, I'm gon' do it tonight, y'all! 'Cause I'm tired an' I'm ugly an' I'm…alone.

(*Picks up the bottle of wine. Looks at it a long time, then wipes her lips with the back of her hand.*)

Later For My Drawers!!!!

(*She starts wailing uncontrollably and guzzles the wine straight out of the bottle. She puts it down, quickly picks up the razor and slashes at her wrist, but just as she is about to pierce her skin with the razor, she hesitates and pulls the razor away. She repeats this several times. Then, she nicks herself ever so slightly with the razor. Having done this, she steels herself for one last attempt. Still crying, she raises the razor and aims it toward her wrist. Suddenly, the razor is lowered, and we notice that her sobs have turned to a kind of forlorn laughter, both at and with herself. Looks directly up into the light.*)

Shit, I ain't crazy.

Scene Five

Lights come up on DUANE *sitting alone in the living room listening to music when* MAVIS *enters. It is some hours later.*

DUANE: Hi.

(MAVIS *stares at* DUANE *a long time saying nothing.* DUANE *rises, goes to her, takes her in his arms, and attempts to kiss her. She turns her face so that he is only able to kiss her on the cheek and pushes herself clear of him.*)

MAVIS: Well, this damn sure is a surprise.

DUANE: I knew it would be. Wow, you don't look like you hardly changed at all.

MAVIS: You been waitin' long?

DUANE: Coupla hours, I guess. Looked in on Delores. She's sure growin' into one beautiful little mama.

MAVIS: Yea. In a coupla more years, she'll be just ripe for pickin'.

DUANE: So...uh...how you been?

MAVIS: All right. Makin' a livin'.

DUANE: Yea, you got a pretty nice place here.

MAVIS: It beats Ferry Street. Remember them days?

DUANE: Yea.

(*Both fall into an uneasy silence.*)

MAVIS: Um...well, can I fix you a drink?

DUANE: No, I don't think so.

MAVIS: Still the health freak, huh? No drinkin' an' smokin'.

DUANE: Can't break old habits, baby.

MAVIS: Well, how about some food? You look thin. I remember you used to be a husky dude.

DUANE: Went on a diet an' I stopped eatin' meat, too. I feel a hundred times better.

MAVIS: Oh.

DUANE: Lemme have a cold drink like soda, if you got it. That'll hold me.

(MAVIS *goes off and returns with a soda.* DUANE *takes it.*)

Thanks.

(*Sips.*)

This is good.

(*Pause.*)

MAVIS: Duane...why are you here?

DUANE: (*Caught off guard.*) For you and Delores.

MAVIS: Why?

DUANE: Why you think, baby?

MAVIS: Ten years you been outa my life. Now, you just gon' come on the set an act like you only been on an overnight trip.

DUANE: Don't be that way, Mavis. This ain't easy.

MAVIS: Shit. I should hope not.

DUANE: There ain't nothin' here for you, Mavis. Not a damn thing.

MAVIS: A doctor wants to marry me.

DUANE: You gonna do it?

MAVIS: I dunno maybe. He been mighty good to me.

DUANE: Where the hell you ever meet a doctor?

MAVIS: (*Tensely.*) Whatchu mean by that?

DUANE: Nothin'.

MAVIS: I met him at church.

DUANE: You still go to church?

MAVIS: (*Lying through her teeth.*) Occasionally.

DUANE: Yea, I remember you in the old days…you used to sing in the choir and help organize the outings. The Perfect Little Angel.

MAVIS: That was a long time ago.

DUANE: High school days.

MAVIS: Uh-huh. The happiest time of my life.

DUANE: My greatest ambition then was to make all-state in basketball.

MAVIS: And get between the legs of every girl in sight.

DUANE: (*Laughing.*) Oh, wow, baby, why you wanna take me there?

MAVIS: 'Cause it's true.

DUANE: Maybe. But I've changed now.

MAVIS: Nigguhs don't change.

DUANE: Why don't you give yourself a chance to find out?

MAVIS: Duane, I found out all I needed to know from you ten years ago.

DUANE: I was a *boy*, then.

MAVIS: You was man enough to ask me to marry you. Man enough to make a baby.

DUANE: And boy enough to have failed you, baby. That's why I'm tryin' to come back if you would only let me.

MAVIS: You know what it's like to walk down the street for two weeks lyin' to everybody, tellin' 'em that you went down south to visit some relatives 'cause I couldn't face the fact that you left me? You ever sit in a welfare office and watch those pinched up face bitches ask you about your personal life and like you ain't shit? Huh? You got any idea what livin' on a food stamp is like, Duane? Let you come back?! Shit! You can crawl the hell on back to where you came from for all I care. I had to feed Delores by myself on chump change when your little pint-sized checks stopped comin'. You ever see a child goin' to school hungry day after day after day an' knowin' ain't nothin' you can do about it?

DUANE: And what good would it have done for me to have stayed around? I wasn't doin' nothin'. My job wasn't payin'. You got better care from the city than you ever got from me.

MAVIS: But I was happy with you, Duane. Didn't nuthin' else count.

DUANE: That's the way you saw it, baby. I saw it differently.

MAVIS: And now look at the result.

DUANE: Look, I finally got that music thing together. I got my own group an' I'm doin' real well playin' gigs around the country. We tour with all the big names and we get lots of recording dates. I got money now, baby. Alla the things I couldn't give you before I can give you now. That's why I'm back.

MAVIS: Forget it, Duane. Hey, why don't you send us a check every now and then. Like you used to do. Remember?

DUANE: Mavis?...

MAVIS: So where you livin' now?

DUANE: Atlanta.

MAVIS: No kiddin'? I hear it's real nice down there.

DUANE: Yea, it's a beautiful place. 'Course the rest of Georgia's kind of a drag.

MAVIS: What're the women like? I hear they're real man-getters.

DUANE: They got a lotta Southern charm an' they really know how to work them roots on the man they want.

MAVIS: How come ain't nunna them got you?

DUANE: I was too busy. I had work to do.

MAVIS: Well, at least I ain't the only woman you've fucked over with that line.

DUANE: I was tryin' to get my thing together to get back to you, Mavis. My leavin' an' stayin' away ain't never had nothin' to do with no other woman.

(MAVIS *says nothing.*)

MAVIS: So…you a big-time musician, now? Shoulda' known you'd be somethin' with that horn someday.

DUANE: I ain't no John Coltrane, but I can handle myself pretty good.

MAVIS: No kiddin'. You need a singer in your group?

DUANE: Oh, you a singer now.

MAVIS: I've done a few clubs around here on the weekends. Did pretty good, too.

DUANE: Well, sorry, Mavis, I can get a singer any time. What I need is a wife.

MAVIS: Hey, I thought I had steered us clear of that conversation.

DUANE: It's too important to be covered over by small talk.

MAVIS: Duane, I'm free. My life is my own. I do what I want, go where I want, and be what I want to be. I ain't givin' it all up.

DUANE: I ain't askin' you to give up nothin'. I'm askin' you to come back to Atlanta with me.

MAVIS: You know, Duane, sometimes I get these flashes of rage. Like I wanna hurt people. For no reason other than to see them hurt like I been hurtin' alla this time. You don't want me back, man. You don't even know me.

DUANE: I been waitin' ten years to be together enough to deserve you, baby. I don't hear a word you sayin'.

MAVIS: No. I ain't goin' back.

DUANE: Whatchu gonna do, spend the rest of your life strugglin' to make ends meet? And for what? To satisfy some jive notion of false pride. Damn, Mavis, be serious.

MAVIS: Whatever I am an' whatever I'm gonna be couldna' never happened if it hadn't been for you, my man.

DUANE: Wow. Okay, so alla your misery is my fault. But I ain't denyin' it. I been insistin' on it ever since I got here. Okay, but look around, baby. You got this crowded little four room crib an' maybe you payin' about $150 a month for it. So what? What the hell is that? I betcha you scuffle to make that rent. An' that overcrowded school down the street? Is that where Delores goes? Is that where you sendin' my daughter to school? How many clothes she got? You got any credit cards anywhere? If she get sick can you afford the hospital bills? When you walk in a store do motherfuckahs fall all over themselves to wait on you 'cause you somebody? No! So, watchu tellin' me, actin' all sanctimonious an' shit. Hey, just where the hell do you think you're comin' from with me? Duane Carter. Duane *Carter!* You mention that name anywhere in the music business and people go crazy 'cause I'm one of the best side men there is. Go look on the back of your record albums over there and check out the personnel. That "D. Carter" you see is me, baby. I play the best clubs in the top cities in the county. Down in Atlanta I'm a personal friend of everybody that's anybody. You understand? Don't a week go by that I ain't pullin' in big bucks. Hey, look at me, woman! I ain't no wayward nigguh who just happened to make good because he hit the number. I spent ten years of my life buildin' somethin' that's gonna last. It may sound like pie-in-the-sky to you, but I ain't jivin'. Mavis, I can offer you the world 'cause I can *give* you the world.

MAVIS: Yea. You givin' me everything but yourself. That's why I know can't nothin' be real between us.

DUANE: Then, don't forgive me. Hate me. But just come back. Everything I got is yours. What we had has always been real for me, Mavis.

MAVIS: That why you left me an' Delores?

DUANE: Look, I couldn't do nothin' here, I was stiflin'. Workin' as a short order cook, an' knowin' all the time I was better than that. Knowin' all the time I was a young man who had the talent to be *somebody*. I couldn't see bringin' Delores up like we was brought up. But you. All you wanted was security. Nothin' else. To hell with my dreams and ambitions.

MAVIS: Security can mean a lot to a woman who ain't never had none.

DUANE: Just one word of encouragement from you was all I needed. That job wasn't no good for me.

MAVIS: You was makin' good money. Why should I have to give that up for somethin' I wasn't even sure could work.

DUANE: You coulda at least give me a chance.

MAVIS: I couldn't *afford* to. I was happier than I ever coulda imagined. I couldn't throw alla that away for a pipe dream.

DUANE: Except now you see it wasn't no pipe dream.

MAVIS: Yea...now, I see.

DUANE: Baby, I had to have more than what we had then. I knew I had to grow up, I knew I had to provide for you, I knew I had to be somebody, or die. I tried to make you understand, but you wouldn't listen.

MAVIS: It was a beautiful time for us, despite the hassles.

DUANE: It was hell for me. I don't never wanna see those days again. But now, I'm satisfied, 'cause I got everything I went after.

MAVIS: Yea, but you lost me, Duane, 'cause where I'm at today don't even include you.

DUANE: You really mean that, don't you?

MAVIS: You had no choices? Well, neither do I.

DUANE: At least live there, baby.

MAVIS: You know that it wouldn't work out.

DUANE: Then, ain't no reason for me to stay around here.

(*Rises to leave.*)

MAVIS: It's late, Duane. Why don't you spend the night an' drive back tomorrow? The sun'll be up an' you'll be fresh. Besides, you can see Delores.

DUANE: Thanks, but I'll be all right. It's best that I split. Seein' Delores woulda been nice, but, well… it would just make things worse, you know? 'Sides, Mavis, I don't dig sleepin' in no strange beds.

MAVIS: (*Without emotion.*) I can send Delores down to see you on summa the holidays an' durin' the summers.

DUANE: I'll keep a lookout for her.

MAVIS: She oughta enjoy herself. By the way, you got any other kids?

DUANE: Yea. A son in Baltimore.

MAVIS: Oh.

(*Smiles.*)

Well, someday you can take Delores to see him. She's always wanted a brother or sister.

(*Lights a cigarette and begins to smoke.* DUANE *stands watching her a long time.*)

DUANE: Baby—

MAVIS: Goodbye, Duane.

(DUANE *goes out without a word as* MAVIS *continues sitting on the sofa staring straight ahead. A spot picks up* BETTY *in another part of the stage.*)

BETTY: Aunt Mavis! Aunt Mavis! Bobby gave me his fraternity ring an' he says I'm gonna be his forever. He said when he gets outa school he's gonna come back an' marry me. We're gonna be so happy. You'll see. I love him so much. We gonna have lotsa kids an' Bobby's gonna work hard an' make everything sweet for us. Everything's gonna work out. You'll see. You'll see.

(*Light fades on* BETTY *and picks up on* PEPPER.)

PEPPER: I told you! I told you I'd be offa this block. Me an' your truck driver friend's gon' hook up. That's right! Live with it, broad. Look at that ring. Coulda been your ring, but it's mine now. An' I'm gonna be a good wife to him, too, 'cause I got everything to lose.

(*Light fades on* PEPPER *as* MAVIS *continues sitting, although her face now reflects loneliness, bitterness, and resignation. She rises, slips off her dress, and tosses it casually away from her. The cigarette dangles from her lips as she saunters across the stage to a bed and falls upon it and lies still almost as though dead.* JOHN 1 *stands near the bed adjusting his clothing as though in the final stages of dressing. He reaches into his pocket and tosses some money on the bed. It lands near* MAVIS *who makes the barest of moves to pick it up.* JOHN 1 *looks at* MAVIS *a moment then exits without a word.* MAVIS *simply lies still, then slowly rises and rolls the money into a tiny roll, places one leg on a chair, and with her back to the audience inserts the money into her vagina. Lights come up on* BETTY *and* PEPPER *who stand at opposite ends of the stage.* MAVIS *stands tired and worn as though the years of what she has been doing have finally caught up with her.* BETTY *and* PEPPER *begin to laugh.*)

MAVIS: Fuck it!!!

(*Breaks into laughter and then tears.*)

You can all kiss my ass!!!

Blackness

THE
Mighty Gents

Notes on *The Mighty Gents*

The first play I wrote after graduating from Howard was a one-act entitled *The Street Corner*. The main characters were all teenagers, and the work reflected my memories of the youngbloods I knew on "the block" when I was growing up in Newark, New Jersey. As I aged, however, moving swiftly through my twenties, the characters in the play began to age with me. In fact, my memories of my teen years became less and less vivid as time went by, perhaps because I was not a true "hard head." I was always on the periphery of thug life, but never really in it. I always knew—somehow, some way, no matter what—that I was headed someplace else. But I was a witness nonetheless to the gradual decline of many of the young men I came up with. They were lost to alcohol, to drugs, to crime, to senseless violence, and in at least two cases, to suicide.

As I moved deeper into my twenties, my approach to the rewrites of *The Street Corner* began to change as the steady drumbeat of news of death, incarceration, or loss to disease among so many of my friends came with increasing frequency. I changed the characters: from eighteen to thirty, the age I was nearing when I developed the final version that would become *The Mighty Gents*; from all male to including a female character; from the children of working class to, with one notable exception, men who were either homeless or barely working poor.

I also wanted to explore the anger, desperation, and lack of direction I was seeing all around me in Newark, Harlem, and the black communities I was visiting across America—wherever my professional career was taking me at the time.

At some point, I changed the title of the play from *The Street Corner* to *The Last Street Play*, a reference to the idea that this would be the last play I'd ever write about life on the block. There were ideas I had, statements about black life I wanted to make, that needed a broader arena. (I'd find them in *The Talented Tenth*, but more about that later.)

I finally settled on the title *The Mighty Gents*. It was evocative of many of the New York–area street gangs of the '50s and '60s, where names that included words like *kings*, *imperial*, and *esquire* were ubiquitous. In Newark during the late '50s and early '60s, the coolest thing you could be was "a gent." We dressed to "the nines," as we used to say. We eschewed jeans and sneakers, unless we were going to play ball somewhere. We knew all the latest styles and top clothiers.

I also remembered a story I'd heard about the Negro leagues, and how many of the teams had gotten their names: in an age when black life in America was so severely circumscribed, the names that were chosen were ones that ascribed a strong sense of self to each team and member. The Chicago American-Giants, the Kansas City Monarchs, the Newark Eagles, the Philadelphia Stars—names like these were about affirmation and aspiration. They were about presence. Hence, "The Mighty Gents": a name clung to by a group of thirty-year-olds who were once the would-be princes of their neighborhoods—warriors who ruled their streets—now homeless, forgotten, and disrespected by young people who have little knowledge and less concern about the notorious street kings these men used to be.

The Last Street Play was first performed at the Urban Arts Corps in the Chelsea section of Manhattan in the spring of 1976. It was produced by the Frank Silvera Writers Workshop. The Manhattan Theater Club produced the play the following year. It opened, again under the title *The Last Street Play*, on May 12, 1977. That production was directed by Tom Bullard, and Roscoe Orman, Yvette Hawkins, Maurice Woods, Morgan Freeman, Gary Bolling, and Richard Gant were featured in the cast. James Lipton produced the play on Broadway, under the title *The Mighty Gents*, in 1978. That production was directed by Harold Scott, and the cast included Dorian Harewood, Starletta DuPois, Morgan Freeman, Howard Rollins, Frank Adu, Brent Jennings, Richard Gant, and Mansoor Najee-Ullah.

The Mighty Gents

Characters

FRANKIE: *Age thirty. The leader.*

TINY, LUCKY, ELDRIDGE: *All are age thirty. All are followers.*

ZEKE: *Age fifty-two, or thereabouts. A man grown old before his time who has seen it all before.*

BRAXTON: *Age twenty-nine. A pimp. A hustler. A smalltime hood.*

FATHER: *Frankie's father.*

RITA: *Age twenty-eight. Frankie's "old lady."*

In memory of all the
Brothers and Sisters
who saw the light at the
end of the tunnel…and
chose the darkness instead.

Scene One

A spot comes up on RITA, *sitting in a rocking chair. She is knitting. She will always be lit and visible throughout the entire play.*

The spot on RITA *dims a bit and lights up on* FRANKIE SOJOURNER, *drinking from a bottle of cheap liquor, standing alone on a street corner.*

A series of slides projected on a rear wall shows photographs of the Mighty Gents, circa 1960.

Sound: A street fight. Shouts, screams. The sounds of the fight fade and are gradually replaced by marching feet.

The slides continue and we hear the Mighty Gents' chant:

VOICE NO. 1: Make way! Step back! Mighty Gents is comin'! Mighty Gents is comin'!

VOICE NO. 2: We're the Mighty Gents.

VOICE NO. 3: Earth-shakers.

VOICE NO. 4: Troublemakers.

VOICE NO. 1: Woof-ticket takers.

ALL: And known to put fire to nigguh's asses.

VOICE NO. 2: We're the Mighty Gents!

VOICE NO. 3: Head-knockers.

VOICE NO. 4: Showstoppers.

VOICE NO. 1: Hard rockers.

ALL: Can you dig it?!!!

VOICE NO. 2: We're the Mighty Gents. We don't take no stuff.

VOICE NO. 3: We're the Mighty Gents. Nigguhs known to be tough!

VOICE NO. 4: We're the Mighty Gents. Known to be lovers supreme.

VOICE NO. 1: We're the Mighty Gents. The baddest dudes on the scene.

ALL: The Mighty Gents. Back up!!

(*There are cheers and boisterous, juvenile laughter, which slowly dies down. The slides disappear and a light remains on* FRANKIE.)

FRANKIE: Once, when I was about fifteen, I met this broad who was around thirty at the time. I was young an' tryin' to be fly and the mysteries of sex still held a certain kind fascination for me. I usedta think that sex with an older woman would make me a man much quicker. The older guys on the block always usedta say that this broad really had it together when it came to gettin' down. I wanted to be more experienced like those guys. I didn't wanna be an ignorant chump alla my life. One day she came up to me an' the next thing I knew I was goin' up to her apartment. We sat down to talk an' listen to some jazz. She taught me about Charlie Parker, Billie Holliday, and Bud Powell—people I had never heard of before. I was really gettin' my mind completely blown. Here I was, bein' made to appreciate some music you couldn't even dance to. She served me this dynamite wine and told me about places she'd been to—places I'd only seen on TV. I really dug her rap. I was learning so much. I just knew this was gonna be my night. We drank some more and then she gave me the first joint I ever smoked. We all were wineheads in those days so a joint was really exotic. It was from Mexico. Outa sight. Then, there was no longer anything to talk about. We both knew why I was there, but she didn't treat me like I was a stud or somethin'. I really dug not bein' made fun of or used 'cause I was young. Yea, so we went into the bedroom an' she told me to lie down on the bed. Then she started to undress me an' when I was naked she took this oil an' began to massage me all over and hummed this tune. She kept tellin' me how beautiful I was. None of the girls I knew could do the things she was doin' to me with her voice and her hands. Hey, man, I was hooked. I thought to myself that the only thing a young girl could do for me was lead me to a grown woman. So, I just lay there tryin' to be cool. You know, talkin' outta the side of my mouth, tryin' to be profound, hopin' she wouldn't see how nervous I was. I had to really concentrate to keep from gettin' an erection. Didn't want her to think I was weak emotionally. You know? Then, she started to get undressed. I wanted to watch but I turned my head 'cause I didn't want her to think I wasn't used to seein' a nekked woman. Soon, she was finished an' she came toward the bed. And then I knew why everything was goin' so well: "She" was more well-hung than I was. I wanted to run but I couldn't. I wanted to bust that freak in his mouth, but I was afraid I might get killed. So, I just lay there and let him do whatever he wanted to. I was there a coupla hours. Seemed like I was never gonna leave. Then, finally I was gone. When I got in the street I threw up. I slept in an alleyway 'cause I was too ashamed to go home. I don't remember much of anything else from that entire month except that I screwed every girl I could and did everything that was considered manly, extra hard. Anything to prove to myself that I wasn't a...well, you know. Yah, then I joined the Mighty Gents an' started a lucrative career as a head-knocker. After I drew first blood against the Zombies, I didn't doubt myself ever again. That freak died of a drug overdose five years ago. I wonder if he ever thought about me.

(*Pause. Lights change.* ZEKE *enters. He stops and stares at* FRANKIE *a moment, smiling ruefully.* FRANKIE *sees him, glares, then looks away in disgust.*)

ZEKE: Frankie...how ya doin'?

FRANKIE: Go 'way, old man.

ZEKE: How 'bout a drink?

FRANKIE: Please, man. I'm busy.

ZEKE: Busy doin' nothing. Ha, ha, ha. Look at you: An exgangbuster, only now you a present-day bum. Tired of it, aincha, youngblood? I know. I been there, too.

FRANKIE: Look, Zeke. You gon' move...or should I?

ZEKE: This a free sidewalk. I can stand where I want.

FRANKIE: Suit yourself.

(FRANKIE *starts off.*)

ZEKE: That's right. Walk on off. Treat me like I'm a nobody. Well, I'm somebody, too. I'm somebody, too.

FRANKIE: Later for you, old man...

ZEKE: (*Looks at FRANKIE.*) Why you dislike me so, Frankie? I ain't never did nothin' to you.

FRANKIE: It's not like I dislike you, Zeke. Just ain't got no use for you, that's all.

ZEKE: That's the trouble with the young folks these days. Ain't got no goddamn respect. In my time, people had respect.

FRANKIE: Your time is past, old man.

ZEKE: Yeah, guess you right. I grew up in Harlem in a time when my old neighborhood was known as the "bloodbucket." Harlem was a punishment tour for the cops in those days. I was a pimp at seventeen. Can you imagine that? At seventeen. Now, that's a distinction few men can claim. But underneath all that, there was love...there was respect...these days...

FRANKIE: These days people are in to survivin'.

ZEKE: Survivin' don't mean nothin'. Winnin' does.

FRANKIE: I'll see you later. Here, knock yourself out.

(FRANKIE *looks disgustedly at ZEKE, who begins gulping the contents of the bottle down.*)

Zeke, you ain't goin' nowhere except to an open grave. An' that's one trip I ain't hardly gon' make with you.

(FRANKIE *turns and exits as* ZEKE *watches him.* ZEKE *laughs wildly for three of four beats, then the laughter stops. He glares in the direction* FRANKIE *has exited and holds the glare while turning to the audience. He eyes the audience sullenly, his eyes darting from here to there. Finally, he will settle on one member of the audience. The scowl melts into a warm and charming smile.*)

ZEKE: Hey, Sport. Got a quarter?

(*There is a blackout of all lights except the spot on* RITA.)

End of Scene One

Scene Two

RITA *continues to rock in her chair and knit.*

An additional light now comes up on another street corner somewhere. We see TINY, LUCKY, *and* ELDRIDGE.... *They are in the middle of a conversation, and also pass around a bottle of cheap liquor.*

They seem bored... devoid of any real purpose. All three are only thirty years of age but project a sense of advancing years. The spark we saw in them in the slides has disappeared long ago. Only a dull flicker illuminates their spirits now.

However, TINY *seems to have the most energy of the group. A certain pragmatic nature, tinged with a sense of cynicism will penetrate his nature. Perhaps it was the war in Vietnam, a wound from which still causes him to limp slightly.* TINY *is sometimes a leader of this motley group when* FRANKIE *is not around.*

ELDRIDGE *is one of those guys who will go along on any ride that will take him somewhere. He is smart without being very bright. He destroyed himself long ago with indulgence in alcohol. He tried drugs at one point, but gave it up when he nearly died from an overdose. He found that suicide was not one of his "trips."*

LUCKY *is highly emotional and somewhat unsure of himself. He never volunteers to do anything, and is one of those people who always expects someone else to take the initiative in something.*

All three were once close. Now, they don't particularly like each other, but remain together because they're outcasts and no one will have them. ELDRIDGE *is pacing.*

ELDRIDGE: Anybody seen Frankie?

LUCKY: He'll be around sooner, or later.

(ELDRIDGE *looks offstage. He sees something that brings a smile to his face.*)

ELDRIDGE: Hey, man, will you check out this "mama," here.

LUCKY: (*Looking in same direction.*) Good God!

(*All begin looking out toward the audience.*)

ELDRIDGE: If she ain't just about the finest "hammer" I have ever seen. Watch this.

(*Shouting toward audience.*)

Hey, sweet thing? Hey, pretty mama. Can I walk along with you? Hey, fine struttin' sistuh. Hey? Hey?!

(*The others guffaw as the unseen woman apparently has kept walking.* ELDRIDGE *stands embarrassed, for a moment, then begins shouting angrily toward the unseen woman.*)

Oh, so you think you into somethin', huh? Well, you ain't, so deal with that, "Miss Hollywood." There're more apples on the tree, an' more fish in the sea, too, for that matter. So, later for you...SKANK!!

LUCKY: Hey, man, why you wanna be like that? Damn!

TINY: Yea, Eldridge. It was her privilege not to speak.

ELDRIDGE: I get tired of these jive-time, stuck-up broads, man. So, I ain't Rockefeller. So what? That don't mean I gotta be so much dirt under her feet. I make a simple greeting an' she act like I offended her by speaking. I hate that, man.

LUCKY: Man, ugly as you look, if I was a broad I'd be offended if you spoke to me.

(TINY *and* LUCKY *break into laughter, as* ELDRIDGE *glares at them, trying to think of a counter-insult.*)

ELDRIDGE: Least I had the heart to speak to her. Least I had that much pride in myself.

LUCKY: Too bad she didn't share your feelins.

(LUCKY *and* TINY *begin laughing again.*)

ELDRIDGE: Oh, later for you two stupid asses.

(*They stand around in silence for two or three beats.*)

TINY: Wonder where Frankie is.

LUCKY: Forget Frankie.

ELDRIDGE: An' what's supposed to happen when he gets here?

LUCKY: (*Laughing.*) He gon' turn that pile of dog shit into gold.

ELDRIDGE: What difference do that make? It'll still stink.

(BRAXTON *enters and walks toward them. They stare at him. He glances at them but walks by without a word. The three men remain silent until he is gone.*)

LUCKY: You know who that was?

TINY: From the minute I saw him.

ELDRIDGE: You think he remembered us?

LUCKY: 'Course he remembered. Sucker just didn't wanna speak, that's all.

TINY: We coulda been like him. The nice clothes...alla that.

ELDRIDGE: Ain't no sense in dreamin' dreams that can't come true.

LUCKY: You got that right. Still, in all...look at him, and look at us. Just can't understand it.

TINY: Maybe Frankie'll have the answer.

LUCKY: Yea...maybe.

ELDRIDGE: (*Begins to pace.*) Somethin' needs to happen, man. I'm tired of this waitin'.

LUCKY: Yea, man...seems like that's all we do now. Wait.

ELDRIDGE: (*Still pacing.*) Where the hell is Frankie? He's s'posed to be here by now.

LUCKY: Frankie's a thinker, man. He knows what's happenin'.

ELDRIDGE: Well, I wish to hell he'd tell me.

LUCKY: Frankie'll find a way out.

ELDRIDGE: Damn right.

(*Pause.*)

What's he supposed to find a way out of?

LUCKY: Damned if I know. Whatever it is we into, right now, I guess.

TINY: An' what happens if Frankie don't find a way?

LUCKY: Hey, man. You know the rules.

TINY: Yea. Yeah, I know the rules.

(*Lights fade.*)

End of Scene Two

Scene Three

Lights change as FRANKIE *enters the apartment belonging to him and* RITA. *It is sparsely furnished, with a cheap stereo phonograph visible, an old used TV, a sofa-bed, threadbare and worn, sagging armchair, faded wallpaper, and a window that reveals nothing on the outside except the window of another apartment.* RITA *still sits in her chair, knitting, and not having very much luck. Her hands tremble nervously. She is a young woman but looks older.* FRANKIE *plops down on the sofa bed.* RITA *barely takes notice of him.*

FRANKIE: Hey, baby.

RITA: Uh, huh.

FRANKIE: How's the knittin' comin'?

RITA: Same as always. I know what it is I want to do and I know what it is I have to do to get what I want, but somehow I just can't do it.

FRANKIE: Yea.

RITA: I went over Martha's today to hold her hand.

FRANKIE: What happened?

RITA: Doctor told her she gon' haveta have an operation on account of her weight. Her blood pressure's slowly killin' her. Doctor told her if she didn't cool out she be lucky to live three more years.

FRANKIE: I figured as much. I see the pain in Lucky's eyes all the time.

RITA: But what hurt was Martha said she didn't really care that much. And I held her hand and cried with her, Frankie, 'cause sometimes I feel the same way.

FRANKIE: Martha'll pull through. She just like the rest of us. She's a fighter.

RITA: (*Shakes her head.*) Not anymore. Her spirit's gone. She just waitin' now. (*Pause.*)

You think that's how come we ain't makin' no babies after ten years of tryin'? 'Cause our spirits are gone, too? Maybe if we find our spirits, Frankie...

FRANKIE: It wouldn't change nothin'. Spirits need places of magic to live in. We ain't that, no more.

RITA: We was magic once.

FRANKIE: (*Smiling.*) Damn right we was. That was the secret of our success.

RITA: We need a baby, Frankie. The circle can't be complete without one.

FRANKIE: Yea, I know.

RITA: We don't have no child then we gon' pass from here without a trace.

FRANKIE: Yea, baby.

RITA: Maybe our kid could be the one who might find the way to make this shawl. Then, maybe the little one could teach us how to be magic again. We can be magic again...can't we?

(FRANKIE *doesn't answer.* RITA *turns away. There is a pause.*)

FRANKIE: Hey, baby?

RITA: I'm listenin'.

FRANKIE: I been havin' this funny dream?

RITA: Funny dream?

FRANKIE: In the dream I'm alone and surrounded by wolves. They're lean, hungry, desperate. They keep starin' at me. Then, they jump me one by one, takin' chunks of flesh outa my body and, despite my screams, I don't die. I lie there, beggin' them to help me. 'Cause I'm a wolf, too, only I'm fat and healthy. They ignore me an' run away, leavin' me lyin' in my own blood. What does it mean?

RITA: Nothin'.

FRANKIE: But—

RITA: You had the dream last night. The past is the past. So, let it lay, honey.

FRANKIE: I can't.

RITA: You ain't got no choice, baby.

FRANKIE: I'll always have a choice. I was one of the baddest dudes who ever walked the streets of this city.

RITA: Yea. You *was* a lotta things, Frankie.

(*Pause.*)

FRANKIE: How's the knittin' comin'?

RITA: Same as always. I know what it is I wanna do and I know what it is I have to do to get what I want, but somehow I just can't do it.

FRANKIE: I can dig it. Hey, baby, I'm goin' out to meet the fellas.

RITA: Frankie?

FRANKIE: Yea, baby?

RITA: I love you.

FRANKIE: I love you, too, baby.

(RITA *hold out her arms to embrace* FRANKIE, *but he rises and walks past her to another part of the stage.* RITA *shrugs her shoulders and goes back to her knitting. Lights fade.*)

End of Scene Three

Scene Four

The street corner. TINY, LUCKY, *and* ELDRIDGE *stand around harmonizing an old '50s "doo-wah" tune.*

TINY: Yea, man, them's was the good ol' days.

LUCKY: People had class, then.

Eldridge: I thought they was gon' last forever.

Lucky: Nothin' last forever 'cept a bad marriage.

Tiny: You should know, man. You been married three times already.

Eldridge: Yea, three times…and to the same broad. Fat Martha. Hahahahahahahahahahaha.

Lucky: Least I got me a woman, Eldridge. Best you could ever do was a wet dream, or two.

Eldridge: Even a wet dream is better than Fat Martha.

Lucky: And Fat Martha is a helluva lot better lookin' than any of the booga bears I seen you with. That last hammer you had, Ruth Eva. Damn! That was a hard-lookin' broad. Hey, man, I heard every summer, she gets in heat an' tries to mate with every Mack truck she sees. That's how hard *she* looks.

(Lucky *and* Tiny *burst into laughter.*)

Eldridge: Aw, man, later for you.

Lucky: And you got a nerve to talk about Martha. Hey, man, Martha a stone winner. You'll never meet as fine a woman as she is, turkey.

Eldridge: Nor as overweight, either.

Lucky: Least my ol' lady don't mate with Mack trucks.

Eldridge: An' at least mine was nevah no junkie "ho," either.

(*Pause. There is silence.* Eldridge *has struck a sore point with* Lucky.)

Lucky: Whatchu say, man?

Eldridge: You heard what I said.

Tiny: Hey, y'all, let's not take it there, okay?

Eldridge: Keep out of it, Tiny. Yea, man, you heard what I said.

Lucky: Pray to your God that I nevah hear you say that again.

Eldridge: Oh, you gon' get warm, now, huh? You like to play but you don't wanna be played with. That it?

Lucky: You don't be draggin' Martha through the mud, man. You don't be don' that with my ol' lady.

Eldridge: It's common knowledge, man.

Lucky: I don't care if it's on the front page of the goddamn *New York Times*, suckah. You ever say that within earshot of me again, we gon' *fight*.

Eldridge: Aw, man—

LUCKY: Aw, man, nothin'. Me an' that woman been through hell together an' we saved each other when nobody else wouldn't lift a finger to help us. I owe that woman my life, nigga, an' you say some weak-ass shit like that? Man, I'll cut your throat!

(LUCKY *and* ELDRIDGE *grapple, but* TINY *pulls them apart.*)

ELDRIDGE: I nevah did like your ass, Lucky. I used to wish for the day when you'd get offed by somebody.

LUCKY: Well, I'm still here an' I'll be here long enough to dance on your grave and scatter your brittle bones to the wind.

ELDRIDGE: You kiss my ass.

LUCKY: Okay.

(LUCKY *leaps at* ELDRIDGE, *grabs his face, and kisses him on the cheeks. Enraged,* ELDRIDGE *tries for* LUCKY *but* LUCKY *dances out of reach laughing for all he's worth.*)

ELDRIDGE: I'm gon' gitchu, man! I'm gon' gitchu! Goddamn homosexual!

(LUCKY *keeps his distance and laughs as* ELDRIDGE *wipes the kiss from his cheek. Just then,* FRANKIE *enters.*)

FRANKIE: Say, why don't you lames cut out alla that noise?

LUCKY: Lanky Frankie, what's hap-nin?!

FRANKIE: Ain't nothin' happenin' but the leaves in the trees an the trees wouldn't be happenin' if there wasn't any breeze.

(FRANKIE *and* LUCKY *laugh, slapping each other "five."*)

TINY: Whatchu doin' for it, Frankie?

FRANKIE: Not a thing, man, and you?

TINY: Nothin', man. Just matchin' wits with these two half-wits, here. That's what's called a monumental task. Outside of that, I spent the rest of the time at my friendly neighborhood unemployment office. Rough. I ain't goin' back in there no more. Find me a job on my own.

ELDRIDGE: Told ya ya shudda come on with me, but, naw, you so hard-headed.

TINY: Man, I wasn't ridin' all the way down to South Jersey to spend the day pickin' peas for chump change. I'm better than that.

ELDRIDGE: Yea, but who got the money in his pocket and who's broke?

TINY: Later for you, man.

FRANKIE: How much you make, Eldridge?

ELDRIDGE: (*Evasive.*) Enough.

TINY: Betcha that turkey's lucky if he made ten dollars.

(TINY *begins to laugh.*)

ELDRIDGE: Well, whatever I got is more than *you* got, Tiny, so you shut up.

TINY: That's okay, man. I got me some money. My veteran's disability check's comin' tomorrow. I'll be richer than alla you chumps put together.

(ELDRIDGE *laughs.*)

FRANKIE: Looks like the war did somebody some good after all.

TINY: Yea, some good.

FRANKIE: Come on, man, you know what I mean.

TINY: Yea…sure.

(*Pause.*)

You shoulda seen me in the unemployment office. I felt like I was in a circus doin' tricks. I hate that place.

ELDRIDGE: Then, why keep goin'? You know if they got no jobs for able-bodied civilians, they ain't hardly holdin' no jobs for war vets with gimpy legs.

TINY: (*Quietly.*) Hey, man, lighten up. You know I don't like to talk about that.

ELDRIDGE: Aw, daggone, Tiny, you ain't dead, man, so—

TINY: So, just quit talkin' about that. Just *quit*.

ELDRIDGE: Aw, man—

TINY: I ain't tellin' you no more, Eldridge.

(*Pause.*)

ELDRIDGE: I'm thinkin' about makin' it down south, man. Maybe to Raleigh. Nothin' more I can do up here.

TINY: Nothin' for you down there, either.

ELDRIDGE: There's thirty acres my mama's livin' on. She always told me I'd be back.

LUCKY: Yea, when you ain't got nothin' else, you still got the land. A good point.

FRANKIE: Aw, man, the only thing south I dig is South America.

Tiny: Is he talkin' about Alabama?

(*All laugh, then, they grow silent again.*)

Frankie: What time is it?

Lucky: I don't know. Late. Who knows?

Tiny: Who cares?

Frankie: Let's sing somethin'.

(*All groan.*)

Tiny: Man, we just got finished doin' that.

Frankie: So what? It's better than standin' around doin' nothin'. Besides an agent might hear us an' sign us to a contract.

(*All laugh. The laughter dies down and there is the dejected silence again.*)

Maybe we can try and sing a cappella at the Half Step Lounge. We could get about $50 apiece for a night's work. Maybe—

Lucky: Maybe you dream too much, Frankie.

(*Angrily,* FRANKIE *turns and walks away from the others.* LUCKY, TINY, *and* ELDRIDGE *exit.*)

Frankie: (*Sulking.*) That's right, go on and walk away. That's about all you good for anyway. I've always known that. Always. That's why I would up bein' a warlord and the eventual leader and all y'all ever got to be was dumb-ass soldiers. Even now, you refuse to see who I am. Damn, ain't nobody ever understood who I am…or was…

(*Lights change. We see* FRANKIE *now assume the mannerisms of a teenager and his father emerges from the shadows.*)

Father: Now look, let's you and me get somethin' straight, boy. This is my house an' I ain't gonna brook no mess outa you, you hear me?!

Frankie: But, Daddy, that fight wasn't my fault. I had to defend myself.

Father: You broke that boy's arm, do you know that?

Frankie: It was either him or me.

Father: You may have to go to jail, an' I'm gonna haveta spend the rest of my life, damn near, payin' for that boy's medical expense.

Frankie: I told ya, he jumped me. I had to fight.

Father: You mean you wanted to fight. You wanted to hurt him. A man jumps you, you fight to get him off you.

Frankie: That's what I did.

FATHER: You had him down, Frankie. You had him beat. And *then* you broke his arm. For no reason. You took a stick and smashed that child's arm. S'pose he's never able to use it again. You ready to take the responsibility for that?

FRANKIE: Aw, c'mon, Daddy, lighten up. It ain't as bad as alla that.

FATHER: What makes you like that? What makes you so cruel that you could deliberately do somethin' like that?

FRANKIE: He gon' 'be all right. He ain't dead. Ain't no sweat.

FATHER: I'm gon' send you down south, that's what I'm gon' do. I'm gon' get you outa this town. Put you where you can learn to be decent.

FRANKIE: I ain't goin'.

FATHER: You'll go, boy, or so help me I'll call the police in here an' have them put your ass away till you ready to act right.

FRANKIE: Hey, man, I know you ain't gonna try to call no cops on me. No, ain't no way you gonna do that to me.

FATHER: You just try me, boy.

(FRANKIE *and his father stare at each other for a while.*)

FRANKIE: Yea, you'd do it, all right. Your perfect chance to get rid of me. You ain't never wanted me around, no way.

FATHER: I wanted a son, not a damn savage. I wanted someone who would grow and take this world like I was never able to do. Someone who was gonna make me proud. Your mother and me spent all our energy tryin' to do the best for you an' we seen our efforts fail. But she's dead, now, thank God. 'Cause she don't haveta hear the kinda conversations you an' I been havin' lately.

FRANKIE: You an' Mama didn't wanna deal with the real world, that's why y'all never been able to deal with me.

FATHER: All I know is, you either goin' south to your grandma's or else you goin' to the reformatory.

FRANKIE: You just don't understand, do you? You ain't never gonna understand. I'm a Mighty Gent.

FATHER: Not any more.

FRANKIE: I'm a Mighty Gent forever.

FATHER: There's only farms in the South. Down there you can be a Farmer Gent.

FRANKIE: I ain't goin'.

FATHER: What?!

(FATHER *moves toward* FRANKIE. FRANKIE *defiantly clenches his fists, ready to fight.* FATHER *seeing this becomes even more angry and menaces* FRANKIE.)

What the...? Put your hands down!!!!

FRANKIE: No! You gon' haveta beat me to get me to leave the Gents. They're all I got. The only family. You ain't nothin' to me. I don't never see you an' you don't even talk to me like you love me. Alla time pushin' me around. You want me to go south, make me.

FATHER: (*Softening.*) Son, listen to me...

FRANKIE: That kid broke the rules. He broke the rules. You got to be strong to be allowed to exist. You got to be able to command some respect and he couldn't do that. He insulted me an' couldn't back up his words. I *had* to hurt him real bad 'cause if I don't I be breakin' the rules, too. You got to stomp a dude when he sounds on you, otherwise you a punk. An' that makes you lower than roach doo-doo in everybody's eyes. I ain't no punk. I'm a Mighty Gent an' if I fail to make people respect me, I ain't got no right to walk the streets. I ain't got no right to live.

FATHER: Frankie...

FRANKIE: No! You ain't got nothin' to say to me.

(FRANKIE *starts out, but his* FATHER *grabs him and pushes him back.*)

FATHER: You ain't goin' nowhere, boy, except to your room to pack.

FRANKIE: Then, you know what you gotta do to get me in that room.

(FRANKIE *starts out of the room again, his* FATHER *grabs him by the arm.* FRANKIE *breaks free, and swings at* FATHER. *Enraged, he slaps* FRANKIE *hard enough to knock him down.* FRANKIE *gets to his feet and tries to leave again.* FATHER *knocks him to the ground.* FRANKIE *rises, fighting back tears, and tries to leave again and is grabbed at the collar by the* FATHER *who is now prepared to strike* FRANKIE *with his fists. This time, though, the* FATHER *stares at his son's defiant, emotionless face, and the cocked fist drops to his side. He pushes* FRANKIE *back away from him. Then, he reaches into his pocket, takes out a few dollars, and tosses them at* FRANKIE*'s feet.*)

FATHER: Take it an' walk on out that door an' don't come back till you ready to act right. Until that time, as far as I'm concerned you don't exist. I swear 'fore God, I think if I had a gun in my hand right now, I'd put it 'side your head an' blow your brains out rather than see you become what I know is in your future. Get outa my sight, boy.

(*Lights change and we are in the present.*)

FRANKIE: I prob'ly woulda gone down south sooner or later, if you hadn't tossed that money at me. You insulted me when you did that. I couldn't back down, then.

FATHER: I know.

FRANKIE: I cried some when you passed away, if that means anything.

FATHER: You destroyed what was left of my family, Frankie. Just smashed my dreams and hopes like they was no more than some cheap china.

FRANKIE: Forgive me...please?

FATHER: I was bitter even when they lowered me into the ground, boy. Ain't nothin' changed, even now. Goodbye, son.

FRANKIE: Goodbye.

(FATHER *disappears into the shadows.* FRANKIE *lights a cigarette, takes a deep drag, savors it, then exhales. He looks at the flickering match, smiles wistfully. Then, blows it out.*)

Blackout

End of Scene Four

Scene Five

Lights up on RITA *in the apartment. She is standing, drinking from a can of beer. The rest of the stage is dark. She takes a long guzzle of beer, then clears her throat. Somewhere in the darkness, the Mighty Gents hum a riff from an old fifties R&B "doo-wah" ballad, but we hear no lyrics.*

RITA: I used to be a street-warrior's woman—a "deb." We never called ourselves "girls." "Girls" went to high school but didn't know nothin' and thought love was like what you read in the magazines and saw in the movies. "Girls" screwed with their clothes on in the back seats of cars, and in the hallways of tenements with their drawers stuffed in their boyfriends' hip pockets while they stood pinned to crumbling walls holding their skirts up...yea...Charlene, Cynthia, Donna, Martha, and me, well, we were women. We belonged to the Mighty Gents, who didn't screw us. They "made love" to us. We was wise enough to know the difference and made sure our men understood what was happenin'. They loved us in their clubhouse on real beds, and let us carry their weapons for them, and took us places, and showed us more things than most of "the girls" could even imagine in their wildest dreams. The Mighty Gents told us we were their queens. We were special, then, and every day was filled with sunshine and light. We wasn't children no more. Just sixteen. Wasn't children no more. Childhood was a drag. Only people I ever saw enjoy bein' kids was those little rich kids on TV with their shining blue eyes and blonde hair, runnin' round sayin' stuff like, "Jeepers" and "Golly" all day. Well, our life was different. you know? I mean…uh…different…well, you know what I mean. I mean, we understood early that the rules was on Monday you was born, and on Tuesday you was grown up. That's just the way it was…"Jeepers"…Ain't that nothin'?

(*She falls silent and takes a swig from the can of beer.*)

Hey, the excitement never seemed to end, though. There was the moonlight bus rides to Bear Mountain on hot summer nights…And the parties at Tiny's house on Bergen Street. One 20-watt red-tinted light bulb in the basement and nothin' but slow records playin' an' everybody clutchin' each other and doin' the Grind. Alla us teenagers holdin' on to each other, clutchin' and clutchin', tryin' to get to somethin' we all knew we didn't feel in the real world, but, still, tryin' to get it from each other. Somehow, hopin' that…hey…that's okay, forget it. Then, there were the fights. Yea, the fights…everybody fought. Men *and* women. Me and my women…well, we was the baddest debs in the city. Fifteen hair-pullers, and we didn't lose nary one. That's right…nary one. The Zombies' debs were the toughest. I still see some of them around. We good friends now. All that stuff is past. Know what I mean?…But, the Mighty Gents and their fight against the Zombies' men…well, that's another story…one I don't like to think about.…I found out a lot about a lotta things after that fight.

(*She falls silent again.*)

…Like the night I carried Frankie to the hospital with that knife stickin' outa his chest…only time I ever really prayed and meant it…yea…it… was…all…so…much…fun. That's right. We were somebody, then. We debs…we women…now…

FRANKIE: (*In the darkness.*) Hey, baby, bring me a can of beer, will ya!!

(*Lights come up to reveal* FRANKIE, TINY, LUCKY, *and* ELDRIDGE *sitting, facing the audience as though crouched in front of a TV screen.* RITA *brings* FRANKIE *the beer and goes back to her chair and the knitting. The other men already have beer in their hands. We can hear muffled sounds coming from the "TV." They are watching a boxing match.* FRANKIE, *to the TV.*)

Stick 'em, man! Stick 'em! Make him bleed!

TINY: Lookit my pretty man dance! Lookit him *dance*!

LUCKY: A true master, ain't he!

ELDRIDGE: And so *pretty*! Even Sugar Ray wasn't *that* pretty!
(*Leaps to his feet.*)
You got him, now! Knock him out! Knock him out!
(*Others cheer and cry out loudly.*)

TINY: Yea, it's just about over now.

FRANKIE: Aw, man, he's lettin' the cat get away! No! No! C'mon, man, stalk him. Stalk him! You done already closed one of his eyes. He can't see no way! Pick him apart!

RITA: Oh, Lord, why don't y'all turn that mess off.

FRANKIE: Aw, Rita, whatchu mean turn it off! This is *art*. The matador and the bull!
(*To the TV.*)
Oh, man! Lookit that!
(*Others shout.*)
Kill him! Kill him!

LUCKY: Oh, wow! He got him wobbly-legged! Take 'im now! Now!

TINY: Yea, that dude can't hold up. He got to come down.

FRANKIE: Come on, sucker! Fall! Quit takin' so many punches!
(*Angrily.*)
Fall, you *chump*!!
(*A bell rings.*)

ELDRIDGE: Oh, man, how you like that? The bell saved the turkey.

RITA: And my nerves.

LUCKY: Don't worry. That fool's gonna fall the next round. He can't hold up against the champ. Even if he don't fall they gon' haveta stop the fight, anyway

ELDRIDGE: That dude's too beat up to last much longer. Look at his face, man. There ain't hardly nothin' left of it.

TINY: Imagine, man. The champ's only a little older than us. You know that? I remember when he started. He been fightin' for better than half his life. Damn, and he's still on top. How do he do it?

Eldridge: Yea. He ain't go the knockout punch no more. His legs ain't nowhere near what they used to be, neither is his stamina. And yet...

Lucky: The cat's a magician.

Tiny: Wish I knew his secret, man.

Frankie: (*Staring hard at the TV.*) You got to have the endurance, man. You got to have the endurance. Know what I mean?

Tiny: Somewhere in the world there's a primitive tribe of natives bein' ruled by a chief who's the same age as me. Know that? You know that?

Lucky: That's heavy.

Eldridge: A chief decides life and death.

(*Pause.*)

Frankie: See, if that cat push himself to the limit against the champ, he'll finish the fight on his feet. But, my man's gon' beat him. Simple as that. He gon' destroy that lame. And that's the way it *should* be.

Tiny: I see young dudes sittin' in restaurants downtown who make decisions that can change the world. They the same age as me, y'all. The same age. Damn.

Lucky: But they was never Mighty Gents. Guess that makes us even, don't it?

Rita: Is the fight over? I got somethin' I wanna watch.

Lucky: It'll be another round, at least.

Rita: I was askin' Frankie.

Frankie: It'll be another round, at least.

Lucky: See, I told you.

Rita: Lucky, you can't tell me nothin'.

(*Pause.* Lucky *looks at* Rita *a moment.*)

Lucky: What's wrong with you?

Rita: You know what's wrong with me. Same thing that's been wrong for years.

Lucky: Look. What's between me an' Martha is between me an' Martha.

Frankie: Please. Don't you two start that mess again.

Lucky: Don't worry, Frankie. I'm cool, man. I'm cool.

Rita: That's your problem. You *too* cool. In fact, you *coolin'* Martha *out.*

Lucky: You bein' unfair to me, Rita. I'm in *your* house, so there ain't much I can say, or do.

Rita: Well, we can step outside and settle it.

Frankie: Now, wait a minute…

Rita: Martha's sick, and Lucky is sittin' up here watchin' two grown men beat each other's brains out.

Lucky: (*Hurt.*) She ain't sick. Martha's gonna be all right!

Rita: Y'all ain't nevah had no sense of proportion. Not in all the years I known you.

Eldridge: Damn, Rita, why you always comin' down on us? Every time we come over here, you got somethin' to say.

Rita: Ya'll the reason I'm knittin'.

Tiny: Uh-uh. Forget *that*. *You're* the reason you're knittin', Rita. Don't put that on *us*!

Lucky: (*Quietly.*) It ain't my fault about Martha. I love that woman. I love her. We was just tryin' to find a way, that's all. That's all. I love that woman.

Rita: (*To TINY.*) I'm gonna learn the secret of what my Gran-mamma told me an' I'm gon' give it to Frankie and we gonna cut alla this aloose! That's why I'm in this chair, knittin'.

Tiny: You in that chair 'cause you scared.

Rita: Not as scared as you, Tiny. Not as scared as you.

Frankie: Okay, hush up!! We missin' the fight!

(*The tension eases a bit as the men settle back into watching the "screen." We hear the sound of a bell and the cheer of the crowd.*)

Okay, here it is!

(*Laughing.*)

Look at my man dance! That's right, champ, stick 'em!

(*Suddenly everyone cheers loudly and leaps to their feet.* Frankie, *pointing to the screen.*)

Oh! Check that! Check that!

Tiny: Haha! Ain't gon' be no getting' away this time!!! Ha, ha, yea!

Lucky: Stick the suckah! Stagger him, cut him, make him bleed! Make him bleed!

(RITA *sits in her chair trying to remain aloof, but the shouting of the men and the fight on TV both make her very nervous and uncomfortable. She is reminded of the gang fights and mayhem of her youth: something she has been striving to forget for years.*)

ELDRIDGE: Stick 'em, stick 'em, he gon' fall any minute!! Come on, champ, do it for me!! Do it for me!!

(ELDRIDGE *is throwing imaginary punches along with the image he sees on TV. The other men are wide-eyed as they gaze into the screen.*)

TINY: Get him, get him!! Beat 'em 'til he can't take no more!! Stomp him!!

(*A loud cheer from all of them.* RITA *watches them with a combination of fear and wonderment on her face. Then, she too, eyes the screen.*)

There he goes!

FRANKIE: He's down! That suckah ain't getting' up! no way! The champ got him. Stomped him into the canvas!! HAHAHAHAHAHA!

ELDRIDGE: (*Admiration and wonderment in his breath.*) Ain't it wonderful? He's a master, a true master. I love him, man; I truly do.

TINY: Lookit him. The winner and still champ!! After all these years! After all the crosses the cat had to bear: the winner and still champ!! Wow.

(*There is a long pause here. The Mighty Gents stand transfixed in front of the "TV set." There is a glazed look in their eyes. Otherwise, their faces are nearly emotionless. We can hear the cheering and shouting coming from the TV. It seems to grow louder as the men simply stand there. The Mighty Gents seem to transcend themselves, becoming for a moment—a fleeting moment—the heroes of their dreams. They bask in this. Then, suddenly,* RITA *leaps to her feet, runs to the "TV," and shuts it off. The cheering and shouting stops. The lights change back to normal. Snapped out of their dream world, the men turn, startled and resentful, to* RITA.)

FRANKIE: Goddammit, Rita! What the hell is the matter with you?!?!

BLACKOUT

End of Scene Five

Scene Six

LUCKY, TINY, *and* ELDRIDGE *are standing alone, as usual, on the corner.*

LUCKY: Damn.

ELDRIDGE: You can say that again.

LUCKY: Damn.

TINY: Need to get me a new suit of clothes, man. Need to get ready for the spring.

ELDRIDGE: You a chump, man. A first-class, grade-A chump.

TINY: Why? 'Cause I want a new suit?

ELDRIDGE: Hell, a new suit ain't gon' change what you is. You the same as the rest of us.

TINY: Man, why you jumpin' on my case?

ELDRIDGE: A new suit. Ha! Ain't you nothin'? A new suit. Broke as you is, as we all is, you got the nerve to stand here in fronna everybody an' dream about gettin' a new suit. You better start dealin' with reality, my man. The only time you gon' get a new suit is when they lower your rusty butt six feet under.

TINY: So whatchu care? It's my dream. If I wanna dream about a new suit, that's my business.

ELDRIDGE: Not when you start paradin' that dream in fronna me.

TINY: Then, go somewhere else when I start paradin', turkey.

ELDRIDGE: YOU go someplace else.

TINY: Make me.

LUCKY: (*Instigating.*) Oh, oh, it looks like a gunfight, y'all.

(ELDRIDGE *and* TINY *stare at one another as* LUCKY *chuckles derisively, but they ignore him and circle each other with fists cocked, prepared to fight.* ELDRIDGE *and* TINY *circle each other, dancing and feinting, resembling two middleweight contenders well past their prime. They become pathetic and comical, almost, when we realize that neither will dare swing at the other.* LUCKY, *laughing.*)

Hey, you two gonna fight, or dance the tango, or what?

ELDRIDGE: (*Interrupting.*) Oh, man, why don't you shut the hell up, you foul-smellin' fool?

LUCKY: Foul-smellin'! Maybe. A fool? Never.

ELDRIDGE: You wanna make somethin' of it?

(*Just then,* ZEKE *enters.*)

ZEKE: Make somethin' of what?

(*All let out an audible groan.*)

TINY: Hiya don', Zeke?

ZEKE: How the hell it look like I'm doin'? How *you* doing?

Lucky: We doin' fine, Zeke.

Zeke: Well, bully for you an' all like that. Where's Frankie at?

Eldridge: We don't know. We ain't his father.

Zeke: Damn good thing, too. If you was he'd be dead by now.

Eldridge: What's that supposed to mean?

Zeke: Nothin'. Just a passin' comment that' all.

Eldridge: Well, why don't you make like your comment and pass on, as well?

Zeke: Why is it, every time I come around somebody tryin' to send me off?

Lucky: (*Facetiously.*) Maybe you got halitosis.

Zeke: What's that?

Lucky: It's a medical name for cirrhosis of the breath.

Zeke: (*Innocently.*) No shit. Maybe I better go an' have it checked on. Huh?

(Lucky *and* Eldridge *can hardly contain their snickers.* Tiny *looks on with pity and disgust.*)

Lucky: Yea, maybe you'd better do that, Zeke.

(Zeke *starts off.*)

Zeke: But the first thing I'm gonna do is get me a drink.

Lucky: Do that, Zeke.

Zeke: See y'all later. Cirrhosis of the breath. Huh? Hmmm.

(Zeke *exits.* Lucky *and* Eldridge *laugh it up.*)

Tiny: Why ya'll wanna do that to him? Why ya'll take advantage of him like that?

Lucky: 'Cause that old man give me the creeps, that's why.

Eldridge: He gets this funny look in his eyes every time he's around us.

Lucky: Like he knows somethin' we don't.

Eldridge: I get tired of him always tryin' to hang. He ain't young no more. His day is past.

Tiny: Hadn't oughta treat him like that.

Eldridge: Hell, I need a drink, too, come to think of it. I need to get plastered. I wanna get so high till I won't even be able to remember who you two lazy chumps are.

LUCKY: (*Laughs.*) Yea, an' you liable to do somethin' stupid like get on the wrong bus an' wind up all the way crosstown with no way to get back. Like the last time. Remember?

ELDRIDGE: Let's not talk about that. Okay?

LUCKY: (*Laughs.*) Man, you was just about the dumbest dude. Hey, Tiny, remember this cat call hisself hoppin' the #1 to go home an' he falls asleep an' rides clear out to the garage on 20th Street?

ELDRIDGE: It wasn't funny, man.

LUCKY: (*Still laughing.*) Oh, yes it was, too. Man, everybody laughed when they heard about it. I heard even the bus people were crackin' up. This big stupid idiot lyin' in the bus slobberin' all over him.

(*Laughs.*)

ELDRIDGE: I told you it wasn't funny, man. I don't like people laughin' at me.

LUCKY: Why not, Eldridge? You a natural-born comedian.

(ELDRIDGE *jumps* LUCKY *and the two men grapple.* TINY *pulls them apart.*)

ELDRIDGE: Who's laughin' now, punk? Who's laughin' now!! I swear I'll kill ya. I mean it. I don't like nobody laughin' at me! I told you about that!!

(TINY *stays between them.*)

LUCKY: You put your hands on me again an' you're guaranteed to lose them.

TINY: Hey, why don't you two calm down?

ELDRIDGE: He ain't had to laugh at me, man.

TINY: Aw, man, it wasn't nothin'.

ELDRIDGE: It was to me! Bad enough I got to be a bum, but laughed at, too? Shit!

LUCKY: I ain't forgettin' this, Eldridge. You an' me gon' take it to the max for real, one of these days.

ELDRIDGE: Now's just as good a time as any!

(*They charge each other again.* TINY *keeps them apart.*)

TINY: What the hell, are ya'll crazy?! You gon' off each other over an insult? Y'all *crazy*?!

ELDRIDGE: I don't care, man. Nobody attacks my honor!

LUCKY: Later for your honor. I want your life, suckah!

(LUCKY *leaps at* ELDRIDGE *again but* TINY *pushes them apart.*)

TINY: Okay, that's enough! That's enough! Forget this! We Mighty Gents, remember? We fight the world, but not each other!

ELDRIDGE: The Mighty Gents was high school days. We grown men now.

TINY: The Mighty Gents is as long as we're together. Remember that. 'Cause that's all cats like us got left.

(ELDRIDGE *and* LUCKY *continue to glare at each other, but back away from each other as* TINY *continues to stand between them. Soon, they have moved to opposite sides of the stage and stand with their backs to each other.*)

What's wrong with us, man? What's wrong?

(*Lights fade.*)

End of Scene Six

Scene Seven

Lights up on RITA *and* FRANKIE *in their apartment.* FRANKIE *seems tired and perplexed as he stares into space and sighs heavily.*

FRANKIE: Yea, baby. Nobody understands who I am … or was …

RITA: I know who you was, Frankie.

FRANKIE: The guys just don't seem to wanna listen …

RITA: Later for them, baby. You don't need them.

FRANKIE: But, I'm responsible … I mean, the Mighty Gents is all we got … just like you and me. …

RITA: Spiderman left. You coulda done the same.

FRANKIE: And look what happened to him. Naw, leavin's not the answer. I got to stick this out.

Got to bring us all out together.

RITA: And what if nobody wants out except you, baby?

FRANKIE: That ain't true, and you know it.

RITA: All I know is I don't want nobody messin' over you, an' I'll do anything to try an' keep you from bein' hurt again. That's the way it is between us. Remember?

FRANKIE: Yea, baby. Me an' you been a real team.

RITA: You was the heart.

FRANKIE: And you was the soul.

RITA: (*Quietly.*) I let you down once.

FRANKIE: That wasn't your fault, baby.

RITA: I shudda been more in tune with where we was and the danger we were in. You almost died, Frankie.

FRANKIE: But, I didn't. I'm right here. Where I always been.

RITA: I remember when we were in the emergency room. I was just bawlin' all over the place. I just knew you was gon' die. Then you looked at me an' reached your hand out toward me. An' you told me that as long as our spirits was one you wasn't gon' die. You said all I had to do was keep on havin' faith and hope in us…together…and you'd always live. Your voice was real mellow-like and your face was so soft and gentle. I'll never forget how you kept reachin' out for me. Just kept reachin' out.

FRANKIE: (*Smiles wistfully and chuckles.*) Yea. That was back in the days when I was immortal.

(*Pause.*)

RITA: Frankie?

FRANKIE: Uh-huh?

RITA: Are you still havin' that dream?

FRANKIE: Yea.

RITA: You figured out its meanin', yet?

FRANKIE: No.

(RITA *sips some beer and looks at her trembling hands.*)

RITA: I need to finish this knittin', Frankie. I need to so bad. It's gon' be a shawl, you know. Gon' wear it to protect myself against the cold.

FRANKIE: I know, baby.

RITA: See, the sun always usedta shine where I was born. It wasn't paradise but it was the closest thing to it. Mama was always there to hug us and Poppa was always there to tell us everything was gonna be all right.

FRANKIE: That was a long time ago, Rita.

RITA: Yea. Then, the change came an' we left the land of the sun. But the old folks said for us to be sure to learn how to knit. Knittin' is the essence of life, you know. Alla that intricate stitchin'. Make shawls, they said. The shawls gon' protect you against your fears and against all things harmful to you. That's what they said. An' when the shawls are finished then we'd be able to find our way back home. I been here alla my life, now, an' remember what was said to me but forgot what it means. If I knew what it means I'd know how to knit and then maybe I'd understand why I am like I am. You think so, Frankie?

FRANKIE: Yea, baby. Rita?

RITA: Yea, Frankie?

FRANKIE: You know as well as I do that you wasn't born in no land of sunshine. You was born right here in Newark, N.J. just like me.

RITA: Oh no. I was born in sunshine. Nothin' but pure sunshine through and through. That's what my mama told me.

FRANKIE: It ain't nothin' but a legend.

RITA: It's the truth, Frankie.

FRANKIE: The only truth we got is each other.

RITA: When I finish this shawl, I'll be able to tell you what your dream means.

FRANKIE: You still the same girl I met when I joined the Mighty Gents.

RITA: I was gonna be a lab technician in a hospital.

FRANKIE: Yea, I remember. You had that ambition.

RITA: Damn right. I wasn't gon' be no grey shadow the rest of my life, like my mama an' all the rest of the women on the block.

FRANKIE: You was one mean, evil little mama in those days.

RITA: That's cause I know what was expected of me: I was s'posed to graduate at the bottom of my class, get an unskilled job, marry some dude no better off than me, have lots of babies, get divorced and wind up on welfare. I was fightin' against that destiny. I wanted to win.

FRANKIE: Well, looks like you still fightin', baby.

RITA: An' someday I'm gonna win. You better believe.

FRANKIE: You were the best lady streetfighter I ever saw. But I cooled you out, made you mine.

RITA: I made you fight to get me.

FRANKIE: You kicked and scratched so much till I began to wonder if it was worth it.

RITA: Those were the rules, Frankie. I was glad when you made me yours. I felt safe with you. You were one strong warrior. Even Spiderman was afraid of you.

FRANKIE: (*Laughing.*) Yea, yea, I sure remember those days. They were beautiful. Now, Spiderman is doing twenty-five to life.

RITA: We debs loved y'all from the beginning. Y'all filled us with a sense of pride…and fear.

FRANKIE: Yea…fear…

RITA: I can remember seein' men who talked down to my mama and spit on my daddy with their eyes and voices, cringe in fear when the Mighty Gents came walkin' 'round. And when they feared the Gents, they feared me…yea.

FRANKIE: Rita?

RITA: Yea, baby?

FRANKIE: I'm scared.

(RITA *looks at him.*)

I feel like we in this race, you know? Where we runin' hard an' we usin' all the knowledge we got to win. Then we find out that the victory wasn't worth the effort. We find out we been playin' by somebody else's rules an' reachin' for somebody else's prize. We got tricked, baby. I'm scared I ain't gon' find a way out. I'm gettin' desperate. Gotta make my own way.

(FRANKIE *buries his head in his hands.* RITA *looks at him for a moment.*)

RITA: Frankie?

FRANKIE: Yea, baby.

RITA: Frankie, make love to me.

FRANKIE: Why, baby?

RITA: Yea, you got a point, Frankie.

(*Pause.* RITA *continues to struggle with her knitting while* FRANKIE *stares wanly into space.*)

FRANKIE: Hey, baby.

RITA: Hey, baby.

FRANKIE: I love you, baby.

RITA: I love you too, Frankie.

(*Lights fade to black as* FRANKIE *and* RITA *continue in their poses.*)

End of Scene Seven

Scene Eight

Lights up on ESSEX BRAXTON, *standing alone. He is smooth, suave, and serenely self-confident. He is dressed in a conservative but expensive-looking three-piece suit.*

BRAXTON: I am the American Dream. I read the *New York Times* and subscribe to the *Wall Street Journal.* I drive a Seville…and a Mercedes. I have a comfortable home in the suburbs and a spacious apartment here in the city for…uh…business purposes. I wear only the finest suits and carry myself in a manner befitting my station as an upwardly mobile young man. I stand at the gates between the cavemen and civilization. My job is to keep them contained; keep them at each other's throats so that they will leave the rest of us alone. You should be grateful to me for what I do. Because of men like me, you never have to see these cave dwellers, unless you happen to venture onto their grounds. Their lives and deaths are meaningless to most of you and well they should be, for these hopeless humans are surplus people in today's world. Logic dictates that they should be killed off in a quick, painless, and sanitary manner; however, that would not be civilized. Hence, the need for men like me. We kill them for you. We are capable of destroying some 50,000 lives a year nationwide. We could double our output, but if we did we might easily put ourselves out of business. With no more cavemen to amuse itself with, civilization might decide that men like me would make charming playthings. Perish the thought. What's this? What are all these frowns and disgusted looks on your faces? Oh, yes, I forgot. You're all innocent…and the innocent are never guilty of anything these days. Not even their own ignorance. Okay, if it'll make you feel better, everything I've said to you is a lie. How's that? Okay? Good. Far be it from me to ruin your evening. After all, my job is to protect you. Not frighten you.

(Pause as BRAXTON *studies the audience.)*

I wish I could be gutless enough to blame my predicament on you, but nobody twisted my arm. I'm just in it for the money. What pisses me off is that none of you appreciate me.

*(*BRAXTON *turns from the audience and moves away as the lights change to reveal* FRANKIE *standing on a corner.)*

FRANKIE: Yo, bro. Spare some change?

BRAXTON: *(Disdainfully.)* Get the hell away from me.

(BRAXTON *continues on his way when* FRANKIE *suddenly recognizes him.*)

FRANKIE: Essex Braxton.

(BRAXTON *turns.*)

You're Essex Braxton.

(BRAXTON *still says nothing.*)

Remember me, man?

BRAXTON: No. Should I?

FRANKIE: Frankie Sojourner, man.

BRAXTON: Who?

FRANKIE: Frankie Sojourner. Frankie Sojourner, the Bad Burner. Warlord for the Mighty Gents.

BRAXTON: Oh, yeah. From my gang-bangin' days. Ancient history. Long time, man. What's happenin'?

FRANKIE: You are, judgin' from those nice vines.

BRAXTON: I manage.

(*Pause.*)

So, what can I do for you?

FRANKIE: Nothin'. Just saw you an' wanted to say hello. For old times' sake.

BRAXTON: What old times? You was a Gent I was a Zombie. You broke my arm once.

FRANKIE: And two years later you put a six-inch knife car across my chest. So, we even.

BRAXTON: Yea, we was barbarians in those days.

FRANKIE: (*Serious.*) We was warriors, man. Warriors.

(*Pause.*)

BRAXTON: Yea. I suppose so…well…later.

FRANKIE: Heard you was a big-time gangster these days, Braxton.

BRAXTON: That what you heard?

FRANKIE: Pimpin', hustlin' gambling'. But, no drugs. What's that, man? An example of your morals?

BRAXTON: Where you been hearin' alla this?

FRANKIE: A little birdie, bro.

BRAXTON: Yea, well, little birdies get their wings clipped pretty often. You outa be careful not to get in the way of slashing blades, my man.

(BRAXTON *turns*.)

FRANKIE: Yea, times sure do change. I used to kick your ass all up and down 18th Avenue. Now, look: you a star, an' I'm a bum.

BRAXTON: That's life, brotherman.

FRANKIE: Ain't always gon' be that way, though. I'm gon' be a star again, too. One of these days.

BRAXTON: Like the song says: everybody is a star.

FRANKIE: You tryin' to be funny, man?

BRAXTON: (*Looks at* FRANKIE *a moment*.) Gotta split.

FRANKIE: How'd you do it, man?

BRAXTON: What?

FRANKIE: Climb so far so fast. I mean—uh, no harm intended—but you ain't all that bright, and you really ain't that tough, either.

BRAXTON: Like I said...I'll see you later.

(BRAXTON *starts to leave again*.)

FRANKIE: Where you goin', man? I mean, you got time to talk to me. I *know* you got time to talk to me. How'd you do it?

BRAXTON: I used my head. I learned that when it's time for a moment in your life to be allowed to pass on, let it pass. You know? When I was a Zombie, I was a Zombie. But, hey, I never deluded myself into thinkin' I was gon' be a Zombie for life. I mean—

FRANKIE: I know whatchu mean, Braxton.

BRAXTON: Then, you understand why I can't be seen with you.

FRANKIE: Say what?

BRAXTON: You a ghost, Frankie Sojourner. I stay around people like you too long an' I'll be a ghost, too.

FRANKIE: You keep talkin' out the side of your mouth like that an' you gon' be a ghost, for real.

BRAXTON: (*Icily*.) You shouldn't let the memory of what you once did to me in some bygone era cloud the reality of what I can do to you, today.

(*Both stare at each other, poised to strike.* FRANKIE *relaxes first*.)

See what I mean? No discipline. That's why I'm alive...and you're dead.

FRANKIE: Not as dead as you think.

(*He lunges at* BRAXTON, *who steps back, draws a gun, and lays the barrel against the center of* FRANKIE'S *forehead*.)

BRAXTON: Deader...later.

(BRAXTON *backs away into the darkness as* FRANKIE *shouts after him*.)

FRANKIE: I ain't dead, yet, suckah! I'm alive!!! I can fight back!! I'm a star, you punk!! And someday you gonna know that!! The whole goddamn world's gonna know that!!

(*Lights fade on* FRANKIE *and come up on* TINY, LUCKY, *and* ELDRIDGE *on the street corner watching life pass them by. For a long time they stand—simply, glumly, and passively. Their faces register little or no emotion. We hear the sound of a car driving by*.)

TINY: What's that? A Mark IV?

LUCKY: Yea.

ELDRIDGE: Dude's prob'ly pullin' in a nice piece of change.

TINY: He don't look no older than thirty. Same age as us.

LUCKY: He got it made, that dude. Hey, look! Check out that Mercedes. Wow, man, that's livin'.

TINY: Hey, y'all, I got a letter from my folks today. Seems my sister's fixin' to graduate from Spellman College. They gon' throw her a party. Mama wants me to come.

LUCKY: You gon' go?

TINY: No. Ain't goin' home 'til I get over up here. What I look like goin' back down home lookin' worse off than when I left.

(*Pause.*)

Ain't that a blip? My sister's gon' join the Black Bourgeoisie. Yea. Hey, there's finally gon' be somebody rich in my family.

LUCKY: Yea, I know the feelin'. My two brothers got a taxi business goin' good for them down in Raleigh. Every time I see them they lookin' sharper an' sharper. Hell, I got way better marks in school than they did.

(*Puzzled.*)

What happened? What the hell happened?

TINY: (*Changing the subject.*) Man, willya look at that Buick?

ELDRIDGE: He really got it customized, too. How much you think it cost him?

TINY: Two grand, easy.

(*Unnoticed by them,* LUCKY *begins to weep.*)

ELDRIDGE: Aw, man, hell no. Eight hundred, at best.

TINY: Two grand, I said.

ELDRIDGE: Aw, man, yo' mama's two grand. Ain't nobody in his right mind gon' pay that kinda money to get his car customized.

TINY: Look, chump, I went to mechanic's school for a while and I tell you that custom job cost that dude at least two grand—and what the hell you mean crackin' on my mama! I don't play that.

ELDRIDGE: You need to play some knowledge, 'cause half the time you don't even know whatchu talkin' about.

TINY: I'm gon' be talkin' about takin' a coupla years off yo' life, you crack on my mother again.

ELDRIDGE: Aw, man. Everybody know you a' orphan. Later for you.

TINY: Yea? Well, later *this*, suckah!

(TINY *slugs* ELDRIDGE *and the two men grapple, then circle each other, looking like two would-be Alis or Sugar Rays well past their prime.* LUCKY *continues to weep. Then:*)

LUCKY: You two stupid asses! We blew it, man! We blew it!

(TINY *and* ELDRIDGE *stare at* LUCKY *as he wipes the tears from his eyes and stares at the ground.*)

TINY: Damn, what the hell is wrong with him?

ELDRIDGE: Damn if I know.

(FRANKIE *enters.*)

FRANKIE: What's happenin'?

TINY: You got it.

FRANKIE: Hey, Lucky, what the hell's wrong with you, man?

LUCKY: Fuckin' change of life. You mind?

FRANKIE: (*Offended.*) Well, excuse me for breathin', crybaby.

(LUCKY *leaps to his feet, ready to fight.* FRANKIE *glares at* LUCKY, *who backs down.* FRANKIE *turns from* LUCKY *disdainfully.*)

All right, now listen up. I think I got us our ticket outa this hellhole life we leadin'.

LUCKY: (*Sarcastically.*) No shit.

(FRANKIE *backhands* LUCKY, *sending him sprawling.*)

FRANKIE: Anybody else?

(LUCKY *rises, humble.*)

LUCKY: What's on your mind, Frankie?

FRANKIE: Every day we see petty gangsters walkin' up an' down these streets, actin' like they own the city. Livin' high off the hog, and spittin' on cats like you and me. Know what I mean?

ELDRIDGE: Yea, Frankie, but hey, man, that' the way it is.

FRANKIE: Well, it don't have to be. Hear? The way I see it, the only way we gon' get us summa this good life that's out here is if we take it…and I'm talkin' about takin' it off the only people who are more despised than us.

ELDRIDGE: Zeke?

FRANKIE: No, you idiot! I mean hittin' them big-time hustlers, that hang out in alla these bars out here. And I'm talkin' about one in particular. Essex Braxton.

LUCKY: Essex Braxton?! You crazy?

FRANKIE: *Insane* for not having seen this move before. The four of us is unknown. The census don't count us and welfare don't even know we alive. Who gon' know to look for us if we make a hit? How you gon' find men who ain't got no known address, whose parents and relatives ain't seen them in months? We can hit these hoods for alla they scratch an' no one would ever know who we was 'cause we don't exist. How they ever gon' find us? All derelicts look alike. Yea, man, we gon' hit Braxton an' take every cent he got on him. Crooks hittin' crooks. Who gon' give a damn? Niggas hittin' niggas. Who even *cares*?

LUCKY: Yea, man, you got a point. Yea, why not?

ELDRIDGE: Don't he carry a piece?

FRANKIE: So what? If he don't get a chance to use it, what good will it do?

ELDRIDGE: But, if he got a piece…

FRANKIE: He'll be knocked cold. When he wakes up his gun'll be gone, too.

ELDRIDGE: But, what's to keep him from getting' another gun an' come lookin' for us. You forget, man. He *knows* us. We do this to him an' he'll *kill* us. Gun, or no gun.

FRANKIE: Whatchall think I am, some kind of amateurish idiot? You think I didn't think of that. We wear masks, man. We hit him over by

Kinney and Prince where it's darkest. He won't be able to see a thing. He'll never know who we are.

TINY: I don't know, man. That gun still worries me.

FRANKIE: Fine, then you just worried yourself outa a chance to make some money tonight, fool.

TINY: Now, wait, I ain't said I wasn't gon' do it.

FRANKIE: Then, shut up. We do it the way I say an' anybody too squeamish can stay home.

LUCKY: So, this is the way out, right, Frankie?

FRANKIE: You damn right it is. Y'all forgettin' what he did to us? What he did to the Gents? He turned us into dinosaurs, man. The cat stabbed me, shot the Spiderman, and took three of our debs an' put them on the block. Y'all forgettin' that? He climbed outa here on our flesh, man! On our flesh! Every day that punk laughs at us. Every day! Now, it's our turn! An' it's the only way we gon' make it!

LUCKY: All these years, an' it comes down to this.

TINY: It's been comin' to this all along, ain't it?

ELDRIDGE: He got everything an' we got nothin'. It's getting' back time, ain't that right?

FRANKIE: There you go.

ELDRIDGE: Yea, this is soundin' better alla time. Sure.

TINY: I can get me some nice clothes.

LUCKY: Me an' Martha can get a nice pad.

ELDRIDGE: An' maybe some woman'll look at me an' have somethin' nice to say, for a change. Like they used to when we was the Mighty Gents.

FRANKIE: We gon' take back all the nice things we used to feel about ourselves. These streets gon' be our world again.

LUCKY: I can dig it.

FRANKIE: We gon' beat that suckah, good too. I want him to suffer. I want him to feel that pain down to his very soul, know what I mean?

ELDRIDGE: What if he puts up a fight?

FRANKIE: (*After a pause.*) Then, we kill him. It's as simple as that.

TINY: Oh, God.

ELDRIDGE: Damn, this is getting' thick. Let's get a drink.

FRANKIE: No, no drinkin'. I don't want nobody messin' up 'cause they high.

TINY: Aw, come on, man. A little taste ain't gon' hurt nobody. Besides, I gotta get my nerves together.

ELDRIDGE: You askin' a lot of us, man. We puttin' our lives on the line.

FRANKIE: (*Pulling a bottle from his hip pocket.*) Okay, okay. All we gon' have is this one pint between us, an' that's it. Understand?

(FRANKIE *takes a gulp and passes the bottle around.*)

ELDRIDGE: One pint? Man, we'll kill that in a minute.

LUCKY: No chance of even the slightest buzz.

FRANKIE: So, whatchu expect? This is important what we're doin'. Aw, man, you guys are hopeless! I shudda split a long time ago 'stead of nursemaidin' you bums along. Y'all can't do nothin' right. That's why you need me!

LUCKY: We don't need you, Frankie. We just follow you.

(FRANKIE *glares at* LUCKY. *Just then,* ZEKE *enters.*)

ZEKE: Well, well, it's the young boys. What the hell y'all doin' out here? That's what I thought. Now, c'mon, tell ol' Zeke. Who y'all gon' bust? Maybe I can give you some pointers on how to waste a cat without no blowbacks.

TINY: Zeke, I think you got the wrong idea.

ZEKE: No, I ain't. No, I ain't. Y'all gon' hit somebody. I can feel it in my bones. Who? Who?

FRANKIE: We may be inclined to hit *you* if you don't get the hell outa here.

(*The young men laugh.* ZEKE *is undaunted. He moves to each of the men and looks into their eyes. Then, he comes to* FRANKIE, *peers, then smiles broadly. He recognizes something he hasn't seen in a long time.* FRANKIE *nervously turns from him.*)

ZEKE: You got that desperation, aincha?

(FRANKIE *and the others look at him.*)

Oh, I can recognize it well enough. You reached that point in life where a man gets desperate. He got to make his mark now, or else he ain't never gon' make it. Got to bust loose, or else get busted up. Right? That's it, ain't it? Time to bust loose.

(*The young men are silent.*)

Lemme bust loose with you, Frankie. Take me along. Okay? Don't lemme just shrivel up an' die. Take the old man along.

FRANKIE: No way, Zeke. This is a young man's trip.

ZEKE: (*Begging.*) Please, Frankie…please…please…I ain't old. I can be young again. I can be strong…please…

(*The young men laugh.*)

That's right. Make fun of ol' Zeke. He a fool. He don't know. Well, lemme tell you somethin'.

(*Suddenly,* FRANKIE *lunges at* ZEKE *and pushes him violently across the stage.*)

FRANKIE: You're not funny anymore, Zeke. You're a pest. Leave…now.

(ZEKE *turns and exits slowly.*)

ZEKE: (*As he goes out, near tears.*) You ain't no better than me, Frankie Sojourner. You may think you are. But, you ain't no better than me!

(ZEKE *is gone.*)

TINY: Sometimes, I feel sorry for the dude, man.

FRANKIE: Sorry?

TINY: Yea, man, I mean, he's got nothin'.

FRANKIE: (*A note of fear in his voice.*) That's because he's weak. Because he's always been like that. That's why he crawls around these streets like a sick roach all the time. The best thing that coulda happened to him is that somebody shoulda put a bullet through his brain thirty years ago. He's a nothin'. God, I hate people like him. They're like leeches, suckin' the strong people dry, livin' offa the garbage the rest of us throw in the streets, then come shufflin' around us with their toothless grins and their hands held out, lookin' for sympathy. Well, there ain't none. Ain't at all. All there is is strugglin'. Constant and never-changin'. An' either you change, or you get changed up. That's all there is to it.

LUCKY: It ain't all like that, Frankie. It can't be.

FRANKIE: Don't tell me, man. I know. I know what it's like. I been studyin' it for years. Checkin' it out on all levels. Bidin' my time, waitin' for the big move to come, waitin' to be showed the way. Well, I found out you gotta make your own escape. Plot your own salvation. Ain't nobody gonna lift a finger to help you. Nobody. Not your mamma, your daddy, or nobody. Y'all understand that?

TINY: Goddamn, Frankie, what hell's the matter with you?

(*Lights change.* BRAXTON *emerges from the shadows.*)

BRAXTON: It happened on my eighteenth birthday. I must've waited about an hour for him to come walking along. Seemed like an eternity. I was tense, but not nervous. The sounds of the summer night swirled all about me: cars, buses, men and women laughing and drinking. Children up past their bedtimes, playing. I heard them but I paid no attention. I knew what I had to do, and I forced my mind to let me think of nothing else. Then, I saw him. His old lady was with him, as usual. She was *always* there. She was his other self and guarded him like a hawk. They were one. That's why he'd never been taken. They were laughing, holding hands; enjoying a happiness that has always eluded me. I envied him in that moment. It was the last time I'd ever allow myself that weakness. I slid from behind the stoop into the street, using parked cars to shield my approach. I reached into my pocket and withdrew my knife. I paused, crouched lower, and waited…waited…then, I ran from behind the car, rushing the last thirty feet toward them. His back was to me as they kissed. As I ran toward him, I realized that this final act would forever place me beyond the community of which I was a part. I was going to enter a phantom zone of human existence, stigmatized forever by what I was about to do, separated from love, from caring, from compassion. It was the end…and I didn't care one bit. Suddenly, her eyes opened. When she caught sight of me she screamed and he turned. It was too late. I had him. The knife came down into his chest. I saw the blood. I was free. She swung wildly at me and I slapped her to the ground. I ran past the shocked stares of the neighborhood and I heard her cries and screams disappearing behind me. I had won. I didn't know whether he was alive or dead. It didn't matter. Word got around to the rest of the Zombies and even they became a little afraid of me, then. I had more than cunning, viciousness, or daring. I had that one gift that separated me from the rest of them and that made me ruler over them all. They bowed down to me after that, Zombies and Mighty Gents alike. For they knew and understood, that I had acquired the gift of mercilessness…and I left their world forever.

(*Lights fade to black on* BRAXTON.)

End of Scene Eight

Scene Nine

Lights up on FRANKIE *and* RITA's *apartment.* RITA *eyes* FRANKIE *forlornly.*

RITA: Want some beer?

FRANKIE: No.

RITA: So, you got a new game plan. Huh?

FRANKIE: At last. I was afraid I was losin' the touch.

RITA: Well, good luck.

FRANKIE: It ain't about luck, baby. It's about execution.

RITA: Frankie, what if you should lose?

FRANKIE: I can't lose.

(*Firmly.*)

I can't lose.

RITA: Me an' the other debs wanted to win, too. That's what made us different from the "girls."

FRANKIE: Rita, please. Not now.

RITA: Nunna it worked out, Frankie. The war's over. It's too late!

FRANKIE: Too late?

RITA: The Mighty Gents are dead!!

FRANKIE: No!

RITA: Baby, listen to me!!!...

FRANKIE: That why you put them down like you did the other day? That why you're always belittlin' them? 'Cause you think the Gents are dead??!!

RITA: Frankie, don't you remember what they did to you? Don't you?

FRANKIE: So, they ran! The Zombies had us outnumbered—

RITA: They ran and left you. I had to fight at your side because your Mighty Gents ran and left you to face the Zombies by yourself!!! Frankie—

FRANKIE: You think I don't know that?! Sure, I remember...every day I'm with them! But, goddammit, Rita, they keep me alive. I'm *somebody* with them. They *need* me out there.

RITA: *I* need you, too, Frankie—

FRANKIE: Baby, you just don't understand. It's not the same kind of need. I'm the leader out there. Somethin' I can't be nowhere else in life.

RITA: But, you're risking your life for them. What they ever done for you?! What they ever risk for you?!

FRANKIE: Look, don't worry. I got it all figured out. Nobody's gonna get hurt.

RITA: Braxton's quicker than you, Frankie. Why you think he's lasted so long?

FRANKIE: Goddammit, Rita, open your eyes! Look at me! Look at us!! We ain't got *nothin'*! All I ever bring you day in and day out is the same, useless, tired, worn-out body, suckin' your life away—beggin' for sympathy, beggin' for understandin'—all the time—beggin', beggin', beggin'!! Don't nobody see me 'cause don't nobody *care*! An' it pounds into my brain every damn day of my life an' I can't escape it! I got to do this!

RITA: But, Braxton's a nobody, too. Why him? He ain't worth it!

FRANKIE: Maybe you're right, but at least he can pretend at bein' somebody. Hell, I can't even do *that*!

RITA: …Then, it's gon' be for me just like it is for all the other debs. I'm gon' watch you walk away from me an'…Noooooooo!!

(*She blocks* FRANKIE's *exit and fights back the tears.*)

Frankie, I ain't gonna let you go. No. If I gotta hold you here all night, I'll do it. I mean it, Frankie. I ain't gon't let you outa this house.

FRANKIE: (*Approaches* RITA.) Come on, now, Rita, you can't hold me here forever.

RITA: No, you get back and stay there!

(*Fighting tears.*)

You got no right to do this, Frankie. I love you. You got no right…

(FRANKIE *grabs her and tries to hold her to him. She begins beating him about the shoulders and chest, crying incessantly, nearly hoarse from fear and desperation in a struggle she knows she is losing.* RITA, *as she struggles.*)

No! I ain't gonna let you do this! I'll fight you, I'll fight you! I'll never let you out this door!! No! No!

(*But,* FRANKIE *is too strong for her as he pins her to him.* RITA *crumples to her knees amidst tears and anguish as she cries out to* FRANKIE.)

Oh, God, Frankie, please! No! Nooo! Please, baby, don't do this! Please! Please!

(FRANKIE *kneels beside her and brings her to her feet and they embrace. He begins to kiss her tears and speak in soft, tender tones.*)

FRANKIE: Shhh…shh…hey, baby. Don't cry. Please…Rita. Don't. You know I can't stand it. Please, baby. There's nothin' to worry about, I'm beyond the reach of the Braxtons of the world. They can't hurt me…now, cheer up, Miss Sweetness. When this is over we gon' split. Just you an' me. We gon' go somewhere where we won't even have to be bothered. Not by nunna this. Okay?

(FRANKIE *kisses her tears and wipes them away with his fingers. They kiss again.* RITA *moves from him and goes back to her knitting. The lights begin to change.*)

Hey, baby?

RITA: Yea, baby?

FRANKIE: How's the knittin' comin'?

RITA: Same as always. I know what it is I want to do and I know what it is I have to do to get what I want, but somehow I just can't do it.

FRANKIE: Yea, baby. I been on that trip all my life.

(*Pause.*)

Hey, baby?

RITA: Yea, baby?

FRANKIE: I love you.

RITA: I love you, too, Frankie.

(FRANKIE *goes to her and kisses her gently, then leaves.* RITA *goes back to her knitting as the lights fade…*)

End of Scene Nine

Scene Ten

Lights up on ZEKE, *standing alone, laughing at the audience, holding a half-empty whiskey bottle in his hand. He is drunk, disheveled, and is the epitome of the person everyone hates to run into on lonely street corners.*

ZEKE: I hate you all, you know that? You *know* that? Yea, you do. I can see it, because now you've turned your heads an' you ain't lookin' at me no more. You don't wanna listen to what I gotta say. Don't nunna you wanna listen. But hey, that's all right. Tain't nothin' to me. I'm just here to let you know that people like me ain't never gon' go away. We always been here an' we always gon' be here. Summa you gon' wind up just like me an' summa you gon' have me passin' judgment on whether or not you oughta be allowed to live. Can't deal with it can ya?

(ZEKE *drinks some more.*)

I see the way you look at me, wishin' I would go some place and die, so wouldn't no decent person haveta see me again. EVER!! Yea, just like that Frankie, and his bunch.

(*Someone has apparently said something to him as he staggers back and forth along the imaginary sidewalk on stage.*)

Yea, yo' mama, too. That's right! You don't scare me, either!! You know why? 'Cause I'm gon' reclaim myself an' enjoy my life just once more before I pass from this place an' leave the rest of you slobs to scramble for your own little bullshit existence. That's right: Bullshit!! Yea, I said it, so whatchu gon' do, call a cop?! I put a curse on alla you affluent Americans. A curse, but I ain't gon' tell you what it is. No! No! Y'all gotta guess. HAHAHAHAHAHAHAHAHAHAHAHA!

(ZEKE *laughs again, the coughs uncontrollably. He staggers a bit, then falls, then gets slowly to his feet.*)

Please...please...don't walk by me. There ain't no hate in me. I love you. I want you to love me. Won't somebody please stop and talk to me? I'm flesh an' blood just like everybody else. I wasn't always like this. Please? Hey, brother; hey, sister. Hey? Hey?!...No, huh?

(ZEKE *drinks again, then stares out toward the audience through half-closed eyes.*)

Once when I was seventeen, back in 1940, I was hungry and needed a place to stay. My father had put me out for the umpteenth time. I can't say I ain't had it comin' 'cause I was very undisciplined when I was a kid. Yea, well, I roamed them Harlem streets lookin' for a place to squat an' finally wound up with this group of junkie dudes and their old ladies; a rare breed in them days since drugs hadn't really hit Harlem, yet. They were very nice to me; let me drink all the wine I wanted, but didn't allow me to touch no drugs 'cause they wanted to protect me. They never bothered nobody, really. Just stayed locked up in our apartment on 127th Street and got high offa all that smack they was gettin'. Yea, an' I stayed with 'em for months, watching them get higher an' higher till finally they didn't talk; they didn't eat; didn't even clean themselves. They just sat lookin' dumb an' noddin' alla time. An' they began to try to get me to shoot up with them. Yea, man, the suckers had become real lotus eaters. But, I refused, man, 'cause my father had always told me to never put nothin' in my head that I could not control. They really igged me after that, an went on 'bout their business. One day, they got hold of this horse that some Cuban dude in the Bronx laid on them, and they all shot up...and one by one they died. The stuff was pure man, an' their bodies couldn't take it. They gagged an' fell on the floor twitchin', their eyes bulgin' outa their sockets, their tongues was stickin' out an' saliva was just flowin' outa their mouths. Well, I sat there for the longest time tryin' my best to deal with what was happenin'. I got drunk and sat some more an' finally, I realized why I hadn't run away. I got up an' propped alla their bodies up in real, dignified manners: legs crossed, heads tilted back, cigarettes in hands. They really looked great around that stove. I decided that if they couldn't have dignity an' respect in life, then I'd see to it that they had it in death. Yea. Then I went to sleep, and when I woke up, rats was eatin' their bodies. Oh God, oh God!!

(*He falls silent again, then speaks.*)

I had to bury them an' you know I did it? I set fire to that old abandoned building. Set fire to it and watched it go up in flames takin' my friends with it, and I swore on that day that no matter how low I sunk in life, no matter how much I got brutalized, I would never allow another man to think that he could control me and control what I am. I am my own man and I don't care how much you hate me, or despise me, or wish that I would go away. I am you. The real you and as long as y'all exist in this place I'm gon' be here.

(ZEKE *turns and moves away from the audience, mumbling in a tone that the audience can just manage to hear.*)

You hear what I said, Frankie? I'm always gon' be here. Always. You ain't gon' run me out. You ain't gon' belittle me. I take low for no man. You hear me, Frankie?! You hear me?!

(*Lights fade to black and* ZEKE *has disappeared.*)

End of Scene Ten

Scene Eleven

Lights come up full on street corner where FRANKIE, TINY, ELDRIDGE, *and* LUCKY *stand laughing and joking. However, when we first see them they are also singing a popular R&B ballad.*

FRANKIE: (*Laughter.*) See, didn't I tell ya we'd pull it off easy. Lookit this wallet. It's bulgin'. Bulgin' with at least $1,200. Can you dig it? That's three yards apiece. C'mon, let's divvy up now an' get rid of this wallet.

(FRANKIE *counts up the money and gives each his share.*)

LUCKY: Frankie, you're outa sight, man. Stone outa sight.

ELDRIDGE: You better believe it. Frankie gon' make us all rich men. Ain't that right, Frankie?

FRANKIE: How can I disappoint my fans?

(*All laugh and slap each other five.*)

TINY: We got it back, man. After all these years, we finally got it back. Ain't it beautiful?

Lucky: Yea, it makes me feel good inside. I'm somebody again.

Eldridge: Hey, you don't think he's dead, do ya?

Frankie: No, but he probably wishes he was. He gon' be hurtin' all week. Good. Let him feel the pain a little while. Let him feel like we been feelin' for the past ten years. Right?

Tiny: Right. No slack!! We the Mighty Gents. We take no prisoners!!!

Lucky: Damn, this cat remembers all the battle cries.

Tiny: The earth used to tremble when we walked the street, man. I can never forget them days. Even the gangs in New York were no match for us. Remember?

Lucky: Yea, those savages over there. Fightin' with chains and zip guns. Real barbarians.

Eldridge: But we beat them. We the only New Jersey gang in history to run a New York gang off the boardwalk at Coney Island. We was the Mighty Gents and didn't nobody mess with us.

Tiny: Yea, those were the days, man. People had heart, then. Not like now. The Mighty Gents used to run the streets and even the cops thought twice about messin' with us. Walkin' the beat in our neighborhood was a punishment tour.

Lucky: We was tested and we came through. The four of us. The last of the Mighty Gents.

Tiny: That's right. The last. We the last. Wow, man, I never realized…

Frankie: No! Don't even think about that. We here! Alive! An' that's all that counts. Just like in the good ol' days.

All:
The Mighty Gents be comin'
Eyes flashin'
And fists hummin'
We here
Some bad fightin' men
Come to take our place in the sun
We here
Some bad fightin' men
We live for the battle
Don't no one see us run!
Mighty Gents!! Aiiiiiieeeeeeeeeeeeeeeeeeeeeeeeeeeeee!!!!!!

(Joyous laughter. Just then ZEKE *enters. He stands looking at them for a moment or two, then slowly approaches. He joins in the laughter and they stop and stare at him sullenly.)*

ZEKE: Well, I see you boys are celebratin'. You musta had good luck.

FRANKIE: I thought we made it clear that we didn't want you around, old man.

ZEKE: Yea, you made it clear. But I'm around anyway.

FRANKIE: Well, leave, okay.

ZEKE: No way.

FRANKIE: Huh?

ZEKE: No way I'm gon' leave.

FRANKIE: What make you think we gon' let you stay?

ZEKE: Y'all ain't gonna mess with me.

FRANKIE: Aw, man, beat it. We ain't got the time—

ZEKE: *(Interrupting.)* Take the time, youngblood.

FRANKIE: Look, man—

ZEKE: No, you look. I'm getting' tired of bein' pushed around by y'all. I ain't goin' nowhere.

FRANKIE: Look, it's been a good night for us. Don't spoil it, old man.

ZEKE: Frankie, you don't scare nobody.

ELDRIDGE: That's okay, Frankie. Lemme handle him.

(Moves toward ZEKE *who backs away.)*

That's right, Zeke, just keep backin' up 'til you've backed clean outa sight. That's all we want, man. All we want.

ZEKE: No, I ain't goin'nowhere. Y'all gon' haveta deal with me this time.

LUCKY: Man, you must be crazy.

ZEKE: Hell, no. I ain't crazy. If I wasn't here, then I'd be crazy. 'Cause you nigguhs done hit the jackpot tonight an' I'm here to be in on it.

FRANKIE: Whatchu talkin' about? What jackpot? Ain't nobody here hit the number.

*(*ZEKE *bursts into laughter.)*

ZEKE: Man, you really got a sense of humor, Frankie boy. You oughta be on television.

FRANKIE: Zeke, I'm gonna put my foot square through your chest.

(*Menaces* ZEKE *who backs away.*)

ZEKE: Frankie, you better come to your senses and stop showin' off for your buddies here. In fact alla y'all better be cool. Besides, you got somethin' I want.

FRANKIE: What?

ZEKE: The scratch you took offa Essex Braxton.

FRANKIE: You're crazy.

ZEKE: I followed y'all an' watched what happened. Y'all are pretty good. Even better than me an' my boys were in our day.

TINY: You ain't getting' a damn thing, sucker.

ZEKE: I'll get that money one way or the other, Tiny. Alla y'all been takin' advantage of me long enough. Now it's my turn. Gimme that dust. Now! All of it! I ain't playin'.

FRANKIE: Man, you take one step toward me an' I'll be on your back like white on rice.

TINY: You must think you a kung-fu expert or somethin', come woofin' at the four of us, old as you are.

FRANKIE: We gon' bury you, old man.

ZEKE: Y'all better be cool.

FRANKIE: I'm gon' be cool all right.

(*The four men move toward* ZEKE *who immediately pulls a gun.*)

TINY: Oh shit, he got a gun!

LUCKY: Tiny, I thought you was gonna take that gun offa Braxton.

TINY: Man, I thought Eldridge had it covered.

ELDRIDGE: I thought the both of *y'all* had it under control. Damn, man!

FRANKIE: Shut up!! Alla you!

ZEKE: That's right. Just shut up and gimme that money. Give it up!

(TINY, LUCKY, *and* ELDRIDGE, *frightened, quickly throw their money to the ground in front of* ZEKE, *who stoops and gathers it up. But* FRANKIE *stands defiant.*)

What's your problem, Frankie?

FRANKIE: I ain't givin' nothin' up.

LUCKY: Frankie, you crazy?! That man's ready to kill.

FRANKIE: Then I must be ready to die, 'cause I'll be goddamned if he gets that money while I breathe.

TINY: Frankie, it ain't worth it, man!

ZEKE: You better listen to your boys, Frankie. They know I mean business.

LUCKY: Frankie—

FRANKIE: Shut up, allay ya. Y'all let me down, man. This is our lives he's askin' for an' he gets it from you without a fight. Y'all *crazy*? No, man, that's not the way it's gonna go down with me. No way. Take my money, Zeke, if you can.

(ZEKE *aims the gun squarely at* FRANKIE's *head as* FRANKIE *walks toward him.* ZEKE's *aim begins to waver. He seems frightened by* FRANKIE's *determination and willingness to die more than* ZEKE *is willing to kill him. Finally,* FRANKIE *is close enough to grab the gun. He tries but* ZEKE *is surprisingly strong and challenges* FRANKIE *for the gun. As they grapple the gun goes off and* FRANKIE *crumples to the ground. He lies on the ground severely wounded and moans in pain, calling to his friends for help.* ZEKE *panics and flees with the money.* ELDRIDGE, LUCKY, *and* TINY *stand around the moaning* FRANKIE.)

TINY: Hey, man, I think he's gonna die.

LUCKY: Yea, man, Frankie, we sorry, man, but you know how it is.

ELDRIDGE: Oh, wow, Frankie, I'd give anything if it didn't have to be you.

FRANKIE: Help me. Help me.

ELDRIDGE: Ain't no help, brotherman. You know the rules.

FRANKIE: Please. Please.

(ELDRIDGE *begins to cry, then kneels and takes a ring from* FRANKIE's *finger.* LUCKY *takes* FRANKIE's *shoes.* TINY *takes the money from* FRANKIE's *pockets. All of this goes on over* FRANKIE's *anguished protests. The three young men rush offstage as* FRANKIE *calls after them and writhes in pain onstage.*)

Hey, you guys! Hey, you guys! We the Mighty Gents!! You hear me?! The Mighty Gents! The Mighty Gents! Oh, my God, please! Please!

(*Lights come up on* RITA *still struggling with her knitting.*)

Oh, baby. I had it, baby. I had it all. Goddamn! Goddamn!

(FRANKIE *reaches out toward* RITA. *A spot lights* FRANKIE, *another,* RITA.)

RITA: If I could only remember the proper stitch. If I only could…

(*Both lights fade to:*)

BLACKNESS

THE
Talented Tenth

Notes on *The Talented Tenth*

The Black Power movement effectively ended sometime around 1974, and in its wake a new strain of black leadership elites emerged. They came from the business sector and the more traditional urban-ward politics sector. They eschewed the confrontational antiestablishment posture of Black Power, played down any overt identification with the African diaspora, and positioned themselves, basically, as centrist pragmatists. They might present an Afrocentric façade when it suited them—wearing a dashiki here, quoting Malcolm or Martin there—but for the most part, they saw themselves part of the system, as much a part of the "American way of life" as any other citizens.

The Black Power movement, in many ways, had cleared their path. Nearly a decade and a half of successful efforts at raising consciousness among black people and working to consolidate what little economic and political resources there were within the community made it possible for this new class to emerge, particularly when the Black Power movement withered as the result of COINTELPRO, national weariness with the excesses of the radical left, and the arrests, incarceration, and/or forced or self-imposed exile of many of the radical left's leaders.

The Public Accommodations Act was passed in 1964, the Voting Rights Act in 1965. Malcolm X and Martin Luther King were both dead and safely elevated to a sainthood that rendered their memories powerless and therefore nonthreatening. Suddenly, the question became "Where do we go from here?" And while that question was being pondered by millions of black Americans, a new generation of black leadership quickly stepped forward to seize the reins of power in black America. Some were well-educated graduates of schools like Harvard or Wharton. Others were veterans of the Black Power movement, and still others emerged from the backrooms of ward politics in the big cities or the corporate boardrooms of large corporations. They may have come from different backgrounds, but they all had many things in common, particularly erudition, intelligence, and ambition. They had labored long and hard in the background and had been patient. And now, in the aftermath of the hard-won social changes of the 1960s and 1970s, they were enjoying previously undreamed of levels of success. I was a part of many of those circles, and had been since my very first day as a freshman at Howard.

By 1980, I was a man in his mid-thirties; married, with children; a homeowner and in the middle of a successful professional career. I had not stood on a street corner with a crew since I was seventeen years old, and even then I had only been marginal. I would never know thug life the way Jay-Z or Biggie or Easy E would later come to exemplify. But I noticed that there was not much discussion on our stages about the "other half" of American black life—the middle class, the professional classes—and this observation was what led me to write a play that would address some of my observations about the emergence of this new class of leadership.

I originally intended for Essex Braxton, a major character in *The Mighty Gents*, to be a protagonist in the new play. The new play would occur on the very night that Braxton is assaulted by Frankie, Lucky, Tiny, and Eldridge. I imagined that, seeking to move up from being a mere criminal to being recognized as a successful businessman and investor, Braxton was on his way home from a party hosted by a well-heeled black professional. But I soon abandoned the idea altogether. I wanted to move in another direction.

The task would take me nearly ten years. I had to grow as a person as well as a writer. There were nuances of business practices, political deal making, and even interpersonal relationships that I needed to understand, both on the micro and the macro level.

The Talented Tenth became my take on what had happened to the former young soldiers of the Black Power movement of the '60s and early '70s who now found themselves in their forties and successfully integrated into the American Dream. They had spacious homes, the requisite expensive cars, overseas vacations, excellent pension packages, and political connections—and still, something was missing. The bridge between the past and the present—between generations, social classes, interpretations of history, mother and daughter, father and son—has always been important to me. It is a theme that reverberates through every play I have ever written, but *Tenth* may have been the first time since my one-act play *The Past Is the Past* that I was so overt with it.

By the end of the 1970s, it was clear to everyone that an initial phase of the Black Power movement had run its course. There was not going to be a "revolution" in the streets. "The System" was not going to be overthrown and replaced by a more humane democratic socialism. That "fire in the belly" that had driven us in our youthful twenties and early thirties had now given way to a more practical sense of reality. The playwright Ed Bullins once said, "The most revolutionary thing any black man in America could do was to take care of his family." The truth of Ed's comment was borne out not only in statistics chronicling the deteriorating living conditions so many black Americans were facing at the time, but also in the police assassinations and arrests of scores of "militant black leaders and followers," as well as the personal failings of some of those leaders (cronyism, misogyny, and greed). And there was another factor equally important: fatigue—intellectual as well as physical and spiritual—giving way to cynicism and even despair. A new kind of strength was needed, a new vision. We came to realize that we were not going to save the world—at least, not yet.

One day, sometime in 1980-81, I was invited by a good friend to attend the photography exhibition opening of another good friend (and former Howard classmate) who had developed a fine career for himself as a photographer. It was to be held in a suburban town just outside Newark, New Jersey. While I was there, chatting and talking with guests and friends, I suddenly became very aware of just who these people were: professionals in education, government, business, medicine, law, and law enforcement. Some of them came from families that had been established in the black communities of Essex County, New Jersey, for generations. And here I was, a working class kid from Newark, rubbing shoulders with them. I'd only seen most from afar, or perhaps I'd read about them or heard them discussed while growing up. I may even have partied with some of their children in earlier years, but I never expected to really know much about them. But there I was. And just as comfortable and at ease as if I'd been with them all my life.

Ten years before, I'd have dismissed them as the "Black Bourgeoisie" and "Enemies of the Revolution." But the revolution had ended—or had it? Many of the young people in the room had marched, attended rallies; a few had even joined the Black Panthers. Others had actually lived in Africa, something I'd never done. Some of the young women there had straightened their hair; others still wore it *au naturel*. Some of the men wore dashikis, while others preferred Brooks Brothers.

Howard University, the Movement, and a professional writing career that had allowed me to travel all over the country and to points overseas had all combined to mature me, and expose me to possibilities many other young black men my age were never destined to see. As I stood in that gallery on that long-ago day, I realized that I needed to write about these "new Negroes," because I was one of them.

The deaths of Malcolm X and Martin Luther King, combined with the end of "Black Power," created a leadership vacuum in the black American body politic. Into this stepped a new wave of young (and not so young), educated, sophisticated, and ambitious men and women, who saw themselves as less ideological than their forebears and more practical and pragmatic. They didn't want to destroy the system or overturn it. They wanted to assimilate into it.

Black Americans were as American as anyone else. All of the *Strurm und Drang* of the '60s was about just that. Our ancestors were in America centuries before the forebears of more than 70 percent of all the white people who called themselves Americans. Only the Native Americans had a greater claim to the American ideal than we did. We didn't need to go back to Africa. As James Brown famously said, "America is our home."

I decided to write a play about black, middle-class professionals, all of them former activists, who had settled into comfortable lives and were reaping the benefits of successful professional careers. But something is missing, and one of them, our protagonist Bernard, is determined to find that "something," so that he can reclaim the part of his life he feels he has lost.

W. E. B. DuBois, in his seminal 1903 book *"The Souls of Black Folk,"* discussed the creation and elevation of a university-educated leadership class—roughly 10 percent of the black population of the country, steeped in the liberal arts, enlightened philosophy, and science—who would lead the black masses to a stronger position in American society. They would establish the infrastructure for a newfound freedom. Realizing almost immediately how elitist this idea appeared, DuBois abandoned it and never sought to promote it. But the "talented tenth" became part of the language of black communities for the next century. When I arrived at Howard in 1963, just one year after DuBois's death, I remember some of my classmates and myself joking, upon realizing that so many of us were the first members of our families to go to college and that great expectations were held for all of us, that we were "The Talented Tenth."

I spent the entire decade of the '80s writing and rewriting this play. It was finished and placed into production—first at the Manhattan Theater Club in 1989, and later, in 1990, at the Alliance Theater in Atlanta as part of the National Black Arts Festival. Productions have followed all over the country since then. It would be the last full-length play I'd write for more than twenty years.

The Talented Tenth opened at the Manhattan Theater Club in 1989, directed by Neema Barnette. The cast included Roscoe Orman, Marie Thomas, LaTanya Richardson, Elain Graham, Akousua Busia, Richard Gant Ronnie Clanton, and J. E. Gaines.

The Talented Tenth

Characters

BERNARD: *African American; late thirties, early forties.*
PAM: *light-skinned African American; late thirties, early forties.*
MARVIN: *African American; late thirties, early forties.*
ROWENA: *African American; late thirties, early forties.*
RON: *African American; late thirties, early forties.*
TANYA: *African American; mid-twenties.*
GRIGGS: *African American; sixty-five to seventy years of age.*

Scene One

The early 1990s. Lights up on a beach in Jamaica. BERNARD, PAM, MARVIN, ROWENA, *and* RON, *all black and fortyish, relax in the sun.*

BERNARD *stands apart from the others. Lights change and we enter* BERNARD'*s memory.* GRIGGS, *black, in his mid-fifties, appears, dressed in a business suit.*

GRIGGS: Says here you went to Howard University.

BERNARD: (*Prideful smile.*) Just graduated.

GRIGGS: Fine school. Lotta good people have come out of there. You know Professor Spaulding?

BERNARD: History Department?

GRIGGS: Yes.

BERNARD: I know of him. Never had him as a teacher.

GRIGGS: Good man, Spaulding. His father and I served in World War II together.

BERNARD: I didn't know that.

GRIGGS: 'Course you didn't. It's not important. Tell me, Evans, what are your goals in life?

BERNARD: My goals?

GRIGGS: Yes. I mean, what do you plan to do with your life?

BERNARD: *(Thinks a moment.)* Be a success.

GRIGGS: And?

BERNARD: Make lots of money.

GRIGGS: So I should hire you because you want to make lots of money.

BERNARD: Well, uh—

GRIGGS: See, what you're talking about is a desire; it's not a goal. You have no concrete plan in place. Just some vague notion about lots of money, and you expect me to be the one to give it to you.

BERNARD: Well, no, Mr. Griggs. You see—

GRIGGS: Don't tell me, boy. I know what I see: Just one more pie-in-the-sky youngblood. "Be a success." "Make lots of money." I've heard that kind of talk before. It's Negroes daydreaming, that's all. Fantasizing. And fantasizing's dangerous for black people. Especially when they're young, like you. You want to work for me, you learn to look at this world with hard, cold eyes.

BERNARD: I think I understand, Mr. Griggs.

GRIGGS: Make sure you do, Mr. Evans, because school days are over. I run a successful business precisely because I have always understood how this world we live in is constructed. Especially for our people.

BERNARD: Things are changing, Mr. Griggs.

GRIGGS: And how would you know, youngblood? You just got here.

BERNARD: Well, sir, I know I can relax more in my life than my parents could in theirs.

GRIGGS: Relax? Hmph. Relax. So, that's what all our struggling has come down to: so you kids can relax.

BERNARD: Messed up again, didn't I?

GRIGGS: Hopeless. Just hopeless. The Race is in trouble. What is the primary arena in which our people's struggle must be won?

BERNARD: Civil Rights.

GRIGGS: Wrong. Generals who persist in using the tactics of the last war are doomed to defeat in the present one. Remember that. The correct answer is Economics, boy. Money begets power, and power can make anything possible in America.

BERNARD: Yes, Mr. Griggs.

GRIGGS: You don't believe me, but what I'm telling you is the truth. No individual in this country is more powerful than the ethnic group from which he comes. Don't you ever forget that. As long as the Negro is an economic cripple in America, I don't care how many laws are passed telling him what rights he has; I don't care how many of you colored whiz kids come dancing out of the Howards and Harvards of the world, it won't mean a thing if the majority of our people are outside the economic mainstream. Our job as Negro businessmen is to make money, be successful, and be a springboard for whatever is to follow. We have to be practical…and willing to hold on to our heads while everyone else around us is losing theirs. You understand what I'm saying to you?

BERNARD: I think so, Mr. Griggs.

GRIGGS: I'm talking about hard work, Mr. Evans. Really hard work. You young Negroes today have to understand that you have no rights, no privileges, no nothing.

BERNARD: Sir?

GRIGGS: All you've got is duty, responsibility, and the self-discipline that goes with it. It's the first seven generations after slavery that will suffer the most. They're the ones who have nothing to look forward to except struggle. They're the ones who have to bear the pain, make the sacrifices, and fight the battles that have to be fought and won. Your trouble will always come when you begin to think that you deserve a good time; when you begin to think that the world is your oyster. You're generation number six, Mr. Evans. Your grandchildren can have the good time. Not you. For you, there's only struggle. Understand?

(*He begins moving away.*)

BERNARD: You frightened me when you said that.

GRIGGS: I know.

BERNARD: I've been frightened ever since.

(GRIGGS *is gone. Lights change.* PAM, ROWENA, MARVIN, *and* RON *sun themselves on beach towels.* BERNARD *remains standing to the side, staring out to sea. Easy listening jazz plays on a portable cassette player.*)

PAM: You say something, honey?

BERNARD: Uh…no. Just thinking out loud.

ROWENA: I just love Negril.

MARVIN: I could stay here forever.

ROWENA: Shoot, you'd still have to work to make a living. Then, it wouldn't be fun here, anymore. Jamaica'd just be another place to work.

MARVIN: I'll take that chance.

PAM: I don't know. The poverty here depresses me. It's so pervasive. I couldn't stand it, every day.

BERNARD: Hmph. Seems like everywhere you go in the world, black people are suffering.

ROWENA: At least here, black folks are in control of their own lives.

BERNARD: No, they're not. The World Bank is.

RON: Actually, the Bahamas is what's happenin'. I'm planning a hook-up with some foreigners I know—an Arab and two Italians. I'm looking at some beachfront property on one of the outer islands—a resort.

ROWENA: But, Ron, you need contacts in the Bahamas, and you don't know anybody in Nassau.

RON: Rowena, there are black folks in Nassau with money and power. Wherever there are black people with money and power, there you will find a Howard graduate. All I need to do is knock on a few doors at Government House and do a little alumni networking.

MARVIN: Smart move.

RON: Only move there is, my man. Only move there is.

PAM: You make it sound so easy.

RON: No, it's not easy. It's hard work. But things have a way of coming together when you know what it is you want and how to go about getting it.

PAM: Business and money. Ugh! Please, we're on vacation. It's so vulgar to talk about that stuff when you're on vacation.

RON: It's in my blood. I can't help it.

ROWENA: We need to get you married off, Ron.

MARVIN: Oh, oh, marriage: the ultimate business entanglement.

ROWENA: Hardy-har-har. Very funny.

RON: I've been that route. No, thanks.

ROWENA: You need an anchor in your life.

RON: In my life, not around my neck.

PAM: What a sexist thing to say.

RON: All I'm saying is, I tried marriage. It was a disaster, for me *and* Irene.

PAM: That was ten years ago.

ROWENA: Then it's time you jumped in the waters again. All these intelligent eligible women out here and you walking around single. It's criminal.

RON: I'm doing fine, y'all.

PAM: Bernard, what do you think?

BERNARD: About what?

RON: They're trying to marry me off again.

BERNARD: (*Disinterested.*) Well, you'll do what you want to do, Ron. You always have.

ROWENA: Don't you want to see little carbon copies of yourself running around?

RON: One of me in the world is enough.

BERNARD: You won't get any argument from me on that score, brother.

(RON *looks at him. Others laugh.*)

Sorry, Ron, but you walked right into that one. I couldn't resist.

RON: I owe you one, Bernard.

BERNARD: I'm sure you'll be paying me back first chance you get.

RON: Count on it.

BERNARD: Hey, let's leave Ron's social life alone. Surely, there must be some more interesting things we can talk about, or do.

ROWENA: Why? We're on vacation. We're not *supposed* to do anything or talk about anything interesting or "relevant." Too taxing.

RON: Yea, Bernard, chill out. Empty your brain, bro. Plenty of time to fill it up once we get back home.

BERNARD: Yea, that's right. Just lie around in this sand all the damned time doing nothing and talking inanities. We do this year after year.

RON: It's never bothered you before.

BERNARD: It bothers me, now.

(*Beat.*)

Listen…I'm sorry.

PAM: Bernard, what is it?

BERNARD: Nothing.

MARVIN: Worried about old man Griggs and your promotion?

BERNARD: (*Evasively.*) It's hot.

MARVIN: Don't worry about that promotion. You'll get it. You're due.

BERNARD: It's not the promotion.

(*Looking away.*)

It's the aftermath.

RON: Aftermath? What's that about?

(BERNARD *says nothing.*)

PAM: Why don't you let me get you something cool to drink?

BERNARD: Don't want a cool drink. I want to get off this damned spot I'm standing on. I want to get off this hot sand. I want to *move.* I want to *do* something.

PAM: Okay, let's do something. Any suggestions?

ROWENA: How about a game of Whist?

BERNARD: (*A little incredulous.*) Whist?

ROWENA: (*Playfully.*) Yes, Bernard. You know, that ancient Negro parlor game.

BERNARD: No, let's drive over to Dunn's River Falls. There's a great restaurant there.

(*Groans from the others.*)

It's only a ninety-minute drive.

ROWENA: More like two hours, Bernard.

RON: Two hours in all this heat? I'm out, man.

ROWENA: Bernard, we've got a villa with our own cook and waiter. Why do we need to ride all that distance for a meal?

MARVIN: Ro's right. Chill, man. We've only got two days left here. Going to Dunn's River's gonna *waste* one off those days.

BERNARD: Negril is tourist Jamaica. It's not real. We need to get out and talk to the people, get to know them.

ROWENA: Get out and talk to the people? About what?

BERNARD: Maybe we can learn something about this lovely little island.

ROWENA: If it's so lovely, why are so many Jamaicans in Brooklyn?

BERNARD: For the same reason so many Alabamans are in Chicago.

(*Beat.*)

We could stop and see things. That's all I meant.

ROWENA: Right. The lovely drive along the North Coast Highway; endless miles of sugar plantations, shacks, outhouses, skinny dogs, goats, and ashy faced children. Not me, honey. I'm staying right here in Negril. This may be tourist Jamaica to you, Bernard, but after paying my share for that villa and airfare and all the rest, this is all of Jamaica I have any interest in seeing. I'm sorry.

MARVIN: I wouldn't put it quite that bluntly, but my wife's got a point.

PAM: Bernard, stop standing over there all by yourself. Come lay beside me.

(BERNARD *comes over to* PAM *and sits beside her. She pulls him down so that his head rests on her belly.*)

BERNARD: (*Sighs.*) Y'all just don't understand.

ROWENA: I understand this sun caressing my body, I'll tell you that. Let me turn over. I intend to be right black when I go back home.

Lights begin to change. Everyone lapses into a nap as the sounds of the surf crashing onto the beach with the seagulls flying overhead can be heard. BERNARD *sits up and stares out to sea.*

Lights continue to change and segue to the next scene, as we…

END SCENE ONE

Scene Two

Lights up on BERNARD, *alone, putting a sweatsuit on over his beachwear.*

BERNARD: It was during my junior year in college. Martin Luther King tried to lead a march across the Edmund Pettus Bridge in Selma, Alabama, but the local authorities had a law against it. Those were the days down south when there were laws against black people doing anything, including being black, if you get my drift. Well, Dr. King decided to march anyway, and the sheriff's people attacked the marchers and threw them in jail. People all over the country called on President Johnson to do something, but Johnson hesitated. Then, Dr. King announced he would march again, this time all the way to Montgomery, the state capital. The Klan started making noises. And Lyndon Johnson still hesitated. So, the Student Nonviolent Coordinating Committee went into action. They had a local chapter down on Rhode Island

Avenue, not that far from the campus and Habiba and I went down there right after philosophy class and signed up together. We were ready, y'all.

I remember my heart was beating a mile a minute. The both of us were so excited. We were finally in the big fight: helping the Race in the Civil Rights Struggle. We were active participants in making History.

The room was filled with nervous energy. People sang civil rights songs and hugged each other and held hands—men and women, black and white.

Then came speeches and pronouncements to get us fired up. Lots of fists clenched in the air. The room was hot and sweaty and filled with cigarette smoke. I felt a little dizzy and reached for Habiba. Someone began singing "Precious Lord Take My Hand" and folks joined in. We all held hands and closed our eyes and let the power of the song take hold of us. Then, Habiba started shaking, gasping for breath, like she was convulsing. Suddenly, she opened her eyes and looked at me, saying she'd had a race memory. She was with a group of runaway slaves. Armed gunmen had chased them through a swamp. They were trapped with no way out. They began to sing, calling out to God, and the more they sang, the stronger they became. She saw the flash of the gunfire. She felt the bullets searing into her flesh. But she kept getting stronger. Then, Habiba screamed. Just like that. A scream like I'd never heard before. Everyone in the room just stopped. It was like we all felt what she felt. People began to moan and shout and chant. Bloods who'd stopped going to church and had sworn off the spirit possession of our parents and grandparents began to rock and shake and tremble—yea, they got the Spirit that night! All that college sophistication we had didn't mean a thing! 'Cause Dr. King needed us! The workers down in Mississippi needed us! Our people needed us! Yes sir! We were gonna press on, that night! Ol' Lyndon Johnson, you better listen to us, man! 'Cause we comin'! Marching around your front lawn tonight, buddy! And you're gonna send those troops down to Selma and you're gonna sign that civil rights bill, too! Our time is at hand! This is the new young America talkin' and you'd better listen! Scream, Habiba! Scream, sister! Let us feel those bullets! Let us feel the lash! Scream! Don't let us forget! Bring us home, sister love! Bring us home! Yes sir! Yes sir! Teach! Teach!

(Pause.)

We marched in shifts, twenty-four hours a day, seven days. Lyndon Johnson sent the troops and Dr. King made his pilgrimage to Montgomery where he gave one of the greatest speeches of his life. Still see that speech from time to time on TV. I was listening to it the other day when my oldest son came in and asked me if I could give him some money for new clothes. School was out and they were having a special holiday sale at the mall. Martin Luther King's Birthday.

END SCENE TWO

Lights come up full to reveal BERNARD *in* TANYA'*s living room as we segue to:*

Scene Three

BERNARD, *alone, wearing a sweatsuit, seated in front of a TV set.*

BERNARD: Come on, come on…get a hit.

ANNOUNCER'S VOICE: Strike! On the outside corner.

BERNARD: Strike?! That ball was outside. Damn!

(TANYA *enters, wearing a negligee. She is in her mid-twenties, dark-complexioned, brown almond-shaped eyes, high cheekbones. She carries a can of beer and sits next to* BERNARD, *who is still absorbed in the game.* TANYA *hands him the beer.*)

BERNARD: Thanks, baby.

TANYA: Thought you were coming back inside.

BERNARD: Yea…I was…but, I flipped on the TV to get the score and…

TANYA: Yes, I know; the rest is history.

(*Disinterested.*)

Who's playing?

BERNARD: Mets and Dodgers.

TANYA: Who's winning?

BERNARD: Tie score, bottom of the ninth. One out. Mets win if my man here hits one out.

TANYA: ʾHe's gonna strike out.

BERNARD: Don't say somethin' like that. You'll jinx him.

TANYA: He's jinxing himself. He's holding his bat too high and too far back. It's gonna take him too long to get the head of the bat through the strike zone.

BERNARD: No way. He always comes through in the clutch.

ANNOUNCER: Swing and a miss, strike three!

TANYA: Told you.

Bernard: I hate it when you show off like that.

Tanya: (*Big grin.*) Yea. I know.

(*She kisses him. He responds, but not with much enthusiasm and immediately gets back into the game.*)

Tanya: Baby, you've got some gray hair.

Bernard: That's not gray. It's lint.

Tanya: You are *too* vain. This is gray hair.

Bernard: Stress. You're wearing me out, baby.

Tanya: Then, why don't you come back inside and drink from my fountain of youth?

(*Bernard smiles, but doesn't move, keeping his eyes on the TV.*)

You know you haven't said anything about your trip to Jamaica.

(*Bernard grunts.*)

Not that I really care.

Bernard: The trip was alright.

Tanya: Nothing happened down there, did it?

Bernard: No.

Tanya: (*Muttering.*) Too bad.

(*Looks at him.*)

You didn't get too tired running, did you?

Bernard: Only three miles. I can do that in my sleep.

(*Into the TV.*)

Hey! Way to go! Do it! Do it!

Tanya: (*Looks at the TV, indifferent.*) A triple. Not bad. The Mets'll win.

Bernard: You never know.

Tanya: Look at that gap between left field and left center. Game over if one falls in there.

Bernard: Tanya…

Announcer: That's quite a big gap in left and left center. A hit over there, Mets win.

Tanya: God, I'm good.

(*To Bernard.*)

When are you going to take me somewhere?

BERNARD: When I get time.

TANYA: You never seem to have any time.

BERNARD: I do the best I can, Tanya.

TANYA: You always have time for Pam.

BERNARD: She's my wife.

TANYA: Hmph.

BERNARD: (*To the TV.*) Come on, lay off that junk stuff and make him throw strikes.

TANYA: You know, I haven't seen you for two weeks. The least you could do is talk to me.

BERNARD: We talked earlier. I want to watch the game. Okay?

TANYA: You can watch the game with your wife.

BERNARD: Pam doesn't like baseball.

TANYA: So, you come here to take up MY time.

BERNARD: Well, the hell with it, then!

TANYA: (*Soothingly.*) Come on, Bernard, I'm only teasin'.

BERNARD: Look, I'm tryin' to relax. Okay? It's been a long day. I like to watch the game.

TANYA: I understand all that. It's alright.

(*Beat.*)

But, you can see my point, can't you?

BERNARD: (*Impatiently.*) Yes, Tanya.

TANYA: I had lunch with an old classmate of mine.

BERNARD: (*Into the game.*) Uh, huh…

TANYA: She's an investment banker, now. Wall Street.

BERNARD: …Good for her…

TANYA: I want to go in with her on a real estate deal she's trying to hook up down south. What do you think?

(BERNARD *says nothing.*)

Look, is that game over?

BERNARD: They're going into extra innings.

TANYA: Lord, deliver me.

BERNARD: Thought you liked baseball.

TANYA: I was hoping we could *talk*.

BERNARD: We've *been* talking, baby.

TANYA: I mean, without interruptions.

BERNARD: Tanya, this is a good game.

(TANYA *goes to the TV.*)

TANYA: Uh-uh. No way. Forget it.

(*She shuts off the TV.*)

BERNARD: Hey! What're you doing?!

TANYA: Later for the game. Touch my bases.

BERNARD: Come on, baby.

TANYA: (*Continuing to block the TV.*) No.

BERNARD: But, the game—

(*She kisses him.*)

That's what I've always liked about you, baby. You know how to put things in their proper perspective.

(*They caress and embrace each other.*)

TANYA: Mmmm…I think these arms must be the most comfortable place in the world. I'm gonna have a law passed: you have to keep these arms around me twenty-four hours a day.

BERNARD: You don't need to get a law passed for that, baby.

TANYA: No. All I need is a ring.

BERNARD: Uh…er…what time is it?

TANYA: About 10:30.

BERNARD: Time for me to get up from here.

TANYA: Will I see you tomorrow?

BERNARD: I don't know.

TANYA: When, then?

BERNARD: I'll call.

TANYA: You're gonna jog the three miles all the way home?

BERNARD: Why not? Ran all the way here, didn't I?

TANYA: It's so late.

BERNARD: No sweat. I can handle it.

TANYA: I can drive you.

BERNARD: No.

TANYA: I'll let you off at the corner. Don't worry. Your wife won't see you…or me.

BERNARD: I said, no.

TANYA: You look sleepy. You ought to rest awhile. Come curl up with me.

BERNARD: You know as well as I do, if I curl up with you, I ain't gon' hardly rest.

TANYA: I won't bother you. Honest. Just stay awhile.

BERNARD: You know I can't. I've got a busy day tomorrow.

TANYA: I'll wake you early enough.

BERNARD: I gotta go to the bathroom. The beer's catching up to me.

TANYA: Why don't you and Pam get a divorce?

BERNARD: Because I love her.

TANYA: Then, why are you here with me?

BERNARD: Because I love *you.*

TANYA: That's immature.

BERNARD: I gotta go pee.

(*He exits.* TANYA *flicks on the TV.*)

TANYA: Bernard, the game's still on.

(*She smiles sardonically, the irony in her statement suddenly striking her.*)

END SCENE THREE

Scene Four

Lights up on TANYA, *alone.*

TANYA: My father is a truck driver. My mother runs a little three-table greasy spoon on Springfield Avenue that I had to help clean up every day from the time I was in the third grade right up until I graduated from college.

I grew up during the sixties and have therefore benefited from the concessions gained in those years without having to endure the hassles. As a result, I have certain expectations and I tend to take things for granted…*a lot.* Because I know how to fight, I know how to make

my expectations come true. You see, I learned early that, being black
and female, I was at the bottom of everybody's pecking order and
consequently, if I didn't grab what I wanted myself, it wouldn't get
got.

I'm sort of a black cultural cybernetic organism. Yea, check that out.
Inside, a strong inner-city core surrounded by the soft flesh of my
parents' middle-class aspirations, my training at Spelman College and
my graduate study at Columbia School of Journalism. Today, I work at
the largest newspaper in New Jersey. I even have a byline. I'm a child of
my generation; a strong believer in the power of the Individual Will. *I* am
indestructible.

In college, a group of us like-minded young indestructible women
clustered ourselves into a little clique we called The Women of
Substance. We wanted to differentiate ourselves from the so-called
popular women, many of them daughters of the black professional
elite. Serious old Negro money. You've all seen them: the ones with
the coquettish smiles and the batting eyelashes. The ones who were
always used to having things. Anything. Anytime, anyplace, anywhere,
anyhow. They didn't know how to fight. They didn't have to. They just
snapped their fingers and...voilà. This was especially true when it came
to men.

We women of substance were everything the so-called popular women
were not. We were well-read, hard-working, studious, dedicated...and
after what they used to call "the high-priced spread." We just couldn't
understand. We were women who could *do* things.

Then it became clear: women who can do things are most prized by
men who can do nothing. And the *men* who can do things want women
who can do *nothing*. Because such women are no competition and are
eternally grateful to these men for giving them station in life. I've
become convinced the male ego is Mother Nature's idea of sick humor.

Thus, here I am: attractive, successful, intelligent, and alone. Kept on
an emotional string by a man married to one of those "high-priced
spreads." All I have to do is tell him it's over. I should, really. But, now,
I've gotten used to having whatever I've wanted. And I want *him*.

This situation has taught me something I never thought it necessary
to learn, being a black woman of substance—Patience. It's more than a
virtue...it's a weapon.

(*Lights.*)

END SCENE FOUR

Scene Five

Lights up on RON, MARVIN, *and* BERNARD *at a bar.*

RON and **MARVIN:** (*Singing.*)
For he's a jolly good fellow!
For he's a jolly good fellow!
For he's a jolly good fellooooooooow!
Who really knows how to throw down!

(BERNARD *stands and acknowledges the toast.*)

BERNARD: Thank you, thank you. I deserve every bit of it.

(*They laugh.*)

RON: Congratulations, homeboy. Vice-President and General Manager. I love the sound of it.

BERNARD: I love the *feel* of it.

RON: And to think, you damned near drove yourself crazy worryin' about that promotion.

MARVIN: Wear it well, buddy-buddy. You're the big cheese, now.

BERNARD: Yea, Control over all four of my company's stations. Got it all, ya'll: programming, news, public affairs—all mine. And it's all gonna change. Starting next month, Negro radio is dead at Griggs Broadcasting.

MARVIN: Don't get too radical, bro.

BERNARD: I've got to get radical. Not one of our stations is ranked in the top ten in any of their markets.

MARVIN: Really? Didn't know things were that bad.

BERNARD: Our stations are ratings disasters. We made money last year, but we don't turn things around, those profits won't mean a thing.

RON: R&B during the day, Quiet Storm in the evening. Never fails.

BERNARD: I'll have music, but not twenty-four hours a day. I want to do confrontational radio. Crime, corruption, police brutality, lack of quality services—things our people think they can't do anything about, we'll teach them they can. Politics, art, culture—not only will we cover them, but we'll define them...on our terms. Cutting-edge radio, Ron. That's what it's all about.

RON: You're off into some form of advocacy, Bernard. A very bad habit I thought you'd gotten out of years ago.

BERNARD: All Griggs has to do is say "yes" and I'll have things turned around in six months.

RON: Whatever you do, use a little diplomacy. Sam Griggs is one of the pioneer black businessmen in the country.

BERNARD: I don't need to be lectured on office etiquette, Ron. I know what I want and I'm going after it.

MARVIN: You might be moving too fast, Bernard.

BERNARD: None of our competitors interprets the news of history or *anything* that goes on in this country through the eyes of the black community or from the *interests* of the black community. It's the world the way white folks see it, whether they mean for it to be that way, or not. *that's* how it comes out. And that's what I'm challenging and that's what I'm changing. The minute that happens Griggs Broadcasting becomes unique and controversial. Controversy attracts people...and dollars. And if we do our jobs right, not *all* the people we attract will be black, either. Gimme credit for having some brains. Okay?

MARVIN: I still don't know...

BERNARD: Damned right, you don't know. Look, it's my responsibility. Let me handle it. Okay?

MARVIN: No need to get upset, my man. I was just voicing my opinion.

BERNARD: The kind of opinion that makes daring, innovation, and risk-taking such dirty words among black businessmen.

RON: Because capital is limited for most of us. Those hungry bankers always seem to lose their appetite when they see black faces. Griggs knows that, even if you don't.

MARVIN: Look, you just got a big promotion. All you gotta do is make the money and relax. That's all: just relax.

BERNARD: Relax? Marvin, I want to be the most restless black man who ever lived.

(*Tosses some bills on the counter.*)

I'm gonna split. Me an' Pam's got plans.

RON: Give her my best.

BERNARD: I'll be sure to.

RON: That's a good woman you got, man. First class all the way.

BERNARD: Yea. She's good people. I'm a lucky man.

(BERNARD *gulps down his drink.*)

RON: (*Laughs.*) Listen to him. I should have married her when I had the chance.

MARVIN: You did have the chance, but she wanted Bernard.

RON: (*To* BERNARD.) Still can't see what she saw in you.

BERNARD: (*Looks at* RON.) Good looks beyond belief.

RON: She's not that shallow.

BERNARD: You guys watch that scotch. You both gotta drive tonight.

(BERNARD *exits.* RON *and* MARVIN'*s eyes follow him.* RON *gulps down another drink.*)

RON: You know he's gonna blow it, don't you? Guys like him always do.

END SCENE FIVE

Scene Six

PAM *and* BERNARD *are having breakfast. She looks through the mail.*

BERNARD: I'm thinking about going out to the Stadium to see the ball game. Want to come?

PAM: Baseball?

BERNARD: Yea.

PAM: Can I think about it?

BERNARD: Sure…

(*He continues eating. She looks through the mail.* BERNARD *looks at her.*)

Anything interesting?

PAM: Just the usual bills…junk mail…

(*Looks at* BERNARD.)

I ran into Sylvia Witherspoon, yesterday.

BERNARD: How's she doing?

PAM: She told me you and her husband had a fight at the station.

BERNARD: It was an argument. Not a fight.

PAM: She said you've been arguing a lot, lately.

BERNARD: There are things I want to do, but can't. He's one of the reasons I can't.

PAM: Is there anyone there you're not fighting with?

BERNARD: Lots of people.

PAM: Bernard?

BERNARD: I had a nice time at the fundraiser last night.

PAM: (*Beat.*) No, you didn't have a nice time. You danced and talked. But you never really said anything to anyone. You did it all night. And, just now, to me. You're effecting a conversation in order to avoid having a real one.

BERNARD: Aw, Pam, come on…

PAM: Silences, changing the subject; empty jokes. All means of keeping people away from you. Everyone likes who they think is you. The dedicated ex-boy wonder who always seems on top of everything. But, I was thinking that, after fifteen years of marriage, I still don't even know what your favorite color is.

BERNARD: You never asked.

PAM: You never told me.

BERNARD: Dark blue. What's yours?

PAM: Pink.

BERNARD: I thought it was yellow.

PAM: It's pink.

BERNARD: I could have sworn it was yellow.

PAM: Pink.

BERNARD: You never even wear pink. Your favorite dress is yellow.

PAM: You see, you're doing it again.

BERNARD: Well, I'll be damned. Pink.

PAM: Bernard, I'm not just talking about pink or yellow or dark blue. Ron noticed it, too.

BERNARD: My alleged distance, I suppose.

PAM: Yes. We were talking.

BERNARD: You were talking about me?

PAM: After all these years he was surprised about how little he knew about you.

BERNARD: You were talking to Ron about me.

PAM: Yes. He's your friend, Bernard.

BERNARD: (*Sarcastic.*) So, he is.

PAM: What's that supposed to mean?

BERNARD: Ron can get to be a bit much, Pam.

PAM: He's a success at what he does. He's happy, Bernard. So few of our people get the kinds of opportunities he's getting. Be glad for him. He's happy for us.

BERNARD: So, how about it?

PAM: What?

BERNARD: You want to go to the ball game with me?

PAM: Bernard, we were talking about—

BERNARD: Come on, Pam. You'll love it. Just give it a chance.

PAM: I hate sports. I don't understand sports. Besides, we're talking about—

BERNARD: The same ol' same ol'. Forget that stuff. I'll behave, next time. I promise. Let's deal with something I want, this time.

PAM: (*Sighs.*) Can we go out to dinner, afterwards?

BERNARD: Sure.

PAM: Then, I guess it'll be alright.

BERNARD: Your enthusiasm is overwhelming.

PAM: In America, it's sports, not religion, that's the opiate of the masses...the male masses, anyway.

BERNARD: Stop grumbling. I've got box seats on the first-base line, baby. Gift from one of our ad clients.

PAM: First-base line. Is that good?

BERNARD: The best seats in the house.

PAM: Somehow the phrase, "best seats in the house," would work much better for me if it was applied to the Met or the Alvin Ailey.

BERNARD: For most of the people where I come from, the Stadium IS the Met.

PAM: Their loss, I'm afraid.

BERNARD: Alright, the hell with it! Forget the ball game. Let's go wherever you want to go! You satisfied?

PAM: Bernard, I didn't mean—

BERNARD: Save it! We'll do whatever you want to do. I'll go get changed into something appropriate. Will a sports coat do, or must it be black tie and goddamned tails! We'll do whatever you want to do! Go wherever you say! After all, you're the one with the taste! You're the one with the sophistication and breeding! You're the one, you're the one, you're the one!!

(BERNARD *slams the newspaper down, gets up, and storms out, leaving* PAM *sitting alone, trembling, confused, angry, and hurt.*)

END SCENE SIX

Scene Seven

TANYA's *apartment, as she massages* BERNARD's *temples.*

TANYA: You've got too much pressure on you, honey. You need to relax.

BERNARD: I don't want to relax. I just—

TANYA: What?

BERNARD: (*Changes subject.*) I'm gonna take a coupla days away, I think. Maybe the Coast. Check on our sister stations.

TANYA: Can I go with you?

BERNARD: No.

TANYA: Is *she* going?

BERNARD: No.

TANYA: Then, why can't I go?

BERNARD: I want to go alone.

TANYA: I see.

BERNARD: Don't start with me, Tanya.

TANYA: I'm not starting anything. You want to go alone. Fine.

BERNARD: Got something I've got to work out.

TANYA: What things?

BERNARD: Let me worry about that.

TANYA: Am I involved?

BERNARD: Tanya…

TANYA: I don't know why you get like this.

BERNARD: I'm sorry I didn't make that party with you.

TANYA: You could have at least called.

BERNARD: It's hard for me to talk on phones.

TANYA: It's hard for you to talk in person.

BERNARD: I didn't want to call and say I wasn't coming. I didn't want to disappoint you. By not calling, I wouldn't have to deal with it.

TANYA: Well, you did disappoint me and you *do* have to deal with it.

BERNARD: I'm sorry.

TANYA: Why didn't you want to come?

BERNARD: It's not that I didn't want to come. I just couldn't.

TANYA: Your wife?

BERNARD: I didn't want to run into someone who knew me...or worse, knew Pam.

TANYA: That's bound to happen, sooner or later, Bernard.

BERNARD: Why let it happen, at all?

TANYA: You know, I'm getting tired of being your best-kept secret.

BERNARD: You have to expect it when you become a married man's mistress, Tanya.

TANYA: Don't you ever say anything like that to me again. I am *not* your mistress.

(*She rises and moves away from him.*)

BERNARD: I'm sorry. I didn't mean to hurt your feelings.

TANYA: I don't know how much longer I can keep this up.

BERNARD: Look, I told you if you wanted to call it quits, it was fine with me. You're a beautiful, intelligent woman—too beautiful and intelligent to be stuck up under a married man.

TANYA: Don't talk to me like I'm some smitten teen queen, Bernard. I'm not stuck up under you. I *chose* to be with you and I *choose* to have you in my life.

BERNARD: You may come to regret that choice.

TANYA: Don't think the thought hasn't occurred to me.

BERNARD: I'm looking for answers, Tanya. I don't even know how I got here, anymore.

TANYA: Where?

BERNARD: Here. This point in my life, remembering that once I was twenty-two, fresh out of college, with an unlimited horizon in front of me. Then, just like that, I was twenty-five, then suddenly thirty, then thirty-five...now, forty-three. How did it happen so fast? Everything in between seems like a haze, sometimes. I remember being skinny with jet black hair and baby smooth skin. It used to take me a whole week just to grow a stubble. I was just twenty-two....Now, it's all these years later and I'm scared and I'm angry because I want to change my life and do some things I've never had a chance to do. But, if I do I could hurt my wife and my children and everyone who depends on me, so I stay where I am and I dream. But, I don't dare *act*. And yet, I *want* to act...I've *got* to act...before it's too late.

TANYA: (*Beat.*) You can talk and philosophize all you want to; you can even pretend that this anxiety you're feeling is some sort of mid-life crisis, but I know what you're really saying: you want to leave Pam.

BERNARD: I've tried to leave her. I can't.

TANYA: I know. You're loyal to her. That's what attracted me to you.

BERNARD: It's more than loyalty. She's a part of me.

TANYA: You love her.

BERNARD: That's what I tell myself.

TANYA: Don't you know?

BERNARD: We've been together seventeen years.

TANYA: You're sick.

BERNARD: Sick?

TANYA: No. Not sick. Selfish.

BERNARD: Because I don't know my own feelings?

TANYA: You know your own feelings, alright. You like the idea that you can be married to one woman while having an affair with another, then expecting both of them to somehow be forgiving because you refuse to choose. Why should you choose? You're having the best of both worlds. Meanwhile, your wife and I suffer.

BERNARD: Then, why do you stay with me?

TANYA: Because I love you.

BERNARD: It's not enough. Take it from one who knows.

TANYA: I don't know anything deeper than love. I haven't lived that long. (*Looks into his eyes.*)

You want it to end between us, don't you?

BERNARD: If you had seen the way I went off on Pam—

TANYA: I don't care about Pam. Don't tell me a damned thing about you and her. I only care about us. You want to end it?

BERNARD: We should. I can't carry this around with me any longer.

TANYA: It hasn't been easy for me, either, Bernard.

BERNARD: I'm sorry.

TANYA: Just like that, huh? I should have seen it coming.

(BERNARD *says nothing.*)

I was never happier with anyone than I was with you.

BERNARD: I'd better go...

TANYA: No! Look me in the face. Tell me you don't love me anymore. Tell me you don't want to be around me anymore.

(BERNARD *comes face to face with her.*)

BERNARD: I don't love you anymore.

TANYA: Just like that.

BERNARD: What other choice do I have? I won't leave my wife and children, and I can't ask you to wait for me, forever. Let's just stop it, now.

TANYA: I know you're right. I know there's no other way.

BERNARD: I'm sorry. It's my fault. I've been a fool.

TANYA: Maybe we've both been fools.

BERNARD: Yes.

TANYA: Goodbye.

BERNARD: Goodbye.

(*He turns to leave. Then suddenly, he turns back and grabs* TANYA *into his arms. They kiss passionately, falling to the floor and making love. The lights dim.*)

END SCENE SEVEN

Scene Eight

Lights up on ROWENA *and* PAM *relaxing in a sauna.* ROWENA *seems content but* PAM *is distracted, distant.*

ROWENA: ...so, I wind up spending the whole morning on the phone with that Tommy Barrett in the City Planner's Office.

PAM: Betty Lee Barrett's son? The Parks Commissioner?

(ROWENA *nods her head.*)

You need to stay away from those Barretts. That's one ignorant family.

ROWENA: I called that boy to talk about the bid I put in for those vacant lots over in Woodlawn, and that little pootbutt tried to give me the runaround.

PAM: I'm not surprised.

ROWENA: Here, I've got the financing together to put up one thousand units of low to moderate income housing and all I get from City Hall is a lot of bureaucratic nonsense about feasibility studies and background checks. Well, I know a background he can *kiss!*

PAM: They've made a deal somewhere, Ro. You've been elbowed out the way.

ROWENA: I know. Rumor has it some suburban big shot with big bucks greased the right palms. Bad enough when white politicians mess over you, but to get done in by one of your own...Damn.

PAM: Well, nothing in the rule books says black politicians have to be any less greedy than the white ones.

ROWENA: My rule book says they do. We put them there to do a job, and make our lives better; not screw us around like everyone else has done.

PAM: I'll remember to tell that to Mayor Mitchell next time I see him.

ROWENA: And while you're at it, ask him about that twenty-two-year-old youth counselor I hear he got pregnant. And ask him about Andy Thompson getting busted in that school jobs kickback scandal. And ask him about those coke sniffers he got on his very staff that he's not willing to do anything about. And then he's got the nerve to let some party hacks' snot-nosed kid block my housing project. I'm just two seconds away from getting the biggest baseball bat I can find and going own to City Hall to do some urban renewal on those stupid Negroes' *heads*!

(ROWENA *and* PAM *have a laugh and exchange "high fives."*)

PAM: Do yourself a favor: next time, forget Tommy Barrett. Go straight to the top and talk to Georgie Mitchell. He's the mayor.

ROWENA: I intend to.

PAM: Watch him, though. He's slick.

ROWENA: Shoot, Georgie doesn't worry me. I always could handle a man who thinks with his little head instead of his big one.

(ROWENA *laughs again.* PAM *is much quieter, this time.*)

Ooowee! Don't get me started, girl.

(*The laughter dies down.* ROWENA *looks at* PAM.)

Well, have we beat around the bush enough, or are you going to talk about what's bothering you?

PAM: Nothing's bothering me. I'm fine.

(ROWENA *looks at her.*)

Am I that transparent?

ROWENA: What's going on, girl?

PAM: I was never raised to air dirty linen in public. It just wasn't done in my family.

(*Beat.*)

Me and Bernard are going through a thing, that's all. It's nothing.

(*Beat; quietly.*)

It's been going on for months. He's been real moody...distant. Snaps at me...sometimes, even the kids. He'll sit at the dinner table and stare off into space—won't even take part in the family discussions...he used to lead them.

ROWENA: Have you talked to him about it?

PAM: I can't *get* him to talk. It's like he's stopped connecting with me. Left me on a little island. I can't figure him anymore. It's like he never says what's really on his mind.

ROWENA: Maybe he does, and you just don't understand him. I do that with Marvin, sometimes.

PAM: I *know* Bernard. We've been married seventeen years. This just isn't like him.

ROWENA: Now, how many women have made *that* mistake. Hmph, I know I have.... "I know my husband." Like I know Marvin better than he knows himself. Really...We devote so much of our time to studying our men, trying to figure out what makes them tick, knowing what they're going to say, how they're going to react in certain situations. And just when we get everything down pat, when we think we have that man arranged just the way we want him, he'll say something, or do something or even worse, do nothing, at all. And then we realize, we never really knew him. We only loved him.

PAM: There are times when I can feel his eyes on me. Going over every inch of my body. What's he looking for? I can feel myself getting older. Sometimes, it seems as though I can feel my hair turning gray; I can feel the natural oils in my skin drying out. And I wonder if that's the reason he looks at me so strangely. Maybe that's why he's changed. And I come to this gym hoping I can turn the clock back and then I see my daughter in all her sixteen-year-old glory and I know it's impossible.

(*Suddenly embarrassed.*)

God, this conversation is so embarrassing.

ROWENA: No, it's not. It's real, honey…very real.

(*Beat.*)

What're you going to do?

PAM: Don't know. I'm scared. And angry.

ROWENA: The kids pick up on any of this?

PAM: I don't know. Maybe. They haven't said anything.

ROWENA: Well, don't do anything rash, girl. Keep your head. Think this thing through.

PAM: I know. But, Bernard's got to help. I'm not going to pull all the weight by myself. There's only so much I'm willing to take.

ROWENA: Anything I can do?

PAM: You listened to me. That's enough.

(*Beat.*)

Keep this conversation in this room?

(*Lights.*)

END SCENE EIGHT

Scene Nine

GRIGGS *is in his office when* BERNARD *enters.*

BERNARD: You wanted to see me, Sam?

GRIGGS: Bernard! Sit down, son.

(BERNARD *sits.* SAM *goes to a small bar.*)

Drink?

BERNARD: *Not on the job. You know me.*

GRIGGS: Well, I sure as hell feel like one.

(*Pours himself a drink.*)

If I hadn't seen it with my own eyes, I wouldn't have believed it.

Bernard: (*Big smile.*) I told you I wouldn't let you down.

Griggs: The Arbitron numbers have been astronomical. To jump those many points in so short a time. And the letters I get. My God. The board is really proud of you, Bernard. But no more than me.

Bernard: Thanks, Sam.

Griggs: I know we've had our differences in the past; you've always been so headstrong about things, but through it all I've always been able to count on you. That's not easy for a man like me.

Bernard: We make a good team, Sam.

Griggs: A fine team, yes, indeed.

Bernard: We still have a ways to go, yet. There're still some areas I need to fine tune.

Griggs: That won't be necessary, just yet.

Bernard: But, we need to keep pushing.

Griggs: That's why I had you come to my office, Bernard. Some things have come up.

Bernard: Things?

Griggs: Well, our success has attracted a lot of attention.

Bernard: I know. Our ad rates are climbing at all six of our stations.

Griggs: That's not what I mean, kid.

Bernard: What do you mean?

Griggs: I've been approached by some people who want to buy my company.

Bernard: Who?

Griggs: Pegasus International.

Bernard: Are you going to do it?

Griggs: Right now, all I'm doing is listening to their offer. Nothing more.

Bernard: I don't think it's a good idea, no matter how much they're offering.

Griggs: It doesn't hurt to know what I'm worth on today's market, now, does it?

Bernard: I wish you had talked to me before you made your move.

GRIGGS: Listen, I want you to see to it that our stations maintain their current ratings. Keep our listeners and advertisers happy. Don't get cute. I want my operations functional and running smoothly.

BERNARD: Wow, Sam…I feel like you're asking me to be nothing more than a caretaker.

GRIGGS: I only want to make the best impression I can.

BERNARD: I finally get things turned around and you hit me with this?

GRIGGS: Now, don't be getting dramatic on me, kid…

BERNARD: Dramatic? Sam…I been with you fifteen years…I've had good offers to go elsewhere…but, I chose to stay…

GRIGGS: I know that, and I appreciate your loyalty, Bernard…

BERNARD: I mean, I knew with your not having any children to pass the business on to…Well, I figured, in time, if I was loyal enough…if I worked hard enough,, I'd earn the right to expect…I mean, Sam, I learned everything from you. I was your right hand!

GRIGGS: Hang with me on this, kid. You won't be sorry.

(*Presses his intercom.*)

Mary, have Al bring the car around.

BERNARD: You can make a lot more money holding on to Griggs Broadcasting than by selling it.

GRIGGS: Who said anything about selling? I haven't made up my mind to do anything.

BERNARD: You seem pretty damned close to me, Sam.

GRIGGS: Well, I'm not. Stop jumping to conclusions and do as I ask.

BERNARD: But, Sam…

GRIGGS: (*Impatient; guilty.*) Whatever move I make, you'll be the first to know. Now, I'll see you later. I've got to do this lunch.

(*Lights.*)

END SCENE NINE

Scene Ten

Lights come up full to reveal PAM, MARVIN, ROWENA, *and* RON *in evening gowns and black tie. We can hear music and voices in the background. They are at an alumni affair and sing the Howard University alma mater.*

CAST: (*Singing.*)
Reared against the eastern sky
Proudly there on hilltop high
Far above the lake so blue
Stands old Howard firm and true.
There she stands for truth and right,
Sending forth her rays of light.
Clad in robes of majesty
(*They raise white handkerchiefs and wave them.*)
Oh, Howard, we sing of thee.

(*Lots of laughter, cheers, and applause.*)

ROWENA: Oh, how I hate coming to these things.

PAM: Oh, Rowena, you need to stop.

ROWENA: Everyone looking to see how fat everyone's gotten. Awful.

(*Waves offstage.*)

Oh, hi, Lois!

(*Under her breath.*)

Bitch.

MARVIN: Careful, baby, don't let her hear you.

ROWENA: I don't care. Never could stand that heifer.

(BERNARD *enters in a tux, carrying two wine glasses.*)

BERNARD: (*Gives one glass to* PAM.) Here you go, honey.

PAM: Wondered where you were. You took so long.

BERNARD: Ran into Harvey Benton at the bar.

MARVIN: Bubbleheaded Harvey?

BERNARD: The same.

MARVIN: Man, that guy had the biggest head I ever saw in my life.

BERNARD: He's still got it.

(*They laugh.*)

ROWENA: You know, Harvey and Charyce are getting a divorce, don't you?

MARVIN: Finally got tired of his mess, huh?

ROWENA: Guess so.

PAM: They got married the same day we did, honey.

BERNARD: Really.

PAM: Poor Charyce.

BERNARD: Poor Harvey...literally. That woman is going to take him to the cleaners.

ROWENA: I won't even dignify that remark with a reply.

PAM: I knew they were drifting apart. Charyce mentioned it to me, once or twice.

ROWENA: Sign of the times.

PAM: (*To* BERNARD.) Harvey never said anything to you?

BERNARD: No, but I can't blame him.

ROWENA: Oh? Why not?

BERNARD: We work in the same business. You never give a competitor an edge against you, even if he is your friend.

ROWENA: This isn't about business. This is something personal.

BERNARD: Personal...or professional, it doesn't matter. If it's a weakness, it's exploitable.

PAM: Charyce and Harvey are friends. I don't see them as competitors.

BERNARD: Alright, maybe it's a male thing; a rule of the pack. I don't know. But, it exists.

PAM: You men should talk to Harvey.

BERNARD: When Harvey wants help, he'll let us know.

RON: Besides, there're at least twenty lawyers in this room. Harvey needs to talk to them more than he needs to talk to us.

(*The men laugh.*)

PAM: That's disgusting.

ROWENA: We should have brought our children. They need to see something like this. There must be close to one hundred million dollars' worth of black people in this room and none of them had to sell drugs, rob, steal, or knock somebody over the head to get that money, either.

RON: You really think there's that much, Ro?

ROWENA: Well...fifty.

RON: Hmmm. Excuse me.

MARVIN: Wait up, Ron.

(Both men wander off, business cards at the ready, intent on "networking.")

ROWENA: I'm thinking about putting my girls in the Jack and Jills.

BERNARD: What?

ROWENA: You heard me, Bernard. You ain't deaf.

PAM: I think it's a wonderful idea. Young girls today need the kind of shaping Jack and Jill can give them.

ROWENA: Don't I know it.

PAM: And what do your daughters think?

ROWENA: They don't want to join, naturally.

PAM: All girls are like that. It's something new and that's one thing teenagers hate: the new and unknown.

ROWENA: Tell me about it.

BERNARD: You oughta be putting those girls in a computer camp or getting them in the Jaycees, or something. Teach them about power and how it shapes people's lives. Need to teach those girls something real.

PAM: Oh, Bernard.

BERNARD: And what made you decide to put your daughters in the Jack and Jill, anyway?

ROWENA: This little rogue my big girl brought home. Little tackhead thing, with twenty-two gold teeth cloggin' up his mouth and his hands stuck all down his pockets and this little hat titched on the side of his head like it was growin' out of his temple, or somethin'.

BERNARD: *(Laughs.)* "Mama, this is Bubba, and I *love* him."

ROWENA: How'd you know? That's *exactly* what she said.

(BERNARD laughs harder.)

It ain't funny. Here me and Marvin are bustin' our butts making all this money to send our kids to the best private schools and buy them the nicest clothes, tryin' to give them the best life has to offer, and what happens? She goes out and brings me a "Bubba" with a mouth fulla more gold than Fort Knox.

BERNARD: Relax. It's just an infatuation. She'll get over it.

ROWENA: For all I know that boy could be one of those drive-by shooters they talk about on TV.

BERNARD: You talk just like one of those middle-class biddies I used to hate when I was a kid.

Rowena: Well, I *am* a middle-class biddie, Bernard. And I'm putting my daughter in the Jack and Jills where she might have a chance to meet some nice young boy who's going to go to college and make something of himself.

Bernard: And the first thing he'll make is your daughter. While you're so busy watching that tackhead, it's that little slickhead in the tuxedo who's got your daughter in the backseat of his Daddy's BMW on cotillion night.

Pam: Don't listen to him, Ro. The Jack and Jills are wonderful. I was in the Jack and Jills and I loved every minute of it.

Bernard: I can remember a time when we wouldn't have been caught dead at a Jack and Jill ball, and now here we are talking about putting one of our children in one.

Pam: We've grown up, thank God.

(*Beat.*)

Getting older.

Rowena: Speak for yourself, Pamela.

Pam: I don't mind, really. Each new birthday brings on something new and exciting. I don't want to be twenty again. Today's kids have too many problems.

Bernard: The times are different. In our day we had heroes who told us we could grab fate and shake its tail. King, Malcolm, the Kennedys—

Rowena: Ella Baker, Fannie Lou Hamer.

Bernard: (*Agreeing.*) Teach. Well, they're all dead, now. And no one's risen to take their places. We came of age in a time when no dream was impossible, and no affliction was so terrible, it couldn't be overcome. Remember?

Rowena: But, it wasn't really like that.

Bernard: We believed in something, then. What do kids believe in, today? Instead, everyone is just out here trying to survive.

Pam: Why dwell on it, Bernard? You can't change anything.

Bernard: Yea, you're right, Pam. You've always had a level head about these things.

(Bernard *and* Pam *exchange glances.* Marvin *sees this and speaks up quickly.*)

Marvin: Come on, let's change the subject and talk about something real.

ROWENA: Okay, let's. Who wants to start?

(*Silence.*)

Let's not all speak at once.

RON: I want some more champagne. That's real. Anybody else?

(RON *starts off.*)

BERNARD: Let's talk about fidelity... or infidelity.

(RON *stops.*)

PAM: What? Why?

BERNARD: Because it's *real*.

RON: I don't know, man.

ROWENA: Who wants to talk about that? We all get along fine.

BERNARD: Well, so did Harvey and Charyce.

PAM: They fell out of love. You need love in a relationship.

BERNARD: That what happened with you and Irene, Ron? Y'all stopped loving each other?

RON: That was a long time ago.

ROWENA: All you need is love, Bernard. Strongest glue there is.

BERNARD: Is it? How many times can one's love stand being tested? How many years of making love the same old way; how many days of the same kinds of conversations; how many nights of sleeping on the same side of the bed, having the same old dreams. Huh?

PAM: If you really love someone, Bernard, that kind of stuff doesn't happen.

BERNARD: I had an uncle who carried on an affair with a woman for some twenty years. All the time he was married. My aunt had six children for him. The other lady had three. He swore he loved both women. Was he lyin'? Was he bored with his life and didn't want to face it? What? Why does a man do something like that?

ROWENA: Suppose you tell us.

BERNARD: I think one day my uncle looked up and saw he was living his life by everyone's expectations except his own. He was scared he had lost himself and one day he broke out by having an affair with another woman.

PAM: Well, things like that can happen sometimes, but it doesn't mean it's right.

Ron: Sometimes, when a man is a failure in one part of his life, he tries to become a success in another. What was he—an ordinary laborer, or something?

Bernard: (*Testy.*) He had money, Ron.

Marvin: Come on, Bernard, he only meant—

Bernard: I *know* what he meant. My uncle had his own business. Owned a house. Got himself a new car every two or three years. Sent all his kids off to school, too. Loved and respected by his neighbors and the folks at church. So, what happened? What made him break like that?

Ron: Biological determinism.

Bernard: What?

Marvin: He's saying your uncle was acting out a primal instinct that resides in every human male.

Rowena: It better not reside in *you*. I do know *that*.

Marvin: 'Course not, baby.

Rowena: Biological determinism. You men will come up with any kind of excuse to camouflage your lack of sexual discipline.

Marvin: Discipline? I didn't know you were into freaky deaky, baby.

(*All laugh, except* Bernard.)

Rowena: (*Playfully.*) Marvin, hush.

(*They laugh again.* Bernard *looks at them.*)

Bernard: We're getting off the subject.

Ron: What is the subject?

(Bernard *looks at him.*)

Oh, yes. Infidelity.

Bernard: It goes beyond infidelity. Look, I'm trying to get at something, here. I feel like we're in a lot of trouble.

Ron: I think the brother's had a little too much to drink.

Bernard: I'm *fine*.

Ron: Then what is the something you're trying to get at? You've been running your mouth all night. Why don't you get down to it?

(Bernard *glares at* Ron *and suddenly blurts out:*)

Bernard: Fuck you, man. *Fuck* you!

Ron: (*Tense.*) I think the brother's had too much to drink.

(BERNARD *starts for* RON. MARVIN *gets between them.*)

MARVIN: Hey, man! Bernard! This is us, remember?

(BERNARD *struggles, but* MARVIN *holds him fast.*)

Remember?!

RON: Excuse me.

(ROWENA *goes after* RON. MARVIN *soon follows.* BERNARD *moves downstage, in another direction.* PAM *moves toward him.*)

BERNARD: Doesn't it ever bother you, Pam? Doesn't it ever get on your nerves? We're so full of shit.

(*Lights.*)

END SCENE TEN

Scene Eleven

BERNARD *stands alone in a spot.*

BERNARD: I knew something was wrong when I began to hate them. It went against everything I had ever come to believe in. People whom I had once viewed as the victims of everything that was wrong with America; the perfect human metaphors for our society's very real failures, now stood before me, an endless parade of poor downtrodden men holding squeegees in their hands, fighting each other over the privilege of wiping my windshield for fifty cents.

What would Du Bois have thought if he could see what the last days of the twentieth century had brought to black people? What would Douglass or Garvey have thought? The sons and daughters of Africa; the descendants of the survivors of the middle passage—the heartiest black people who ever lived—now reduced to standing on street corners selling their bodies for a drug fix and clubbing each other with broom handles for the right to make a couple of quarters washing someone's windshield.

Instead of lamenting their sorry fate, I hated them because I knew there was nothing I could do to change their lives. They would always be there, day after horrible day. Their lives would never change. I had managed to grab the brass ring and I was being pulled up and away from them, floating higher and higher. I would survive the madness and they would not. And I hated them for not surviving, for ensuring that the intelligence they had, the love they were once capable of giving, were to be denied to our people. I came to see that the legacy bequeathed them by the many thousands gone, by all the blood that was shed, had truly been wasted on them. There was no help for them. And I hated them for making me realize that I had to abandon them lest I be pulled down with them.

And that's when I realized that something was wrong. Who gave me the right to judge them? Who gave me the right to feel superior? I act as though there is nothing I can do. But, that can't be true. It just can't be.

(*Lights.*)

END SCENE ELEVEN

Scene Twelve

Lights up on BERNARD *and* GRIGGS *standing on the promontory at Eagle Rock Reservation.*

GRIGGS: I love coming up here.

BERNARD: You used to bring me up here when I first started working for you.

(*He looks at* SAM. *He knows something is up.*)

GRIGGS: You can see all the way to New York. Must be a good twenty miles.

BERNARD: Fourteen. Remember?

GRIGGS: Yes, fourteen. Of course.

(BERNARD *looks at* SAM.)

BERNARD: Why're we up here, Sam?

GRIGGS: Don't want to beat around the bush. Good. You see, I wanted a place where we could really talk. Away from the office. I wanted to explain to you—

BERNARD: You're going to sell to Pegasus.

GRIGGS: Yes.

BERNARD: Then, there's nothing to talk about.

GRIGGS: There's plenty to talk about.

BERNARD: Hey, man, it's your station. You do what you want.

GRIGGS: Don't you take that tone with me.

BERNARD: Why don't you give me some time, Sam? I know I can come up with the backing to make you a very fair offer.

GRIGGS: Bernard, what have our grosses been? In our *best* year? Ten, twelve million? These guys pull down those kinds of bucks in a month! That's the kind of world we live in, now. You can't compete in a world like that, nickel and diming your way along.

BERNARD: I know how to compete in that world, Sam. I've spent a career wading through that world helping you build this company. I didn't do it with mirrors.

GRIGGS: (*Sighs.*) Sorry, Bernard. My mind's made up. I've made provisions for you to stay on. They're going to move you over to their facilities in Fort Lee. Our offices are slated to be torn down and the land cleared for sale.

BERNARD: And you expect me to work for these people?

(*Pause.*)

GRIGGS: They're very impressed with that Urban Cutting Edge Format you've developed. They want you to run things for them during the interim. Of course, one of their guys will be in overall charge, but you know how that is.

BERNARD: Sam, I can't believe this, man.

GRIGGS: They'll want you to diminish that controversial stuff. Politics and black radio don't mix. They'll want you to keep it light. "Infotainment." I think that's the phrase they used.

BERNARD: Dammit, Sam, you had no right to do this. It's my turn. This is *my* shot.

GRIGGS: Make your own shot, Goddammit! Like I had to!

BERNARD: And that's the justification?! You had a hard time, so every young person who comes after you has to do the same? How do we develop an economic base for our people if we keep selling off our businesses in the name of fiscal expediency? How do we encourage our young kids if we block them at every turn and leave them with no institutions to take over after we've gone? Answer me that, Sam?

GRIGGS: There it is: that same smarmy, baby boom self-righteousness I've had to put up with for the past twenty goddamn years! I'm not going to be judged by your expectations, or anyone else's. I'm doing what I think is right!

BERNARD: The black community was changing, Sam! It was up to us to be at the forefront of that change!

GRIGGS: It was too dangerous!

BERNARD: But, that was our job, Sam! There were new voices and ideas out there that needed to be heard. Poets and musicians who might've been able to give our people something more than twenty-four hours of "Ow, ow, ow! Give it to me, Mama, while you shake your thang!" It's never been your station to do as you please, Sam. It belongs to the people. It should have been their voice. Not their sleeping pill.

GRIGGS: Well, I remember things differently, Bernard. Every time something jumped off at the studio I had the FBI, the FCC, and the local police hanging around the station with subpoenas, search warrants, questionnaires, and who knows what else. Every time some militant ran off at the mouth, or some singer warbled a lyric that some scared bureaucrat construed to be a call for black people to riot in the streets. I wasn't going to have that. I wasn't going to have my business go down the tubes on a bullshit tip! Hell, no!

BERNARD: I used to hear dudes lecture about you in school, man. Your name was right up there with Walker, Fuller, Johnson...Lewis and Smith—all the pioneers in black business. I never thought I'd live to see the day when you'd become content to be just another anonymous business transaction on some white man's ledger.

GRIGGS: Look, they're going to be paying you a lot of money. More than I ever paid you. And let me remind you, "Mr. Guardian of the Great Black Consciousness," that the most revolutionary, political act any black man can perform in this country is to successfully take care of his family— because *no one expects him to*!

(*Beat.*)

Look, maybe one day you'll get a chance to do your own thing. But, not right now. This ain't the first time a black man has had to wait his turn. Take the job, Bernard. Go with these guys. Everybody else is.

(BERNARD *turns his back and begins walking away.*)

So, what's it going to be? You going to be a righteous revolutionary with no prospects, or a pragmatic businessman who looked the dragon in the eye...and decided to wear an asbestos suit? I want an answer soon, and it better be the right one.

END SCENE TWELVE

Scene Thirteen

PAM *and* BERNARD *at home.*

PAM: You know, we've got money saved and I'm working.

BERNARD: I know.

PAM: How could they fire you like that? No warning. Nothing. Just fired.

BERNARD: I had warnings.

PAM: (*Looks at him.*) Then, you should have heeded them.

BERNARD: I wasn't going to keep letting those people get on my nerves. Me and Griggs had words. I told him what I thought of his policies and he fired me.

PAM: Well, you know how hot-tempered Griggs is. Go back and talk to him. See if you can get your job back.

BERNARD: Maybe I don't want it back.

PAM: You think that's wise? You need a job, honey.

BERNARD: Right. A job. Not *that* job.

PAM: What are you going to do?

BERNARD: I want to go after Griggs Broadcasting.

PAM: Go after it? You mean buy it?

BERNARD: Yes. It won't be easy. But, I know I can raise the money.

PAM: It takes time to make something like that work.

BERNARD: Griggs'll stall Pegasus, trying to drive the price up. If he waits long enough, that just might give me the time I need.

PAM: That's the future. What about now?

BERNARD: I'll find something.

PAM: You'd be putting quite a strain on yourself. Working full time, plus trying to raise money—

BERNARD: I don't see that I have any other choice.

PAM: Yes, you do. You could try to talk to Griggs.

BERNARD: Too late for that. I want more, now.

PAM: Griggs has already made up his mind. You can't win that fight.

BERNARD: I've got to try.

PAM: If we were in our twenties or early thirties, I might be inclined to say go for it. The children were small, then, but those days are over. You're almost forty-five years old. It's time you put your feet firmly on the ground. We have responsibilities—

BERNARD: You want me to give up?

PAM: I want you to be practical.

BERNARD: *Fuck* being practical, goddammit! Look what being practical for the past twenty years has gotten me!

PAM: Cursing at me is not going to change the reality of the situation, Bernard.

BERNARD: Oh, Pam, I'm not raising my voice at you. It's just that, for the past few months I've felt things closing in on me. Alarm bells are going off inside my head all the time: "Make your move, now, Bernard. Make your move, now."

PAM: Why is it you only see what you haven't accomplished, and completely ignore the good things you've done with your life?

BERNARD: Because I know I'm supposed to be further down the road. That's why.

PAM: I love you, Bernard. But, if you're going to allow everything we've spent all these years building up to come crashing down around our heads, I'll fight you. I swear before God I will fight you tooth and nail.

(*She turns and goes out.* BERNARD *remains onstage.*)

END SCENE THIRTEEN

Scene Fourteen

A golf course in Essex County, New Jersey. PAM, BERNARD, RON, MARVIN, *and* ROWENA *on the links.* PAM *is first off the tee.*

ROWENA: Oh, Pam. Great shot!

PAM: Best I've ever done, I think.

MARVIN: Sliced it too much, if you ask me.

ROWENA: No one did, so hush. You men are always so critical.

RON: Come on, Ro. Your turn.

(ROWENA *steps up to the tee.* MARVIN *looks at* BERNARD.)

MARVIN: Come on, man. Get in the game.

BERNARD: Got my mind on other things.

RON: Better concentrate on this game, bro. The sistuhs are serious about beatin' us, this time.

ROWENA: Damned right.

(*Whack! Ro's shot flies off the tee. Everyone except* BERNARD *oohs and aahs.*)

PAM: Bernard? Your turn, honey.

BERNARD: I need to talk to y'all.

(*He steps to the tee, places his ball down.*)

MARVIN: Yeah, well, talk while you're playing, bro. That's what golf's all about.

(BERNARD *takes his time setting himself and lining up his shot.*)

BERNARD: I'm organizing a counterbid to acquire Griggs Broadcasting. I need y'all to put your money where your friendship is.

(BERNARD *drives a tremendous tee shot.*)

MARVIN: Damn!

BERNARD: Is that a comment on my statement, or my shot?

ROWENA: (*Under her breath.*) Both.

PAM: Honey, I thought you were going to think this thing through before you discussed it with anybody?

BERNARD: I have thought it through. What do y'all think?

ROWENA: Well…uh…it sounds interesting…

MARVIN: (*Steps to the tee.*) Kind of caught me off-guard, Bernard, I mean, hey, I'm playing golf, man.

BERNARD: This is the right move at the right time. Communications is a growth industry. We could—

RON: You don't have to sell us on the virtues of the broadcast business, brother.

MARVIN: That's quite a lot of money you've got to raise, my man.

BERNARD: I've got the will and the expertise, and y'all have got the kinds of contacts I'd need to get things moving. What do you say?

(*Whack!* ROWENA *drives her shot.*)

ROWENA: I like the idea.

PAM: We could organize a dinner party, invite some key people, and get the ball rolling. I can have my office put the prospectus together in no time.

MARVIN: A Limited Partnership would be enticing…

BERNARD: Then, it's agreed. You'll do it.

(*All except* RON *chime in words of agreement.* RON *looks at them all. Then:*)

RON: No.

BERNARD: What?

RON: Sorry, Bernard, I think it's a bad move.

ROWENA: You're wrong.

RON: Think on it: the growth area in communications is not radio. It's cable TV.

BERNARD: Hey, look, I'm the one who has a communications background, not you.

(RON *steps to the tee. As he speaks he places his ball, sets himself, and lines up his shot. Occasionally, he allows himself to make direct eye contact with* BERNARD.)

RON: Then use that knowledge to look ahead. Find a cable franchise that's on the block, then talk to us. Just looking out for your interest, brother. You gotta put your money where it'll do the most good.

ROWENA: Maybe Ron is right.

PAM: I don't know. Maybe Bernard is right. Ron could be wrong about this.

(RON *swings. Whack!*)

RON: It's unlikely. The think tank at my company did some comparative studies, and—

BERNARD: Tell me something, Ron. You ever hear of people taking their portable cable TV to the beach with them? Does cable TV ride around with them in their cars, or go with them when they're out jogging? Or shopping? Or picnicking? Or doing *anything* outside of the house? Radio is *always* there. Instant communication. Instant information. Touching base with our people whenever and wherever. That's what radio offers. That's why it will always be an important component to people's lives. And that's what makes it a sound investment. You sit around listening to some slick Ivy League bean counters running their mouths over some fancy food in a Wall Street restaurant and suddenly you want to stand out here and pontificate as if you have insight into the Great Secrets of Life. I *know* what I'm talking about. I'm not a fool.

RON: Nobody said you were, brother.

BERNARD: Then, shut the hell up, goddammit and stay outa my way!

(BERNARD *moves away. His outburst has made everyone uneasy. Pause.*)

How about the rest of y'all?

ROWENA: I'm sorry, Bernard. But Ron's still given me some food for thought. But, let me see a prospectus.

BERNARD: Sure, and you'll get back to me. Right?

MARVIN: Uh…er…it's starting to cloud up. Let's get a few more holes in before it rains.

ROWENA: Yes, let's go.

(MARVIN *and* ROWENA *move on.* PAM *and* RON *linger with* BERNARD.)

RON: Sorry, Bernard. I wasn't out to hurt your feelings, or anything. I just felt I had to speak my mind.

BERNARD: Your kind of thinking calls itself being careful and prudent, but it's really just a disguise for a lack of vision and the willingness to ACT. I'm going to get Griggs Broadcasting, Ron. I won't let men like you get in my way ever again.

(RON *and* BERNARD *stare each other down. Then:*)

RON: Better watch this next hole, brother. There's a helluva sand trap.

(BERNARD *says nothing as* RON *moves off and* PAM *moves close to him.*)

(*Lights.*)

END SCENE FOURTEEN

Scene Fifteen

The next afternoon. BERNARD *and* TANYA, *in* TANYA's *apartment.*

BERNARD: Just talk to your friends, and have them talk to some of their friends. We'll call a meeting and I'll have a prospectus for them to look at.

TANYA: Bernard, my friends are a pretty conservative bunch. We're very careful at what we do.

BERNARD: You know anything about Pegasus International?

TANYA: They're an up-and-coming communications conglomerate. Not nearly as big as their name implies.

BERNARD: Which means they can be defeated. We're not talking a transcontinental megacorp here.

TANYA: My people'll want a sure thing.

BERNARD: Then, they're crazy. There *are* no sure things in life.

TANYA: The history of our people is filled with dreamers and impulsive people like you. The list of their failures is long.

BERNARD: Then, help me write some new history, Tanya.

TANYA: And what does your wife think?

BERNARD: What do you care about what my wife thinks?

TANYA: Just curious.

BERNARD: Don't play games with me, Tanya.

TANYA: No need to get upset. I just asked a question.

BERNARD: This some kind of litmus test? Give you the wrong answer and you won't help.

TANYA: Did I say that?

BERNARD: It's hard to tell. Women start getting notions in their heads and they stop speaking English. Suddenly, they're speaking metaphors and subtleties.

TANYA: What is it with you?

BERNARD: I'm just tired of bullshit, Tanya. Okay?

TANYA: No, it's not okay. I'm the one on the emotional limb, Bernard. I'm the one who only gets pieces of you, while she enjoys all of you. I'm the one alone on the holidays, I'm the one who remains in the shadows. I'm the one who soothes you and quiets you after she's put you down and hurt you. I think I have a right to ask questions and a right to some answers. You always want my help, but what do I ever receive in return?

BERNARD: Maybe you're right.

TANYA: I know I'm right. Now, what does your wife think?

BERNARD: She thinks I should get my old job back.

TANYA: And you really believe you can outbid Griggs Broadcasting?

BERNARD: Help me, and I'll show you.

TANYA: I'll do whatever I can. I love you, Bernard. I love you.

(*They kiss.* BERNARD *goes into the other room.* TANYA *goes to a telephone and dials. She holds the receiver to her ear a moment, then, as it is still ringing, she hangs the phone up and walks away.*)

END SCENE FIFTEEN

Scene Sixteen

PAM *and* ROWENA *in the sauna.*

ROWENA: Mmmmm, this feels so good.

(PAM *says nothing.*)

So…uh…you find out who the broad is, yet?

PAM: No. I'm not sure I want to.

ROWENA: If it was me, I'd just have to know.

PAM: The fact that he's seeing someone is painful enough without having to know who the woman is.

ROWENA: So, what are you going to do about it?

PAM: I don't know, yet. I mean, I'm not sure.

ROWENA: You're sure.

PAM: I don't understand why he feels the need. What did I do?

ROWENA: Find you somebody.

PAM: I'm not interested in finding somebody.

ROWENA: Get interested.

PAM: I don't want to.

ROWENA: It'll dry up if you don't use it, girl.

PAM: Maybe I should have told him how I felt. Maybe if I had been more giving…more open.

ROWENA: Confront him.

PAM: No. I mean, not yet.

ROWENA: Well, if this marriage is important to you, don't waste time.

PAM: I won't. Don't worry.

(*Beat.*)

Hmph. "The Perfect Couple."

ROWENA: What?

PAM: That's what *Jet* magazine said when we got married; the Perfect Couple.

ROWENA: I remember.

PAM: I didn't like that article. Didn't like us being called that. Bad luck.

ROWENA: Shoot, it was perfect: the daughter of a traditional, old-line black Southern family with money getting' married to a new-generation black militant whose work even white critics liked. It knocked us all out when we first heard it.

PAM: You know, my parents didn't want me to marry him.

ROWENA: You never told me that.

PAM: Well, it's true.

ROWENA: Why?

PAM: I don't want to talk about it.

ROWENA: It wasn't because your folks didn't want no big, black-skinned Negro sleeping with their light-skinned daughter, was it?

PAM: (*Sharply.*) No, that wasn't it, at all.

ROWENA: I thought so.

PAM: Well, you're wrong.

ROWENA: Sure.

(*Beat.*)

PAM: I never thought I would be right for him. You knew me back in those days. I wasn't militant enough for the kind of people you and Bernard used to hang out with. I didn't particularly go for wearing all those African clothes. It seemed so phony. They just weren't practical for use in a Western society. I mean, I'm African descended, but I'm not an African.

(ROWENA *looks at her, then looks away.*)

ROWENA: You weren't supposed to get him, you know. Habiba was.

PAM: Oh, yes. Bessie Johnson. The zoology major. If Bernard was serious about her, he would have let me know.

ROWENA: Well, you were considered one of the most attractive girls on campus. All the men had their eyes on you.

PAM: I used to catch hell for not being black enough. What did that mean? I was as black as any of them.

ROWENA: It wasn't about ethnicity. It was about where your mind was at.

PAM: Well, I am the way I am. I'm not changing for anybody. All that African stuff and hardly any of them understood what it all meant. They were always so right—or "righteous." And I was always so wrong.

Everything about me was wrong. I was too smart…too Western…too
middle class…too pretty…

Rowena: Too light?

Pam: What's my color got to do with it?

Rowena: It helped you beat out Habiba.

Pam: My color is not my fault.

Rowena: A lot of people felt you thought it was a great advantage.

Pam: Is that how you felt?

Rowena: I always felt it was a great burden.

Pam: I'm not sure I know how to take that.

Rowena: Think about it, honey.

(*Beat.*)

Pam: Ro, you really think he married me because of the color of my skin.

(*Looks away.*)

This is the kind of thing that can drive you crazy. Suddenly, you start
questioning everything.

Rowena: Don't drive yourself crazy, girl.

Pam: I caught hell from your old group because I was light-skinned,
didn't I?

Rowena: No, I wouldn't say that.

Pam: I would.

Rowena: Look, Claudia Truitt was as light as you and she didn't have
any problem with us.

Pam: Claudia Truitt had a large flat nose, full lips, and a big behind.
There was never any mistake about her. We all know I'm not like that.

(*Pause*)

His color attracted me, you know. There was something so warm and
sensuous about him. There were times when he positively glistened.

Rowena: He still does, from time to time.

Pam: I wanted that warmth.

Rowena: Who didn't?

Pam: I knew I had to have him. And winning him from all you "relevant"
and "righteous" campus militants felt so good.

ROWENA: Really.

PAM: It was a question of class, too, Rowena. A street boy going to college. All my life I had been shielded from men like him. And now here was one up close. I loved it.

ROWENA: A less sympathetic ear might accuse you of slumming.

PAM: I never felt that way.

ROWENA: You never had to. You stood to benefit from the rules of the game, whether you wanted to or not. It's crazy. We were supposed to have buried this color thing a long time ago. Look, can we change the subject?

PAM: We were just deluding ourselves.

(*Beat.*)

I have a dark-skinned cousin who lives in Newark, not even twenty minutes from here. She hates the sight of me. Won't even speak to me. Hates all light-skinned people…and never lets me forget it. It's all part of something that's been going on in my family since before I was born…I've always been afraid that, somewhere deep in his heart, Bernard hates me.

ROWENA: Hates you?

PAM: Yes. Maybe it was some perverse self-hatred that made him marry me and now, years later, it's starting to surface; he can't suppress it any longer.

ROWENA: Bernard oughta be horsewhipped for what he's doing to you.

PAM: Did you love him?

ROWENA: Who?

PAM: Bernard.

ROWENA: Bernard?

PAM: Yes. At Howard. Did you love him?

ROWENA: Ah…I-I-I-I…

PAM: Well, did you?

ROWENA: Yes, but only in the political sense.

PAM: And you hated me for getting him, didn't you?

ROWENA: What are you talking about? Habiba had him.

PAM: And you all really loved Habiba. Big-butt, dark-skinned, African-looking Habiba. She was one of *you*.

Rowena: Pam—

Pam: And you hated me and you *still* hate me.

Rowena: No more, alright?

Pam: Oh, I've always known how you've felt about me.

Rowena: Will you stop?

Pam: Habiba was part of your little crowd: that tight little dark-skinned women's collective you all had. I moved in and snapped my tapioca fingers and y'all's ebony idol was scooped up, just like that.

Rowena: Now, Just a minute!

Pam: I'm just laying my cards on the table, Ro.

Rowena: Shit! You act like the pain doesn't cut both ways. "Dark-skinned women's collective?" Why do you think that was? Huh?! "Well, honey, you so dark you sure can't be pretty. You'd better be smart." Straightening combs dug so deep down into your scalp till the pain made your eyes water. All from trying to make the hair do something it wasn't meant to do and had no business even trying. Excluded from certain circles; not invited to certain parties. Always waiting to be chosen after y—

(*She doesn't finish the sentence.*)

There were always reasons for "dark-skinned women's collectives," Pam. I can still remember a mural on the wall of a restaurant across the street from the campus. It showed campus life back in the thirties, or whenever it was painted. All the students in the mural looked like you, Pam; none of them looked like me.

Yes, I was angry when you took Bernard. It seemed like a confirmation of every feeling of inferiority that had hounded me since birth.

Pam: I can't help the way I look. There are white people in Richmond with the same family name as mine. Some of them look just like my aunts and uncles. They know who I am. They know my whole family. And yet, when we walk down the street and they see us coming they look the other way like we're not even there. Every year when I take the children down home, all the old folks trip over themselves to see who gets to check my children's hair first. How do you think that makes me feel? And right there in Newark, just twenty minutes away, I've got a black cousin the same age as me with two children I have never seen and she treats me like shit!

Rowena: I've spent most of the last twenty years trying to put all the pain aside.

PAM: Nothing's working out, Ro. It's like all my life has been one right move after the other and now, suddenly, everything is being thrown back in my face and I don't even know why. I'm tired of being the yella bitch and I'm tired of being the tragic mulatto. I hate what whites have done to my family and I hate what my family has done to itself. And I hate what they have ALL done to me.

ROWENA: What about what you've done to yourself?

PAM: Sometimes I hurt so bad. I just hurt.

ROWENA: All black women carry scars, Pam.

PAM: They never go away.

ROWENA: We'll never be able to do anything about the pain others cause us until we do something about the pain we're causing ourself.

(PAM *says nothing. The women sit in silence . . . and quietly reach out to one another.*)

END SCENE SIXTEEN

Scene Seventeen

A week later, BERNARD, RON, *and* MARVIN *at their favorite bar.*

BERNARD and **MARVIN:** Africa?!

RON: Why not? The chance of a lifetime.

MARVIN: You just gonna pack up everything and move over there?

RON: I'm already taking a Berlitz course in Swahili, brother.

BERNARD: Surpised me, man. I never would've expected it of you.

RON: Well, you ought to know me by now, Bernard. I'm full of surprises.

BERNARD: Anyway, I think it's a great idea.

MARVIN: Yea. *You* would.

BERNARD: I was in Africa, once.

MARVIN: Yea, we know: Angola.

BERNARD: It's beautiful, man. You'll love it.

RON: Angola's communist, man. I can't make no money there.

MARVIN: Ron, you know they got that tribalism thing in Africa, man. Everything's fine as long as you hooked up with the right tribe. But, hey, that could all change any minute.

RON: Don't worry. I got it under control.

BERNARD: Kwame hooked this all up?

RON: Told you contacting him would pay off, one day.

BERNARD: Damn.

RON: He's up there in the Minister of Agriculture's office. I'll be livin' out in the bush, man. My own spread, a staff—the works.

(BERNARD *raises his glass to toast* RON. MARVIN *does, also.*)

MARVIN: Looks like you're going to be a pioneer.

RON: And a rich one to boot. I make this irrigation idea of mine work, I'll patent it and market it all over the Continent.

BERNARD: Could be quite a boost to the African economy.

RON: Hey, man, I look like UNESCO to you?

MARVIN: I just hope you'll be careful, Ron. I mean, you're going to be a long way from home and well, this is the first time you've seen Kwame since our college days, man. Who knows how much he's changed.

RON: Not that much. He's ambitious as ever. He's going to run for office.

MARVIN and BERNARD: Kwame?!

RON: He'll win, too. He's very popular. He's got six wives, man.

MARVIN: Damn, you know *that* brother's in shape.

RON: Each from the most powerful villages in his region. So, you know he's got connections, and his father's a chief who sits in the national assembly.

MARVIN: Damn!

RON: Wide open, man. We could make the kind of moves our grandchildren won't even be able to dream about over here.

BERNARD: No wonder you became a Republican.

RON: Yea, well, the Republicans help those who help themselves, and I'm going to help myself to some of the Mother Country.

MARVIN: Like I said, man: don't get in over your head.

RON: Look, I'm forty-one years old, going nowhere fast. Stuck in a middle-management position at my firm, with no prospects of a promotion. I trained two of the people who are now up for vice-president.

MARVIN: Hey, man, there's a lot of us in that boat. It's not your fault. You can't help that.

RON: Yes, I can. I can get the hell outa there. I'm not going to spend the rest of my life being a circus animal—a feature on the sideshow of somebody else's main event. Africa's been making a whole lotta money for everybody else, time she made some for one of her prodigal sons.

BERNARD: Gotta tell you, man: you don't sound like the kind of son Mother Africa wants to see. If all you've got to offer her is one more ripoff mentality then what you need to do is keep your "prodigal" ass here.

RON: Later for you, man. I know what I'm doing.

BERNARD: That's what's so scary. And so sad.

RON: Sorry, man. I refuse to feel guilty about *not* feeling guilty. Know what I'm saying?

BERNARD: Yea. Cecil Rhodes would be real proud of you, Ron.

RON: Kiss my ass, Bernard. Why don't you take that sixties anger and stuff it.

BERNARD: Somebody oughta stuff *you*.

MARVIN: Fellas, this is starting to get a little thick. Why don't we just cool it and go on home?

RON: Good idea.

BERNARD: Y'all go ahead. I don't feel like going home.

MARVIN: I think you've had enough to drink for one night. Pam'll start to worry, man.

BERNARD: Maybe she will. Maybe she won't.

MARVIN: Hey, what's that supposed to mean?

BERNARD: If ya'll are going, go ahead.

RON: What's buggin' you, man?

BERNARD: I think me and Pam's had it, man.

MARVIN: It's that other broad you've been seeing. You're letting her get in the way, man. I told you to cut her loose.

BERNARD: It's all gonna come crashing down, man. Later for it. Whatever happens, happens. It's no use, anymore.

MARVIN: Bernard, are you drunk? What the hell are you talkin' about, man?

BERNARD: There's a point where the line between your professional life and your personal life blurs; where the choices you made in terms of one are a mirror reflection of the choices you made in the other. If you're an honest man and true to your heart and your beliefs, there's no problem. But, if not—

RON: I'm going home. I'll see y'all later.

MARVIN: Wait, don't leave, Ron.

RON: And he's got the nerve to talk about me. No, man, if he wants to act the fool, don't expect me to hang around and watch while he's doing it.

MARVIN: We're supposed to be friends. We should talk.

RON: He should talk to his wife and kids. They're the ones whose lives he's messin' up.

BERNARD: What would you have me do, Ron? Keep up the lies, keep on frontin' my game like everybody else around here?

RON: I don't have an answer for you, Bernard. But I will tell you this: this life we've got right now is all we've got. You understand? Don't ask me to give you advice on how to tear that life apart.

BERNARD: This life we've got is no life at all, Ron. It's a lie!

RON: Then lie to me, baby, 'cause I damn sure am enjoying the *hell* out of *this* untruth.

BERNARD: Thank God, I'm not. I'm tired of the lies. I'm tired of being a role model. I have no real wealth, no power, and, ultimately, no respect. And if that's the life I'm offering to my kids, then I'm damned well pleased to be "messing" it up.

RON: You make me nervous, Bernard. You ask too many questions. You push too hard. Always been your downfall. You need to learn to do like me, brother. I'm gonna go home, put some Coltrane on the box, sip some scotch, and then go to sleep and dream about Africa and a lot of money, and wake up tomorrow and know that all is right with the world.

(RON *starts out.*)

Don't be a fool, Bernard. Don't be a fool.

BERNARD: (*Looks at MARVIN.*) That the way you feel, too? I'm a fool?

(MARVIN *says nothing.*)

Y'all just don't understand, man.

MARVIN: And Pam, does she understand?

BERNARD: No.

MARVIN: (*Takes a drink.*) I used to envy you.

Bernard: I used to envy me, too.

Marvin: I remember when ya'll hooked up in school. Couldn't figure out how a Papa Booga Bear like you managed to end up with the foxiest mama in the junior class.

Bernard: She was as mysterious as Habiba was predictable.

Marvin: Oh, yeah…

(*Looks at* Bernard.)

You need to forget about Habiba, Bernard. There's nothing you can do or say to her. She's been dead, for years.

Bernard: If I only could have explained to her—

Marvin: Look, she was the one who made the decision to go to Angola. You didn't have anything to do with that.

Bernard: Angola was all me and her used to talk about. We took that liberating the Continent stuff seriously, man. Fighting for justice for black people wherever they are. All a that. We used to sit up till all hours talking about that.

Marvin: I told the both of you, then, you were crazy. The Angolans could take care of themselves. The last thing in the world they needed was to have some starry-eyed young colored kids from the U.S. running around over there getting' in the way.

Bernard: We didn't used to think like that.

Marvin: Maybe that was our problem. Besides, what was Habiba gonna do for you with her five-year-old sandals, long no-shape-to-them dresses, hair braided-up, no make-up wearin' self?

Bernard: You loved her, too. Remember?

Marvin: Damned right, I loved her. Still do. But, she's dead…and so are the days she lived in.

Bernard: If those days are dead, they're dead because we let them die.

Marvin: They died because they had to.

Bernard: I was a good writer. With a little polish I might have been a great one. Now, all I am is an out-of-work vice-president of a radio station who's spent the past fifteen years selling dog food to people I once tried to move to political change.

Marvin: Oh, boo-hoo, boo-hoo. I can see your tear-stained face driving your BMW all the way to the bank.

BERNARD: Sound like Pam.

MARVIN: That's because Pam's got a lot of sense. She knows you can't help the poor by being poor yourself.

BERNARD: I think that's what I understood about her right from the start. She was used to things. She *expected* things.

MARVIN: That's what good upbringing does for you.

BERNARD: It made her regal in my poor inner-city eyes.

MARVIN: You wanted Pam, Bernard. Habiba knew that. That's why she didn't put up a fight for you.

BERNARD: But, I married an illusion, a dream.

MARVIN: Habiba was the illusion, brother.

BERNARD: I lied to Habiba. I lied to Pam. I've lied to myself. Whatever happens, happens, I don't care anymore.

MARVIN: You know what's bugging you? You're ashamed to admit that you preferred Pam because she was pretty, rich, and had light skin. You feel guilty because you rejected dark Habiba. That's it, isn't it? *Isn't it?*

(BERNARD *says nothing.*)

You think you're the first? Shit, I can promise you you won't be the last. Oh, man, it wasn't just her skin color. It was everything about her. Her taste. Her *class*, brother. That's what attracted you. In the long run, you knew you could take Pam anywhere. She has the flexibility to be anything and look any kind of way. That's why you wanted her. She can fit in. Need her to be the perfect hostess for the sales reps coming to see you at your home, she can do that; want to go see a Broadway musical that hasn't a thing to do with the race problem, Pam'll be right there. Need that perfect wife to razzle dazzle the corporate execs at the next Broadcasters Convention, hey, Pam'll be johnny on the spot. Habiba didn't have that flexibility. You knew it even back then. That's why you left her, man. You were becoming too sophisticated to get locked into doing things one way, and one way only.

BERNARD: She died, man. Killed fighting a revolution; fighting for a cause. That was no illusion. That was real.

MARVIN: Her reality, not yours. You have to be practical, Bernard. Even if your big house and social status seem insignificant right now, you just remember that you didn't even have that much back in those good old days you want to run back to. Whether you admit it or not, all that talk we did about freedom, justice, and equality—all that marching an singing; all those sacrifices, the injuries—all those *deaths*—pointed to just one thing: not black nationhood, but a nice home in a nice neighborhood, two cars, a fine family, money in the bank, and a chance at the good life.

And if you think I'm lying, just take a look at how all your great revolutionary leaders in Africa live once they get to power. Show me one successful black American leader who still lives in the ghetto. Show me one welfare mother who wouldn't leap at the chance to escape the inner city Habiba loved so much if she could just get her hands on half the money you make in just one year. Pam understands that, and that's why you went after her. 'Cause she's got the class and she's got the knowledge. And face it, brotha, that's what you wanted all along, isn't it? That's what any sensible man wants. Isn't it, brotha? Isn't it?... Well, isn't it?

BERNARD: No. A purpose, Marvin. Something worth living for, fighting for and, if need be, worth dying for. That's what any sensible man wants. Especially any sensible black man.

(BERNARD *gulps down his drink, slams the glass down on the bar, and exits, leaving* MARVIN *to ponder.*)

END SCENE SEVENTEEN

Scene Eighteen

Lights up on TANYA's *apartment.* PAM *appears at the door and rings the doorbell.* TANYA *answers it and comes face to face with* PAM.

PAM: Tanya Blakely?

TANYA: Look, I don't want any trouble...

PAM: Then you know who I am.

TANYA: Yes.

PAM: May I come in?

TANYA: I told you, I don't want any trouble.

PAM: It's a little late to be worrying about causing any trouble, isn't it? May I come in?

(TANYA *steps back and* PAM *enters.*)

May I sit down?

TANYA: Oh, you plan to be here that long?

PAM: May I sit down?

(*She sits.* TANYA *sits across from her.*)

TANYA: Well?

PAM: Looking at you, I see why my husband is so taken with you. I may as well admit it. He's probably in love with you.

TANYA: Yes, he probably is.

PAM: Are you in love with him?

TANYA: Yes. I am.

PAM: Then we have a problem.

TANYA: We don't have a problem. He's not in love with you, anymore.

PAM: He's told you that?

TANYA: He will.

PAM: You have a lot to learn about Bernard, my dear.

TANYA: How did you find me?

PAM: Sometimes it's necessary to invade your husband's privacy to learn more about him.

(TANYA *says nothing.*)

I'm here to tell you that I'm not giving him up.

TANYA: I consider myself warned. Now, if you'll excuse me—

PAM: You and I are not through, yet.

TANYA: Oh yes we are—

PAM: Sit down.

TANYA: What makes you think you can boss me around in my own house?

PAM: There are rules, Miss Blakely. You know them as well as I do. I'm not the one trying to steal somebody's husband.

(TANYA *sits.*)

TANYA: I don't have to steal him. He'll come willingly.

PAM: And how long will he stay? Do you really think he'll give you the same number of years he gave me?

TANYA: The same, and more.

PAM: What are you? Twenty-four? Twenty-five?

TANYA: Old enough.

PAM: I'm forty-one. I've stood with him at the funerals of both his parents and had him at my side when each of our four children were born. I gave him the money to publish his first book of poetry and flew to Africa with him and stood at the grave of the only woman I think he ever truly loved. I've watched him suffer the indignities of being subordinate to people who didn't have one-tenth his talent or intellect. I've forgotten more about him than you'll ever learn.

TANYA: So?

PAM: I'm here to tell you you're in way over your head.

TANYA: Am I? All I ever had to do was be patient and the man was mine. He's been primed to leave you for years. He was just waiting for the right woman to come along.

PAM: And you think you're that woman?

TANYA: I *know* I am. And I'll have babies for him, too. And hold his hands and do everything for him you did, and more.

PAM: I'll bet you would if you had the chance.

TANYA: I will have the chance. Or else you wouldn't be here.

PAM: (*Rises.*) How far will you go for him, Tanya? Tell me that? How much of yourself will you give up? How much pain can you stand? I look at you and I wonder…

TANYA: You don't have to wonder about me. Anything you can do, I can do. Anything you know, I know, too. Alright?

PAM: See, that's not even what I'm talking about. I see a strong will, but I don't see character. Do you know what pressure is, honey?

TANYA: Go home.

PAM: Disappointment, perhaps? I mean, real disappointment—not just a canceled gold card or some other buppie shit. But real disappointment. What do you really know about Bernard besides that sliver of meat that hangs between his legs?

TANYA: Get out.

PAM: Do you know about the torment that burns inside their souls? Can you go into that white heat and cool it down? You'll have to do that a lot with Bernard, you know.

TANYA: Get out, I said.

PAM: I was frightened, coming here. I want you to know that. Terribly frightened.

Tanya: I don't give a damn. You need to be frightened.

Pam: Then, I saw you and it all came together. I know, now, I don't have to be afraid any longer. You'll send him back to me.

Tanya: All my life I've had to deal with stuck-up yella bitches like you. Y'all think you're God's gift, with your sense of tradition and your money, and your mixed heritage and all that other shit. I've watched you all get by on nothing more than your looks. What blondes are to brunettes you bitches are to us. Well, I got your man, honey. Little old black-as-night me and I'm gonna keep him. I don't care how much you know about him, or how many kids y'all got. I don't care if you win every penny in the divorce settlement. I'll still have *him*. And whatever he loses I'll build back up for him *double*. And that means twice as much money, twice as many kids, and twice as much *woman*.

(Pam *says nothing. She rises and goes to the door. She stops and turns.*)

Pam: It's not a new woman he's looking for, Tanya. Ask him about Habiba.

(Pam *turns and goes out.* Tanya *stands watching, puzzled by the comment. She picks up a pillow and throws it with all her might in the direction* Pam *has exited.*)

(*Lights.*)

End Scene Eighteen

Scene Nineteen

Lights up on Pam *and* Bernard. *At home.*

Bernard: So I'm signing over the bulk of our stock portfolio to you; all of our jointly held accounts and the money market accounts. If it's alright with you, I want to keep the savings account and the mutual bonds for myself.

Pam: Will we need lawyers?

Bernard: That's up to you.

Pam: And how do we explain this to the children?

Bernard: I don't know. Tell them the truth, I guess.

Pam: And just what is the truth, Bernard?

Bernard: I don't love you anymore.

Pam: Did you ever love me?

BERNARD: Yes.

PAM: Why did you stop?

BERNARD: I was lost. I had to find my way.

PAM: And Tanya's the way?

BERNARD: You had no right to go see her, Pam.

PAM: Don't tell me about what's right, Bernard.

BERNARD: I'm the one causing you pain, not her.

PAM: Don't you stand there and defend that bitch to me. Don't you dare!

BERNARD: We never should have been married. We're too different.

PAM: We're exactly what the other wanted.

BERNARD: I was wrong.

PAM: I was right.

BERNARD: Pamela—

PAM: Maybe I should let you go. Maybe I'm just holding on out of false pride, or ego, or maybe I'm just in some weird state of shock.

BERNARD: I'm sorry.

PAM: I just don't understand how you could have done it.

BERNARD: Look, let's just stop it here. I don't want to go any further into this.

PAM: Well, I do.

BERNARD: Pam—

PAM: No! Seventeen years of my life went into this marriage. And of every day of those seventeen years I proceeded on the assumption that I had your love and that I could trust you. My faith was tied up in our loving each other; in the idea that ours was a commitment to each other, to our children, to our very future. Everything you've done, everything you've said to me over these years is called into question now because you've lied, Bernard. It's all been lies. You're sorry? That's not good enough.

BERNARD: What else can I say?

PAM: I don't know.

BERNARD: Look, I didn't deliberately plot to marry you, deceive you for seventeen years, and then suddenly run off at the age of forty-one with another woman. I didn't sit down one day and plot that scenario out.

PAM: No. You didn't plot anything. You've just allowed things to happen. I can see that.

BERNARD: So, you hate me.

PAM: I pity you.

BERNARD: Look, Pam, this isn't getting us anywhere. I don't want to argue.

PAM: I do.

BERNARD: Pam—

PAM: No, I want to know the truth. For once in your life, look me in the face and tell me everything. No lies, no metaphors, no little jokes, no pleasantries, no Mr. Nice Guy Bernard—just the *truth*!

BERNARD: Alright. I'm a coward. You're right. I couldn't tell you about my feelings because I didn't see how I had the right. A man is responsible to his family. A man is supposed to protect his own; provide for them. His family is his life. His family is the chain that binds him to his past and to his future. That's what I was taught. That's the way I was raised. You don't just walk up to your wife one day without provocation and announce that you're seeing someone else and you've fallen in love with that person, and you're going to leave to be with that other person. On what grounds?

You were never hateful, you were not unfaithful. There is not a single concrete reason I had in my mind for leaving you, no matter how I felt about Tanya. I have a seventeen-year investment in love, sacrifice, and blood here in this family. You don't turn your back on that. So, even after our oldest was born and I knew that I didn't love you as much as I should have, I figured that, in time, I would love you as much as I needed to. So, I waited and I tried and three more kids came. And my career started to take off—and suddenly I had money, status, position, a beautiful wife, four lovely kids, a great house, two cars, the picket fence, the whole works! And there was nothing left of me! Pamela, I didn't get fired from the station. I resigned. I no longer had my own life. I was living your life and the kids' life, and the life that our families expected me to live. I had to find a way out. I couldn't take it anymore. I didn't have the guts to come right out and say it so I created a set of circumstances in which the destruction of all this was inevitable. That's why I never really tried to find another job; that's why I never lifted a finger to do anything that would get that yoke back around my neck. I destroyed everything and out of those ashes, maybe I can start over again. I'm going to rebuild my life, the way I intended to in the beginning. And maybe this time I won't be such a coward. Maybe this time I'll be able to look the world right in the eye for a change.

PAM: (*After a beat.*) How I hate you. When I think of all that I was prepared to go through to keep you...

BERNARD: Don't try to make me out to be the villain in all this, Pam. You did a lot of playacting yourself. You're not entirely blameless in this.

PAM: No, I'm not. In my case, it's an error of judgment. And that poor little Tanya, she just let her behind overrule her mind, but you—you knew every step of the way, exactly what was happening and exactly what you were doing. I guess that's why, when I saw her, I realized that you didn't love Tanya, either. No matter what you say, Bernard. You don't love her.

BERNARD: How do you know what I feel?

PAM: Didn't you just hear what I said? I saw her. Think about it. How do you think she'll feel when she finds out?

BERNARD: (*Tense.*) Finds out what?

PAM: She's the spitting image of Habiba.

(BERNARD *says nothing.*)

She'll hate you for trying to turn her into something she's not. And you can't make up for Habiba no matter how hard you try.

BERNARD: I'm not trying to make up for anything.

PAM: Will you have children?

BERNARD: I don't know if I want children.

PAM: I'll bet she does. That fool girl has no idea what she's getting herself into.

BERNARD: I don't need to hear this.

PAM: Men never do. Men love their illusions. It's women who have to deal with the truth, because we have to live with the consequences of male folly. We're the ones who have to clean up the messes you make. We wipe your asses when you're babies and cover your asses when you're grown.

BERNARD: That's enough!

PAM: Yes. Finally, it is, isn't it?

BERNARD: I'm going upstairs...talk to the kids...

PAM: They love you very much. Don't cut yourself out of their lives.

BERNARD: I won't.

PAM: You can come see them whenever you want. I won't stand in your way.

BERNARD: Goodbye, Pam.

PAM: Bernard?…

(*He turns.*)

Be happy…Be happy…

(*Lights.*)

END SCENE NINETEEN

Scene Twenty

Two months later. TANYA'*s apartment.* BERNARD *is hard at work, going over papers scattered around him. He consults a few notes, then makes an entry on a laptop computer.*

TANYA *enters from outside, carrying a briefcase and elegantly dressed in a business suit.* BERNARD *gives no notice of her presence. She watches him in silence before continuing into the room.*

TANYA: Hi.

BERNARD: (*Looking up.*) Oh. Hey, baby. Didn't hear you come in.

TANYA: Tired.

BERNARD: Long day, huh?

TANYA: Something like that.

(BERNARD *grunts a reply and goes deeper into his work.* TANYA *kicks off her shoes, tosses off her coat, and lays her briefcase aside.*)

I hope that's a resume you're typing.

BERNARD: You just got home and you want to start, already?

TANYA: I'm really tired of this: you haven't worked in two months, Bernard.

BERNARD: I've got money saved. I need time to work my plans out.

TANYA: Rent and expenses are going up.

BERNARD: I've *got* money.

(BERNARD *continues writing.* TANYA *stares at him.*)

TANYA: I know your divorce is putting a lot of pressure on you—the separation from your kids and all—but you and I are supposed to be building a life together and—

BERNARD: Here. Read this.

(*He motions her over to the computer and she studies the screen.*)

It's a proposal. I'm flying down to New Orleans to present it at the African-American Commerce Convention.

TANYA: The Diaspora Group?

BERNARD: That's what I'm going to call the consortium that I'll put together to challenge for control of Griggs Broadcasting.

TANYA: Oh...

(*Moving away.*)

I would have thought you'd given up on that by now.

BERNARD: It's worth fighting for, Tanya.

TANYA: So is our relationship.

BERNARD: What's that supposed to mean?

TANYA: You're spending money you don't have to go down to New Orleans to present a proposal for a business arrangement that's hopeless, at best.

BERNARD: It's not hopeless. Griggs hasn't signed, yet.

TANYA: It's just a matter of time.

BERNARD: Then I'll make the most of whatever time I have.

TANYA: Fine. Do whatever you want.

(*She sits away from him, staring off.* BERNARD *goes back to his work, then looks up. He watches her in silence for a moment, rises, and goes to a closet. He removes a package from the closet.*)

BERNARD: I bought this for you.

(*He brings the package to her.*)

TANYA: What is it?

BERNARD: Open it.

(*She opens the package. It is several yards of kente cloth. An African fabric.* TANYA *tenses.*)

TANYA: (*Half-hearted.*) It's beautiful, Bernard...so expensive...

BERNARD: Don't worry about it, baby. Just enjoy it. Hold still.

(*He starts to wrap it around her waist. She tries to back away.*)

Wait...

(*He finishes.* TANYA *is quite agitated, but says nothing.*)

There. You look beautiful.

TANYA: Your wife told me you had a friend who died in Africa. You went to her funeral.

BERNARD: Yes, that's true.

TANYA: Can I take it off, now?

BERNARD: No. Wear it awhile.

TANYA: (*Emphatic.*) I want if off. Now!

(TANYA *undoes the dress and moves away from him.*)

BERNARD: Now, what's wrong?

(TANYA *picks up the kente cloth and holds it out to him.*)

TANYA: You think I don't know what this represents...and who?

BERNARD: It's just a dress.

TANYA: A funeral in Africa...the Diaspora Group...Kente cloth...I will not be the surrogate for a dead woman, Bernard!

BERNARD: Is that what you think?

TANYA: What else am I supposed to think?!

BERNARD: I admit I wish you could be like her, but I have never wanted you to be her.

TANYA: I have given you everything. I have torn out my guts for you. I have withstood all of your hang-ups, your temper tantrums, the changes you went through with your wife—and now you do me like this!

BERNARD: Tanya, calm down...

TANYA: No!

BERNARD: Calm down, I said.

TANYA: I have memories, too, Bernard! But your halcyon days were not mine! I carry the memories of a seven-year-old girl in Newark standing in food lines because rioters burned down the only supermarket our people had. I had to crawl around the floor on my stomach because the state troopers were shooting through the windows of our apartment, thinking we were snipers. A cousin of mine was killed on the street. *Friends* of mine were killed. And all during that time, I didn't see one dashiki. Not one headwrap. Not one militant brother and sister in the streets, prepared to lead us, or risk anything for us. After all their spouting ideology, all their rantings and ravings about "whitey" and smashing the "power structure," when crunch time came, it was the brothers in the do-rags and the sisters in the miniskirts and clog shoes who did the dying while all the revolutionaries were safely hidden away.

And so that seven-year-old girl made up her mind, and went to school and got her degree. And she presses her hair and goes to work every day and keeps her mouth shut…because *that's* how you get ahead…and *that's* how you stay alive in this white man's country.

(*Looks at the kente cloth again.*)

Why is she so important? She's dead! She can't love you. She can't hold you. She can't comfort you. There's nothing she can do for you. A dead woman with dead ideas! She failed you, Bernard. All those days were a failure. Nothing was accomplished. *Nothing!*

BERNARD: Everything I ever started out to be in my life is tied up in Habiba's memory, Tanya. I won't give her up.

TANYA: You talk as though you think you owe her something. What? What do you owe her? Everything you've done with your life, you've done on your own. The same with me. This is OUR life, Bernard. We're free to live it the way we want to. We've worked hard—

BERNARD: We all have to give back. Sooner or later. No matter how far, or how fast we climb. It's always been that way. We're the lucky ones. Dr. Du Bois called us The Talented Tenth; the ones who were expected to build the ladder for our people to climb. The old folks used to talk about Race Men and Race Women. It didn't matter where you went to school, or how rich you became. You could even become President of the United States, or sit on the Supreme Court. The bottom line was always the same: helping the Race. Making our people's lives better. When my children look into my face I wonder what they see. I was supposed to have passed on a legacy to them. I'm not sure I did my job, Tanya. Malcolm and Dr. King died for something more than BMWs and la bon vie…And if you can't understand that…

TANYA: Oh, like Pam understood? Let you use me up for the next seventeen years till one day you run into some young broad who looks like your friendly ghost and you decide to leave me for her?

BERNARD: You haven't heard a word I've said.

TANYA: I will not have my life sucked up by a ghost. Either you see me for who I am or leave me the hell alone!

BERNARD: I know the difference between fantasy and reality, Tanya. I see you…maybe too well…

TANYA: And I see you, too: a middle-aged man, filling his head up with a whole lot of stupid dreams and ideas, trying to relive his youth!

BERNARD: If those words were meant to hurt me, you've succeeded.

TANYA: I don't know what I ever saw in you.

BERNARD: Then we're both the poorer for it, Tanya.

TANYA: Damn you! Goddamn you!

(*She pulls the engagement ring from her finger and hurls it at him, then turns and flees the room.*)

(*Lights shift.*)

END SCENE TWENTY

(*Segue to:*)

Scene Twenty-One

A few weeks later, GRIGGS *and* BERNARD *at Eagle Rock.*

BERNARD: Thanks for agreeing to see me.

GRIGGS: Talk to me. This is a nice view, but I've seen it before.

BERNARD: I hear you haven't closed with Pegasus.

GRIGGS: Just a matter of time.

BERNARD: Don't. Make the deal with me, instead.

GRIGGS: We've been through this.

BERNARD: Then, we'll go through it again.

GRIGGS: That won't be necessary.

BERNARD: It'll be as necessary as I want it to be, goddammit. If anybody's gonna run Griggs Broadcasting after you, it's gonna be me.

GRIGGS: I hear emotion, I hear rhetoric. I don't hear reality. You're wasting my time, Bernard.

(*Starts off.*)

BERNARD: I've got the Diaspora Group behind me, Sam. We're prepared to match the offer from Pegasus...and we'll go higher, if we have to.

(SAM *stops, turns.*)

GRIGGS: Why should I give up a bird in the hand for some idealistic Negroes in the bush?

BERNARD: Pegasus will erase every memory of you once they get their hands on your company, and you know it. And you didn't build that business for that to happen.

GRIGGS: And neither did I build my business to be run by an insufferable, idealistic, sentimental, hot-tempered pain in the ass.

BERNARD: Yes, but I'm *your* idealistic, sentimental, hot-tempered pain the ass, and that's why you'll make this deal with me. Because you know I'll remember every lesson you ever taught me and I'll do anything to keep our legacy alive…and when the time comes, I'll pass it on to the *next* idealistic, sentimental, hot-tempered pain in the ass. Now, you tell me: will Pegasus make you the same promise?

GRIGGS: God, how I want to believe you, Bernard…but you made a mess of your life—both professional and personal.

BERNARD: It's a price I had to pay. Somewhere along the line I forgot I was generation number six. But now I want to think all the pain and tears were worth it, if for no other reason than I finally found out what it was I always wanted: that sense of commitment to something beyond myself. It feels good to do that again…

There was a woman I loved very deeply. The same year she died the Movement died. All the values we believed in, all the youthful fire, all the innocence—just seemed to disappear. We all became willing to settle for just a little bit less; willing to compromise just to be able to have some peace and quiet.

And for twenty years we've been lost. I've been lost. Not anymore. Through her, I've made my peace. With my past, with my present. I know who I am, I know what I want and I know where I'm going…

GRIGGS: Maybe it's a trip we can make together.

(GRIGGS *comes to* BERNARD *and extends his hand. They shake. They have a deal.*)

(*Lights.*)

END SCENE TWENTY-ONE

Scene Twenty-Two

Lights up on BERNARD's *office at Griggs Broadcasting.* BERNARD *goes over some papers as* A YOUNG BLACK MAN, *about twenty-two years old, enters.*

BERNARD: Graduated top of your class in Howard's "B" school. Outstanding.

YOUNG MAN: You didn't come to the graduation party. I missed you.

BERNARD: Your mom and me... Well, it might have been awkward... You get my present?

YOUNG MAN: Yes.

(*Beat.*)

That doctor's pressing her to marry him.

BERNARD: No one pressures your mother into anything. Whatever decision she makes will be the right one.

YOUNG MAN: You should tell her that, Dad. I think she'd like to hear it from you.

BERNARD: Your mother and I talk... It's always good to hear her voice.

YOUNG MAN: You're like a legend in Howard's "B" school. I was proud.

BERNARD: I'm too young to be a legend. I'm putting you in the sales department, selling air time.

YOUNG MAN: Coolie work?! I'm your son. How'm I gonna make any money?

BERNARD: That's your goal in life?

YOUNG MAN: It better be.

BERNARD: It's a desire, not a goal.

YOUNG MAN: Sometimes, for black people, our desires and our goals have to be one and the same.

(BERNARD *looks at him.*)

Don't look at me like that. It's a new age, Dad. These days, people may be race conscious, but they're just not as race-oriented as they were in your day. Big difference. You know?

BERNARD: And how would you know, Peachfuzz? You just got here.

YOUNG MAN: I know I can relax a lot more in my life than you and Mom could in yours.

BERNARD: Now, you listen to me: you're the seventh generation since slavery. You're the smartest, fastest, most educated generation we've produced yet. But you're not free... and you can't relax. Your trouble will always come when you begin to think that you deserve a good time, when you begin to think that this world is your oyster. Your children can have the good time, not you. For you, there's only struggle. Understand?

(*Lights change.* BERNARD *steps back into the darkness. A spot begins shining on the* YOUNG MAN.)

YOUNG MAN: You scared me when you said that.

BERNARD: (*Receding into the darkness.*) I know.

YOUNG MAN: I've been scared ever since.

BERNARD: Well, don't be scared, youngblood. Just be ready.

BERNARD *disappears into the darkness, leaving the* YOUNG MAN *in the spot. Then the spot fades to:*

BLACKNESS

Autumn

Notes on *Autumn*

I began thinking about writing a play featuring black politicians almost as soon as I completed *The Talented Tenth*. By 1989, when *Tenth* was first being presented, there had been black mayors of large cities in America for close to twenty years. Ken Gibson had been elected the first black mayor of Newark, New Jersey, in 1970; Richard Hatcher of Gary, Indiana, a few years before that. And there were black mayors in Detroit, Cleveland, and Baltimore, and there had been black mayors in Los Angeles and Philadelphia as well. All of these mayors, with the exception of Tom Bradley in Los Angeles (where the black population does not have a voting majority), had succeeded in developing strong political organizations that could mobilize voters to return them to office one election cycle after another. The more effective their political organization, the greater were their chances of being reelected. My hometown of Newark, for instance, has only had four mayors from 1970 through 2014. Four black mayors across forty-four years of history. Two of them served as chief executive for thirty-five of those forty-four years. The loyalty and support provided by layers of ward chairmen represented a rise of black political power only dreamed of in previous generations. In cities where thousands of manufacturing jobs had disappeared, these municipal positions moved thousands of black people into the middle class, providing them jobs and livelihoods that had been previously closed to many of them. I leave it for others to debate the relative merits of patronage as a part of political life. There can be no denying that for hundreds of black politicians across the country, a major goal for black political empowerment in America had been achieved.

And yet…

The parade of black politicians driven from office, because of failure in their character, or by their own greed, blind ambition or cronyism, soon became dismaying. Was this what Fred Hampton died for? Was this the reward for Robert Williams's years of self-exile? What would Martin Luther King or Malcolm think, now? After all of the idealism, all of the pain and sacrifice, all of the marches and years-long struggle, "Black Power" seemed reduced to a gaggle of opportunists across the country, getting theirs in the name of the People. Hard-working, honest politicians not only saw their efforts overshadowed by the media coverage given to the failings of transgressors, but just as often found their work blunted or marginalized by the necessary compromises and horse trading that is a part of every political negotiation. Other times, black political momentum was lost and/or dissipated by fractious internecine battles initiated by various rivalries within the black community itself.

I began to wonder what had happened, what had changed in our communities and in the minds and hearts of so many black politicians. I supposed the Irish, the Italians, and the Latinos, for instance, would certainly have their own tales of disappointment to tell. Weren't *The Last Hurrah* and *All The Kings Men* such cautionary tales? Why should African-American politicians be any different?

After Barack Obama became President of the United States, I became more determined than ever to write a play about urban black politics—specifically, the struggle between an old guard of black politicians who came of age during the Civil Rights struggle, cutting their teeth during the height of the Black Power movement and then riding to political power at the beginning of the post–Civil Rights era. But that was all during the final years of the twentieth century. It is now the twenty-first century, and the first generation of black politicians who were born after Civil Rights and Black Power are beginning to emerge. They are better educated, more comfortable with all the new technologies, more worldly, more ecumenical in their relationships beyond the black community, sleeker, and faster than any generation of African Americans before them. And they want their day in the sun. But what price are they are willing to pay, and what price will the communities they represent will be forced to pay in order for these individuals to realize their ambitions?

In the twenty-first century, the strides toward freedom continue, but the character and quality of the individuals and the construction of the vehicles to get African Americans there remain in question.

Autumn had its world premiere at the Crossroads Theater in New Brunswick, New Jersey, on April 25, 2015. The play was directed by Seret Scott, and the cast included Jerome Preston Bates, Stephanie Berry, Michael Chenevert, Terria Joseph, Joseph Mancuso, Count Stovall, and Kim Weston-Moran. The set design was by Chris Cumberbatch, costumes by Ali Turns, lighting design by Ves Weaver, and sound design by Matt Bittner. The production stage manager was Zoya Kachadurian, and the property master was Sadae Hori. Amie S. Bajalieh was the associate producer; Ricardo Khan, co-founder and creative advisor; and Marshall Jones III, producing artistic director of the Crossroads Theater. The Crossroads Theater also acknowledged special assistance from Woodie King, Jr.

Autumn

Characters

FRANKLYN LONGLEY: *African American, male, about sixty years old.*
GOVERNOR: *White, female, between fifty and sixty-five years of age.*
ZACK DRAYTON: *African American, male, about sixty years of age.*
CALABRESE: *White, male, slightly younger than* FRANKLYN.
TRICIA JOHNSON: *African American, female, between thirty-five and forty years of age.*
MELISSA LONGLEY: *African American, female, a few years younger than* FRANKLYN.
RONALD DRAYTON: *African American, male, in his early to mid-forties.*

Scene One

Lights up in the Governor's Mansion in the State Capitol. FRANKLYN LONGLEY *meets with the* GOVERNOR.

FRANKLYN: Governor, you said you had something confidential?

GOVERNOR: It's no secret there's going to be a lot of upheaval in the Party next election.

FRANKLYN: Your term as Governor ends and you're running for the Senate. With you out of the State House everybody is nervous about where they'll be standing.

GOVERNOR: Except you're not nervous, are you?

FRANKLYN: Should I be?

GOVERNOR: I'm not going to run for the Senate, Frank.

FRANKLYN: What?

GOVERNOR: I've had enough. I want to retire from politics.

FRANKLYN: But you're the frontrunner.

(*The* GOVERNOR *smiles and shrugs.*)

GOVERNOR: So I'm out. Good for me, not so good for our party. We'll need a strong advocate in Washington, Frank. Our party, as well as our State.

FRANKLYN: Agreed.

GOVERNOR: Then you'd be interested?

FRANKLYN: Sitting in Congress? No.

GOVERNOR: Well, that sure as hell wasn't the answer I expected.

FRANKLYN: Governor, I run the biggest city in the state. I'm a two-time president of the National Council of Mayors. I've been wielding power for sixteen years. Why would I give that up to be a sixty-year-old *junior senator* in Washington?

GOVERNOR: Your party needs you, Frank.

FRANKLYN: I'm happy to serve my party, but not in Washington.

GOVERNOR: I'm hoping I can persuade you.

FRANKLYN: I'd go with Bill Horan. He's been in the House three terms, people like him and he's a mainstream kind of guy.

GOVERNOR: Congressman Horan?

FRANKLYN: Bill's been waiting a long time to move up. He'd leap at the chance.

GOVERNOR: I'll keep that in mind. Something else.

FRANKLYN: Yes, Governor.

GOVERNOR: I had an interesting dinner conversation with Harold MacMannis a few nights ago.

FRANKLYN: (*Eyes narrowing.*) You did?

GOVERNOR: He told me about a pitch you made to him and the other Big Four CEOs to redevelop your central business district. They are very excited about it.

FRANKLYN: I'm glad to hear that.

GOVERNOR: I was surprised you never approached me.

FRANKLYN: Well, I still have to get a few ducks lined up. I'm surprised MacMannis brought it up. I'd asked that it be kept quiet.

GOVERNOR: Well, you know how it is: a great meal, a lot of Chardonnay, and my natural charm. Nothing stays secret for long.

(*Not amused,* FRANKLYN *looks away.*)

Now that old Harold has let the cat out of the bag, why don't you fill me in?

(FRANKLYN *hesitates.*)

Don't worry, Frank. This is confidential, too.

FRANKLYN: It's simple, really: I re-zone the central business district so I can close down all those bargain stores, low-end retail outlets, and other marginal businesses there and move them up to Baxter Avenue in Hilltop.

GOVERNOR: Hilltop? It's the most depressed neighborhood in the city, and all the shootings and drugs there. Jesus, Frank.

FRANKLYN: The real problem is, there're no jobs. No life to the place; just an area where people exist. I can turn Baxter Avenue into a major shopping zone, and use the newly opened land downtown to lure new businesses—bigger, *better* businesses.

GOVERNOR: That could take years. Meanwhile, you've taken a ton of tax revenue off the table.

FRANKLYN: I'll cut down blight and increase job opportunities—give everybody up there something to feel good about. No revenues lost—just shifted from one end of the city to another.

GOVERNOR: You still have a nasty crime problem. All those gun deaths.

FRANKLYN: Give me more funding. I can hire more cops.

GOVERNOR: There's no money in our current budget, but maybe our state could get a larger piece of federal funding with a forceful advocate in the Senate.

FRANKLYN: Yes, I could get that money.

GOVERNOR: Good. You're coming around.

FRANKLYN: I could get that money more effectively if I was Governor.

GOVERNOR: Excuse me?

FRANKLYN: The right Governor can be stronger than a Senator.

GOVERNOR: More surprises from you....

FRANKLYN: I'm the best-known politician in the State—besides you, of course.

GOVERNOR: You step on toes, Frank. You hurt people; a part of the game, but you take too much pleasure in it.

FRANKLYN: Endorse me, and a lot of those toes get out of the way. I can win the Statehouse, Governor, and my coattails will be wide enough for us to keep the Assembly.

GOVERNOR: I owe a lot of people, Frank.

FRANKLYN: All of our big city mayors will back me, and some of the larger towns, too.

GOVERNOR: A lot of good people want the job.

FRANKLYN: My coalition was key to your getting a second term and keeping our party in the majority.

GOVERNOR: As I said, it's too early for me to put my hand on anyone's shoulder.

FRANKLYN: MacMannis and those other CEOs will back me, and that's a lot of cash.

GOVERNOR: You really think you can win?

FRANKLYN: I'm the best man for the job. Tell me to my face that I'm not.

GOVERNOR: You and I will speak again.

FRANKLYN: I look forward to it.

(*They shake hands.*)

Lights. End of Scene One.

Scene Two

Lights up on FRANKLYN *and* JEFFREY CALABRESE *studying a planning map spread out across a conference table. Upstage,* ZACK DRAYTON *stares, concerned, out of a window. There is a disturbance from the street below that threatens to distract.*

TRICIA JOHNSON: (*Offstage.*) Mr. Mayor! Mr. Mayor! Help me! Help me!

CALABRESE: You know, Mr. Mayor, I grew up in this city. I have a lot of fond memories here.

TRICIA JOHNSON: (*Offstage.*) I need a place to live! Help me, somebody! Somebody, help me!

FRANKLYN: Really? What part of town?

TRICIA JOHNSON: (*Offstage.*) I know you up there. I see you peekin' out the window! You got to help me!

(FRANKLYN *gestures to* ZACK, *who shrugs his shoulders and lifts his hands, palms up, in a gesture of seeming helplessness.* FRANKLYN *glares, then quickly turns back to listen further to* CALABRESE.)

CALABRESE: Laurel Gardens.

FRANKLYN: I'll be damned. I taught there in the '80s. Chancellor High School.

Calabrese: No kidding? You taught school?

Franklyn: Ten years. Civics.

Tricia Johnson: (*Offstage.*) I've got nothing. I've got nobody! Mr. Mayor, please help me! I ain't never hurt nobody! I'm doing the best I can out here!

Calabrese: (*Indicating* Tricia Johnson *outside.*) I saw that lady on the news. Looks like you've got a one-woman protest going on.

Franklyn: We're handling it.

(Franklyn *looks at* Zack, *who pulls his cell phone from his pocket and makes a frantic and angry call.*)

Tricia Johnson: (*Offstage.*) I need to live! It ain't right what's happening to me! It ain't right!

Franklyn: I have these kinds of flare-ups all the time. Comes with the territory. Sorry for the disturbance.

Calabrese: No. No problem at all.

Franklyn: Good. You were telling me that you went to Chancellor High.

Calabrese: A good forty years ago. I wonder, was Mr. Braverman still around when you were there?

Tricia Johnson: (*Offstage.*) I'm doing the best I can, and I—

(*Suddenly, she is silenced in mid-sentence.*)

Franklyn: George Braverman? Yes, he was. But I caught him just as he was nearing retirement. Really nice guy.

Calabrese: Ball-buster in the classroom, though.

Franklyn: Yea. Old George could be very demanding. I remember your time. You were there in the last of the golden era.

Calabrese: Chancellor High was a quite a place back then. Ranked among the top five high schools in the country. And that included private and parochial as well as public.

Franklyn: Yea, growing up, I used hear a lot about that whole Laurel Gardens neighborhood. First time I ever went over there was when I was on my high school's sports teams and we had to play against Chancellor. Houses with lawns and backyards. Not something you see every day in a city.

Calabrese: Quite true. Chancellor had honors classes in Mandarin and classic Greek lit. I got college credit for those courses.

FRANKLYN: I went to East District High. We didn't have courses like those.

CALABRESE: Don't feel so bad. Look where you wound up.

FRANKLYN: Believe me, I look all the time.

CALABRESE: Of course, things have changed since then.

FRANKLYN: Yea, those glory days are so far in the past, hardly anyone remembers them. The same could be said for this city. Only the old people talked about the glory years. What was worse, they were the only ones who seemed to care. For the young, living in this city meant only one thing: Waiting for the day when you could get the hell out.

CALABRESE: Well, a lot of suburban kids feel the same way about their towns.

FRANKLYN: They have a lot more choices than the kids here.

CALABRESE: You ask me, politics and idealism are a toxic combination. One always gets in the way of the other.

FRANKLYN: Run this city, you learn how to be nimble.

CALABRESE: A lot of people like the way you run this city.

FRANKLYN: I've gotten my fair share of praise. And attention. Yes.

CALABRESE: But you're not really as cynical as you pretend to be.

FRANKLYN: Tell you a story: This was when I was still at Chancellor. I was talking to my class and, in an effort to get them inspired about their lives and their future, gave them the old blah, blah, blah about how all doors could be open to them and how there was nothing in this world they couldn't accomplish. They could be businessmen, I said; they could even become Mayor one day. And you know what? Those kids looked at me like I was crazy.

CALABRESE: Sometimes, life can beat the hell out of you when you're young.

FRANKLYN: To hell with that. Nah, those kids didn't have their faces all scrunched up because they thought I was lying. They looked at me like that because they were asking themselves who in the world would want to be the Mayor of *this* city. All their young lives, the city was always broke. There were no resources for anything. There had always been a black mayor and still, as far as they could see, the poorest, most desperate people were black and, the way things were going, it was *always* going to be that way.

ZACK: Bit by bit, over the years, a city losing its will to live.

FRANKLYN: Exactly. And the more I thought about that, the more determined I became to do something about it. And that's when I decided to run for City Council. And look at me now. All my life, I've known I was destined to do great things. Every move I ever made was designed to point me in that direction. I'm always full in; I don't half step. That's why the people of my city like me. That's why they elected me. Nothing happens to me if I don't make things happen for me. Are we clear?

CALABRESE: I think so, Mayor Longley: And my office towers are just what you need to help you along the way.

ZACK: Those are the Mayor's office towers. You just want to build them.

CALABRESE: I stand corrected, Mr. Longley. But mine is still the company you need.

FRANKLYN: I have lower bids than yours.

CALABRESE: Perhaps. But you won't have the efficiency, you won't have the professionalism, and you certainly won't have those towers as quickly.

FRANKLYN: Well, there is nothing I can do. I am required by law to go with the lowest bid.

CALABRESE: You've traveled to other cities. You've seen my work.

ZACK: Your bid is too high.

CALABRESE: Right now, only you and I know that.

ZACK: The law is a pretty hard thing to ignore.

CALABRESE: I never ignore the law.

FRANKLYN: Neither do I.

CALABRESE: But I was born and raised here. I have deep roots in this city and I still love it. I'm prepared to do whatever it takes to demonstrate my concern to you.

FRANKLYN: I don't need a builder's concern. I just need him to complete the work he's contracted for. I can take care of my city.

CALABRESE: A few extra dollars in the city coffers could help you do that.

ZACK: Excuse me?

CALABRESE: It might help you build a small park; a playground, maybe; the kind of thing voters remember around election time.

ZACK: This conversation ends, right now.

CALABRESE: Wait, you have me all wrong.

FRANKLYN: No, he doesn't.

CALABRESE: Look, these are tough times out here. I have hardworking employees who have families. I'm in an industry that's trying to keep afloat and you're in a city that's trying to keep afloat. I'm only saying I think we can help each other out here.

FRANKLYN: The question is how. I need those buildings up by the next election cycle.

CALABRESE: I can do that. You and I both know those others can't.

FRANKLYN: And it would be ridiculous to accept a bid from vendors who couldn't give me what I need, wouldn't it?

CALABRESE: Well, I'm not a man to disparage respected competitors.

ZACK: So, where are we?

(FRANKLYN *discreetly steps aside to make a call on his cell phone.*)

CALABRESE: (*To* ZACK.) You mentioned an election?

ZACK: Two years from now.

CALABRESE: I'd like to make a campaign contribution.

ZACK: The Mayor couldn't accept it.

CALABRESE: I have a friend who—

ZACK: (*Interrupting.*) Conflict of interest.

CALABRESE: Of course.

FRANKLYN: We're not interested in anything that can be construed as a bribe.

CALABRESE: My company can make a donation to a nonprofit organization; a youth program, a senior citizens' group. That helps the city, doesn't it?

ZACK: How much help are we discussing?

(CALABRESE *writes a figure on a piece of paper and shows it to* ZACK.)

There is a man named Clarence Johnson, Jr. He is the director of a nonprofit called Future of the City. They give out scholarships to college; send kids to camp in the summer, and run sports programs all over town. He's been doing this for years. He's having a lot of trouble with funding.

CALABRESE: I'll look him up.

ZACK: I think that's a good idea.

(ZACK *looks to* FRANKLYN, *who pockets his cell phone and moves back over to* ZACK *and* CALABRESE.)

CALABRESE: I can have a check to Mr. Johnson within the next two weeks.

FRANKLYN: I appreciate businesses that demonstrate real concern for the youth of my city.

CALABRESE: I grew up in a pretty rough neighborhood myself. It's good to help someone who wants to help himself.

FRANKLYN: We'll have a final decision in about...*two weeks.*

CALABRESE: I'll get moving on the permits within a month after that.

FRANKLYN: That's very good to know.

ZACK: If that's it, we have a few more appointments.

CALABRESE: Of course.

FRANKLYN: Thank you, Mr. Calabrese.

CALABRESE: Jeffrey.

FRANKLYN: Jeff, call me, Franklyn.

CALABRESE: (*Extending his hand to* FRANKLYN.) Nice doing business with you, Franklyn.

FRANKLYN: Let's talk again, Jeff. Say, in two weeks?

CALABRESE: I'll be here.

(CALABRESE *shakes hands with* FRANKLYN *and exits.* FRANKLYN *immediately turns to* ZACK.)

FRANKLYN: I need to be on the phone with Clarence Johnson as soon as you can make it happen.

ZACK: Understood.

FRANKLYN: I know that little weasel: He'll have that check cashed and spent the minute it hits his hands. By the way, thanks for handling that "noise machine" outside my window.

ZACK: I've got her in an office downstairs. How do you want to handle it? I'm looking into bringing charges for trespassing.

FRANKLYN: Hell, no. Especially not now.

ZACK: Frank, she's been out there living in a tent on the City Hall steps, making us look like fools. We've got to do something.

FRANKLYN: Get her in here.

ZACK: What? In here?

FRANKLYN: Right now.

ZACK: (*Into his cell phone.*) Yea. Bring her up to the mayor's office.

(*To* FRANKLYN.)

She's on her way.

FRANKLYN: What do you think about Calabrese? Can we trust him?

ZACK: Time will tell.

FRANKLYN: If things work out, there might be a bigger bone we can throw his way.

ZACK: The downtown revamp?

FRANKLYN: Yea. You go over it?

ZACK: I did.

FRANKLYN: And?

ZACK: There will be serious pushback from the City Council.

FRANKLYN: Then you push back harder. I want those votes, Zack.

ZACK: Armando Coutinho might see this as a threat to business in his district. A lot of people from Hilltop shop there.

FRANKLYN: They shop downtown, too. He never complained then. No reason to say anything now. Who else?

ZACK: Efrain Rodriguez. You're giving something to Hilltop; he's going to want something for Garside.

FRANKLYN: That means he's getable. Next?

ZACK: Gary Sutton of Laurel Gardens.

FRANKLYN: Tell him I better have his vote in my hip pocket or it'll be *two* cold days in hell before Laurel Gardens sees another urban renewal *penny* coming out of my city treasury. And that goes for all of them.

ZACK: Maybe you can pull the City Council along, but we've got four big city corporations based downtown.

FRANKLYN: I've already talked to the Big Four. They like what I have in mind.

ZACK: You talked with them?

FRANKLYN: I've been in discussions for a couple of weeks, now.

ZACK: How come I didn't know about this?

FRANKLYN: I didn't want to waste time with you trying to talk me out of it.

ZACK: I'm your Chief of Staff, Frank.

(*Off* FRANKLYN's *stare.*)

I'm also your friend. We've trusted each other a long time.

FRANKLYN: The opportunity was there and I took it. That's all there is to it. By the way, the Governor knows, too.

ZACK: Then I definitely should have been included.

FRANKLYN: Like I said, I had a decision to make.

ZACK: Long as we've been together—

FRANKLYN: I wasn't trying to disrespect you.

ZACK: I see the Big Four every week, Frank. The Governor, too. I'm talking to them, doing the city's business, acting in the name of the Mayor—your name—and these people have inside information I don't have. I don't like looking like a fool.

FRANKLYN: Duly noted. Let's move on.

ZACK: No!

FRANKLYN: *No?!*

ZACK: This could kill your political career, and I go down with you.

FRANKLYN: Goddammit, Zack, I'm the Mayor of this city, not you! This is *my* book! Either get on my page, or get the hell out of my story!

(*Pause.*)

See? This is why—

(FRANKLYN *doesn't finish the sentence. He knows he has gone too far with his old friend. There is a silence, as the two men stand apart. Then:*)

ZACK: Frank, you ain't got to talk to me like that.

FRANKLYN: I'm sorry, man. I—

(FRANKLYN *falls silent again. The two men stand apart. After another beat,* FRANKLYN *moves over to* ZACK *and extends his hand. Slowly,* ZACK *takes it.* FRANKLYN *pulls* ZACK *to him and embraces him. After a brief hesitation,* ZACK *returns the embrace. Satisfied he has won* ZACK *back,* FRANKLYN *steps away from* ZACK, *who composes himself and immediately gets back to business.*)

ZACK: What about the people of Hilltop?

FRANKLYN: What about them?

ZACK: This gentrification we're doing—because that's what it is—is essentially telling them they're not good enough to be in your new downtown.

FRANKLYN: You and me both grew up in Hilltop. Those are our people. I owe my political career to them. I won't forget them. But we both know there're going to be some winners and losers here. This won't be the first time. But whatever happens, you and me, we're going to be on the winning side. You know you can count on that.

ZACK: Yes, I know, Frank. But I don't have too many more political campaigns left in me.

FRANKLYN: I know, Zack.

(*Softly.*)

I know.

ZACK: This is going to be my legacy, too. I want this to be something that leaves a good taste in people's mouths at the end of the day.

FRANKLYN: I won't let you down, Zack. Count on that.

INTERCOM: Mr. Mayor?

FRANKLYN: Yes, Keisha?

INTERCOM: That lady is here.

FRANKLYN: Thank you. Send her in.

(ZACK *moves to the door, gestures, and* TRICIA JOHNSON *bursts in and goes straight to* FRANKLYN.)

TRICIA JOHNSON: Finally! I been callin' for you all mornin'!

ZACK: Miss, Security has asked you numerous times to leave those steps. This is city property.

TRICIA JOHNSON: Yea, well, you got Security says I got to go.

(*Pointing outside the window.*)

But now I got all these people lookin' on, and all those TV cameras down there that say I can stay!

ZACK: Miss, if you don't have shelter, there is a city agency inside—

TRICIA JOHNSON: (*Interrupting.*) I've been to the Housing Authority. They got me on a wait list. For months! Mr. Mayor, you supposed to be the man of the people. Our hero! Help me, Mr. Mayor! You said you would be there for people like me. Well, here I am, me and my kids. What you gonna do for us?

ZACK: (*Whispering.*) Frank, this is why I advised you against bringing her in here.

FRANKLYN: It's alright. Ms.—uhm—Ms.

Tricia Johnson: Tricia Johnson.

Franklyn: Well, Ms. Johnson—may I call you Tricia?

Tricia Johnson: Give me a place to live; you can call me "grateful."

Franklyn: That's fine, because I think we have a solution to your problem, Tricia.

Tricia Johnson: See, now, you trying to run a game on me. I just got in here good and suddenly, just like that, you done found a "solution."

Franklyn: Wait now. If that's the way it came off, then you have my sincerest apology. That was not my intention. But what do you think I've been doing all morning, all those hours you've been on these steps calling me out? I've been upstairs in my office, making calls, going over my records. I wanted to be sure that what I'm about to say is clear and backed up by actual fact. Okay?

Tricia Johnson: Okay.

Franklyn: We do have a place for you. A nice garden apartment, near good schools, and near enough to public transportation so you can get to just about any place in the city. There's also a brand-new supermarket that just opened up. You're eligible for several government and state aid programs, and we are looking into job training you could qualify for.

(*Handing her a card.*)

Call the number on this card. Tell the man who answers that I asked you to get in touch with him. He'll take care of all the arrangements after that.

Tricia Johnson: Ain't got no phone. The phone company cut me off.

Franklyn: No problem. We have phones inside. Now, I'm going to have some people help you and your children take that pup tent and those bedrolls from the City Hall steps. Is that alright?

Tricia Johnson: (*Near tears.*) You did all this for me?

Franklyn: You need help, Tricia. We all need help every once in a while. All of us.

Tricia Johnson: Thank you, Mr. Mayor. Thank you so much.

(Tricia Johnson *moves close to* Franklyn, *and he embraces her. Flashbulbs go off, and* Zack *stands aside, gauging the moment with a cool analytical eye.* Franklyn *lets Ms. Johnson go and she recedes into the darkness.* Zack *and* Franklyn *are alone.*)

Zack: You think that was wise, Frank?

FRANKLYN: I said we were going to give her an apartment. What's so wrong with that?

ZACK: Nothing, except there's not a housing project in the city that fits the description you just gave.

FRANKLYN: She's not going to the projects.

ZACK: You just said—

FRANKLYN: I know what I said.

ZACK: (*Suddenly realizing.*) Oh no, you're not talking about the Essex Heights complex?

FRANKLYN: Tell Freddy to expect that woman's call.

ZACK: Frank, that's brand-new housing. For teachers, bus drivers, sales clerks. Paycheck people—the ones we're trying to keep in the city.

FRANKLYN: It's a mixed-income complex, Zack. A woman like her can qualify.

ZACK: But we've got waiting lists thousands of people long for one of those apartments, and you just got yourself on the eleven o'clock news giving one away to a—

FRANKLYN: (*Interrupting.*) What, a poor, struggling single mother, trying to make it in this world? When they show this on the six o'clock news what people will see won't be another one of those sad day in the life of an inner-city mayor stories; instead they'll get another day in the life of a mayor who solves problems instead of crying like a little bitch. Call Freddy and make it so.

ZACK: But Essex Heights is full. Every last one of those apartments is accounted for.

FRANKLYN: Zack, you're my Chief of Staff. Find a way to make a way.

ZACK: Well, there're about one hundred names on the list—people who owe you favors.

FRANKLYN: And?

ZACK: Maybe I can find a name on there, the one who is the weakest and tell him if he falls on his sword for us this time, we will definitely take care of him the next time around.

FRANKLYN: See? Now, that's why you make the big bucks. Make the call, Zack.

INTERCOM: Mr. Mayor, the Governor is on the phone.

FRANKLYN: Thank you, Keisha.

ZACK: The Governor? What does she want?

FRANKLYN: Just sit back and watch me work, buddy-buddy.

Lights. End of Scene Two.

Scene Three

The Mayor's Mansion. Lights up on MELISSA LONGLEY *as she pours drinks for* FRANKLYN, ZACK, *and then herself.*

ZACK: Jack Del Grosso.

FRANKLYN: Not a factor. That thing with the real estate loan is already in the papers.

ZACK: Swanson.

FRANKLYN: Nah. He's downstate. Those downstate guys can't win up here.

ZACK: Joe Shannon.

FRANKLYN: (*Laughs.*) You kidding me? Joe's got about as much charisma as a rock.

ZACK: (*Raising a glass in toast.*) A toast: To our next Governor.

FRANKLYN: That hasn't been decided. There's a long road between here and the Governor's Mansion.

MELISSA: It's still hard for me to believe.

ZACK: Life is full of surprises. Wonderful surprises.

MELISSA: Franklyn, you and the Governor have been at each other's throats for years, and now this?

FRANKLYN: The Governor is looking for a successor. Nothing's been decided. I've got a great shot at getting the endorsement.

ZACK: Thank God for term limits.

MELISSA: (*To* FRANKLYN.) Last I heard, you weren't even sure if you wanted to stay in politics.

FRANKLYN: Well, that wasn't exactly what I said.

(MELISSA *looks at* FRANKLYN, *but he avoids her gaze.*)

ZACK: You're going to be at the top of the ticket in November, Frank. Everybody knows it. You're the best candidate in the state.

FRANKLYN: Let's not go overboard.

ZACK: I'm only telling the truth, Frank.

FRANKLYN: I'm sure there are others who—

MELISSA: (*Interrupting.*) Now, honey, don't do that. False modesty can be just as bad as shameless bragging.

FRANKLYN: I'm only being honest, Mel.

MELISSA: Refill, anyone?

(*Everyone holds their glasses aloft and* MELISSA *refills them. The smile on her face disappears when she approaches her husband. She quickly fills his glass and then moves away when he reaches out to her.*)

FRANKLYN: I just don't want to count my chickens before they hatch. This is an important step. I want to do things just right. I know how this game is played.

MELISSA: Maybe you're trying to fight a battle when the war has already been won.

FRANKLYN: Meaning?

MELISSA: You can't keep going through life with your fist balled up, Frank.

FRANKLYN: The minute I relax and start thinking I've got things figured out I'm going to get my teeth kicked in.

ZACK: Oldest political maxim there is.

FRANKLYN: Exactly. I know how this game is going to be played. This nomination process is about me. I'm the star of this show, and I'm not bragging, it's Big City vs. the Suburbs, Upstate against Downstate, and it's race.

ZACK: Race? Bite your tongue. This is the Age of Obama.

FRANKLYN: I am *not* Obama. I'm that "other" Negro. I have no illusions.

ZACK: We'll just have to work hard to make sure, that's all; a real get out the vote. Just like back in the day when we got Reggie Mitchell elected. Nobody thought it could be done and, suddenly, BAM! The city's first black mayor.

MELISSA: Yes, we worked very hard for Reggie.

FRANKLYN: Sometimes, I think he never should've been elected.

ZACK: People just didn't want to give him a chance. The level of expectation was so great. He carried the weight of every black person in the city on his back. And a whole bunch of white liberals, too.

Franklyn: Man, I'm through hearing that.

Ronald: So you're blaming him?

Franklyn: My whole career's been reminding people that I am not Reggie Mitchell.

Melissa: You've practically rubbed it in people's faces, particularly the press.

Franklyn: I don't apologize for that. It's part of my charm.

Melissa: It's the way you've ignored his memory, Frank. It's like you've just trampled him underfoot.

Franklyn: I got things done, Mel. That's why he's a forgotten man. People too busy looking at the good I'm doing in this city to remember all the shit he didn't do. We—all of us—busted our asses to get him into office so he could make changes. And as soon as he got in there good, all he wanted to do was "increment" his way through his term in office: a little change here, a minor adjustment there; get what you could, when you could, but never think big, never go all out.

Zack: Oh man, come on, now.

Franklyn: "Don't get the black folks upset. They got the votes." "Don't get the white folks upset. They got the money." "Don't get the Latinos upset. They got the numbers." All I'm saying is, if you want to be a leader, then lead. With Reggie, if you had an argument among people who wanted a choice between sunup and sundown, he'd waste half the day trying to convince everybody to settle for twilight.

Zack: I'm proud of him. I know what he means to the history of this city, and to our people. So I'll stand by him.

Franklyn: You're an enabler.

Melissa: Frank, you, of all people, ought to be able to appreciate what it means to sit in that office and have to deal with all the things anyone in that position has to deal with.

Franklyn: It's not that I'm ungrateful. I know how fortunate I am. I'm restless, I guess.

Melissa: And impatient and judgmental.

Franklyn: Yea, that too.

Zack: The buppie curse.

Franklyn: I expected more.

MELISSA: And I say, considering how much further along we are than our parents ever dreamed possible in their time, we shouldn't complain so much.

FRANKLYN: I'll complain all I want. Everyone from my parents to the pastor in church to my teachers in school taught me to have these expectations, so excuse the hell out of me if I bitch, kvetch, complain, and shout from the rooftops to my heart's content about how pissed off I am that I've had to wait nearly fifteen years to get the statewide recognition that so easily goes to every curly headed wonder boy who crawls up out of some suburban backwater and makes public noises as if he had sophistication and wit.

RONALD: Damn, don't hold back, Frank. Let us know how you really feel. But you better keep that attitude behind closed doors.

MELISSA: No need to worry about that. My husband is very good at keeping doors locked.

FRANKLYN: What?

MELISSA: You're starting to worry people, honey.

ZACK: Well, I sure hope you plan to keep that caustic streak under control on the campaign trail. An angry black man is only acceptable when he's playing linebacker for your favorite team.

FRANKLYN: I've decided that one of the upsides of being past sixty is the right to no longer bite my tongue.

ZACK: Yea, but just be careful not to bite off more than you can chew while you're at it.

FRANKLYN: Y'all think I'm a fool. Y'all think I'm just one more knucklehead off the block who got lucky.

ZACK: Oh, Lord, there's that bourbon talking.

FRANKLYN: Hell no, it's not bourbon! The country is on the brink! High is low, right is wrong, the climate is a mess, and things people take for granted no longer hold true. Some people are happy as hell about that and some people are scared to death. And I'm smack in the middle of it. Because I *know*. I know I got what it takes. I *know*.

(*Pause. Everyone sips in silence.*)

Yea, that's right. Y'all think about that.

(MELISSA *looks at* FRANKLYN *a moment. then:*)

MELISSA: What kind of Governor will you be?

FRANKLYN: What?

MELISSA: You heard me.

FRANKLYN: Melissa, come on—

MELISSA: No. I'm serious. What kind of Governor will you be?

FRANKLYN: A *good* Governor.

MELISSA: I said I was serious.

FRANKLYN: I plan to be as effective a Governor as I've been this city's Mayor.

MELISSA: And what does that mean?

FRANKLYN: It means effective leadership. It means appointing the right people to each key position. It means making improvements. It means doing the job I was elected to do.

MELISSA: But what does it all *mean*?

(FRANKLYN *looks at her.*)

For you, for the state, for the people; how will it change their lives? Make their lives better?

FRANKLYN: I think I just told you that, honey.

MELISSA: You haven't told me anything, Frank. You haven't told me where you want to take this state.

ELLA: Come on, Mel. I think Frank has answered the question.

MELISSA: Has he, Zack? Really? If Franklyn is going to run for this office, he needs to think—you both need to think—about a real vision for where you want this state to be after four years, and how you plan to lead us there. It bothers me that I haven't heard it.

FRANKLYN: Mel, this is the twenty-first century. People don't want visions anymore. No, I take that back: it's not that they don't want their leaders to have vision; it's they want their leaders to have ideas that can work; that make sense. And that takes practical thinking, and both feet on the ground.

MELISSA: Frank, you want to make history. It doesn't matter if that's the most important thing about this campaign or not. It's an inescapable fact. And people are going to have expectations, high ones. You can't meet those expectations being a manager. And you won't meet them for sure if you're simply a politician. Just like Reggie was.

FRANKLYN: See? I was right. Y'all don't understand me, at all.

MELISSA: I understand you, perfectly.

(*Pause.*)

ZACK: Hey, y'all, I think I'm gonna call it a night. We've got a long day tomorrow.

FRANKLYN: Yea, man. Fine.

MELISSA: Thanks for stopping by, Zack. It's always good to see you.

ZACK: You too, Mel.

FRANKLYN: Tomorrow morning, man.

ZACK: See ya.

(ZACK *embraces* MELISSA, *waves to* FRANK, *and exits.* MELISSA *steels herself against* FRANKLYN's *angry glare. They begin to clean up in silence. She pointedly ignores him as she moves about the room. Finally:*)

FRANKLYN: What the hell did you think you were doing?

MELISSA: Don't start with me.

FRANKLYN: I asked you a question.

MELISSA: No. I'll ask you a question: Why was tonight the first time I'm hearing that you plan to run for Governor?

FRANKLYN: Well, I—

MELISSA: (*Interrupting.*) A week ago you weren't even sure if you wanted to stay in politics.

FRANKLYN: You knew I planned to go after the nomination.

MELISSA: We agreed you'd think about it.

FRANKLYN: And I made my decision.

MELISSA: As usual, without telling me.

FRANKLYN: Things are happening fast, Melissa.

MELISSA: You're not hearing me—another "as usual."

FRANKLYN: You're going to stand there pissed off because I want to give you a chance to be the First Lady of the State?

MELISSA: You may think it's a gift. I don't!

FRANKLYN: Your behavior doesn't make any sense.

MELISSA: You're the one not making sense if you think these white people are going to let you be Governor—

FRANKLYN: No one's going to "let" me be anything. The Governor will choose me to succeed him because I earned that distinction.

MELISSA: And every reporter in the state will be digging through your record, looking, peeking, probing, and peering, and they won't stop until they lay everything and anything they find right out there for the public to see. It's been going on for twenty years. Haven't you had enough? I have.

FRANKLYN: Let them dig. I've got nothing to hide.

MELISSA: Franklyn—

FRANKLYN: (*Interrupting.*) I've got nothing to hide.

MELISSA: That's not the point.

FRANKLYN: It's all that matters.

MELISSA: Frank, please—

FRANKLYN: Now you listen to me: I need to know you are going to see this through. I need you with me on this, Melissa. Just like you've always been.

MELISSA: I don't need a pep talk, Franklyn. I know what my role is. Do you really understand yours?

FRANKLYN: Enough. I can handle the drama out there. But I can't have drama in my own household. I won't. Hear me? I won't.

MELISSA: I'll go through this campaign with you. I'll be at your side for everything. I promise.

FRANKLYN: That's all I ask.

MELISSA: But after election night—win or lose—I'm leaving you.

Lights. End of Scene Three.

Scene Four

Lights up on TRICIA JOHNSON.

TRICIA JOHNSON: Maleek! Maleek! Come here! No! Come here, now!...I'll talk to your narrow ass anyway I damn well please, long as you livin' in my house!...Why am I trippin'?

(*Holds out a fist full of cash.*)

This is why! Where'd you get this money? Whose is it?...Yea, I looked through your stuff....I'm your mother, that's why. I'll look through your musty drawers if I got a mind to. Where'd this money come from?...Whatchu mean, this is *your* money?...Stop lyin' to me! You

ain't never had this much money before. I know the street game. You
don't get this much money bein' no lookout....A promotion? King
Supreme said all you had to do is stand in a doorway and keep
watch....Right. So he like you 'cause you smart and dependable. Where
have I heard *that* before?...So you could go to jail, that's what. Or
worse!...You're my big boy, Maleek; my first born....*You* are *not* a man.
You're only fifteen years old....*I* depend on you. Your brothers and
sisters do, too....Yes, I know you're trying to do right by your family,
Maleek, but—...*You ain't got nothin' under control!*...If the Housing
Authority finds out you sellin' on the street, they gon' evict alla us.
What then? What am I gonna do? Your daddy's already locked up....I
been in the hospital three times in the past year and my mama already
got your aunt's kids, she ain't got no room for y'all, an' here you doin'
mess like *this*?! I swear, I'm at my breakin' point, boy!...I don't care
what he promised. You can't count on that King Supreme....He's a
liar....I *know*, that's how I know. He's one of them Boltons....All of
them Boltons is liars. The whole damn family. Me and that boy's
mama been knowin' each other since kindergarten; she the biggest
bitch of them all, and she raised her kids to be just like her. Lowlifes
and gangsters, that's all any of them Boltons ever been, and now they
tryin' to pull you down with them....Don't interfere? You my son.
You—...I *know* I ain't paid the rent in five months. But I got the Mayor
to get us a new place, didn't I? You ain't gotta—...Dammit, forget who
I owe what. Ain't none of your damned business, no way. And—say
what? *You're* tired of bein' poor? Who the hell do you think you're
talkin' to?! Boy, I'll slap the black off you and paint you another
color!...

(*Softer.*)

I know, Maleek. I know you tryin' to help me. I know you tryin' to do the
right thing....I don't know when I'm going to get another job.... Don't
tell me how long it's been. I know how long it's been....If you would just
get back in school....You just got to live with the headaches a little while
longer. The doctor said you probably need glasses. That's all them
headaches is....So be bored. It's school. You can't be nothin' without an
education!...I know....I'm just ventin'....Yes...yes, I hear you....King
Supreme got you now. He ain't gon' let you go....Ain't no way you can
get away from him, unless you get on a bus and leave town....

(*Resigned.*)

Yes…I know.…You gon' do what you gon' do, Maleek. I know it's your life now.…I got to let you be who you gon' be.…I just ask that you be careful. Just don't be stupid.…

(*Looks at the money in her hand.*)

…I'll use this to get those shoes LaRhonda needs.

Lights. End of Scene Four.

Scene Five

Lights up on the Mayor's Office.

Intercom: Mr. Mayor?

Franklyn: Yes, Keisha?

Intercom: Your two o'clock with Assemblyman Drayton, sir.

Franklyn: Thank you.

(*After a beat,* Ronald *enters through the main door.*)

Franklyn: Ronald, come on in.

Ronald: Hi, Frank.

Franklyn: Sit right down.

Ronald: Thank you.

Franklyn: Things going well in the Assembly?

Ronald: Need you ask?

Franklyn: No. Not really.

(*They both laugh. A pause. Then:*)

I should be asking about your dad.

Ronald: My dad around?

Franklyn: Just left. You know how he is. He doesn't want to appear like he's watching over your shoulder all the time. How's he doing? He won't tell me a thing.

Ronald: Dad's hanging in there. But it's only a matter of time.

Franklyn: The doctors are sure?

Ronald: Yes. We're going to lose him.

Franklyn: Your mother alright?

RONALD: Mom's handling it. Being strong for the rest of us. But—well, you know.

FRANKLYN: Listen, if there's anything you need from this office. Anything. You just let me know.

RONALD: Thanks, Frank. You've been a real friend to my family. I really appreciate it. We all do.

FRANKLYN: Think nothing of it. Black politics wouldn't even exist in this state without men like your dad. Reggie Mitchell and me, we both owe so much to your father. I'm standing on his shoulders, and I know it.

RONALD: Thank you, sir.

FRANKLYN: As much as I love your dad, though, this meeting is not about him. It's about you.

RONALD: If it's about working in your campaign, you know you don't have to ask me twice.

FRANKLYN: Well, in truth, I already know who I want to have on my staff. You're not one of them, son.

RONALD: (Clearly disappointed.) Mr. Mayor, I'd like you to reconsider. I can really help, sir. I can go into the wards and find the votes you need. I can—

FRANKLYN: (Interrupting.) Wait, whoa. Slow down. Hear me out, first.

RONALD: I'm sorry, I—

FRANKLYN: I have other plans for you.

RONALD: Other plans?

FRANKLYN: Ronald, I want you to run for Mayor.

RONALD: Sir?

FRANKLYN: Say yes. That's all I need from you.

RONALD: Mayor? Me? But what about the Assembly?

FRANKLYN: Please. The Assembly is where politicians with promise go to die. You want power, don't you?

RONALD: I want to do what's best.

FRANKLYN: Then you want power. Take the big seat in City Hall. That's how you get to do what's best.

RONALD: I'm not so sure it's that easy.

FRANKLYN: I'm sure, because I've been there. Your dad was sure. That's why he worked to put me here.

Ronald: With all due respect, Mr. Mayor, I think my dad was about a little more than that.

Franklyn: Well, I'm not trying to disrespect to your father, but I am telling you what's real out here: Political careers are not about what's right; they're about what's possible. And whatever you make possible, *that* becomes what's right.

Ronald: Why me? You've already got people who are far more deserving. You've got Charlie Williams in the Central District, Freddie Johnson over in the South, and Efrain Rodriguez in the North; especially Efrain. He goes back to the beginning with you and my dad. You're going to raise me up over all those guys? I don't know...

Franklyn: You let me worry about them.

Ronald: They're proud men, Frank.

Franklyn: If those guys had any talent, one of them would have been Mayor by now. Aside from that, not one of them has had an original thought in the last twenty years. Not only do I tell them what to think, I tell them when to think it. And I'm damned tired of it. On the other hand, there's you. What are you, forty-three? Forty-four? Just young enough to be old enough, and you don't carry all that baggage from the old days. You got all that experience in the Assembly, you've got the training your dad gave you, and just as important, you've got his Rolodex. No, kid, if anyone's going to sit in my City Hall, it's going to be you. I'll do for you what your dad did for me.

Ronald: But my Assembly seat.

Franklyn: Oh, Jesus! You're like a broken record with that Assembly shit. There's nothing in the statutes that prevents you from being both the Mayor and a State Assemblyman.

Ronald: Maybe, but a lot of us don't think it's ethical.

Franklyn: Fine. Think about who you want to replace you, and name him. Or her.

Ronald: You make it all seem so easy.

Franklyn: Ron, this is going to be my last campaign. Governor. That's it for me. With the right people in key offices around the state, I can make good things happen for years to come. My legacy. This is my way of giving back. *You're* my way of giving back. You were born and raised in this city, Ronald. I want you to be in position to be its greatest son. I know I can be a great Governor. I know it. But I'm going to need help to reach that greatness. Please. Help me. Help our city. Help our state.

Ronald: Wow. When you want something, you really turn on the juice, don't you?

Franklyn: Don't think of it as "juice." Kool-Aid. It's summertime. Just drink.

(Franklyn *extends his hand. After a beat,* Ronald *takes* Franklyn's *hand. The deal is sealed.*)

Lights. End of Scene Five.

Scene Six

Ronald *and* Zack.

Zack: You need to be absolutely sure it's something you want to do.

Ronald: I can tell you this: The Mayor's Mansion is a helluva lot better than living in that apartment in the state capitol.

Zack: Agreed.

Ronald: Here in the city, we'd be back home. The kids would love that.

Zack: So why is that knot in your brow?

Ronald: I'm fine.

Zack: You're not jumping up and down. And you should be.

Ronald: I don't like the way he talks about it being "his city."

Zack: How you make it your city, is the challenge.

Ronald: But I don't want this to be "my city" the way it's been "Frank's city." You know?

Zack: Well, that's up to you, isn't it?

Ronald: I owe Frank a lot, Zack. I don't know how much I want to be in opposition to him.

Zack: There are going to be times when you'll have to say no to him.

Ronald: I just have to be careful about it, that's all.

Zack: Then maybe you shouldn't have agreed to run.

Ronald: No, I want this. Franklyn's right. I can get way more visibility as a Mayor than I ever could in the Assembly.

Zack: Then go with this opportunity, Ron. Run with it.

Ronald: I didn't get it on my own. It's being handed to me.

Zack: So that's what's bugging you.

Ronald: I don't want to be a member of Frank's "crew" the way—

Zack: The way I am. It's alright. You can say it. I've said it to myself enough times over the years. Frank and I have our own history. It doesn't mean your history with him has to be the same.

Ronald: This conversation is going around and around.

Zack: You go out there half-stepping and mess this thing up, Franklyn will never trust you again, and neither will your old friends in the Assembly. You need to stop with this doubt and make a firm decision.

Ronald: I thought I already did.

Zack: Then stick by it.

Ronald: After all these years, he still treats you like you're his errand boy. He never gives you any respect, Dad.

Zack: Don't use my experience with him as a crutch. Whatever decision you make, you make on your own. I've got nothing to do with it.

Ronald: You may have loved campaigning for him, but I know you didn't love having to cover Frank's ass in City Hall. Everybody knows he's got dirt on him.

Zack: He's not the only one.

Ronald: You and he had a big argument back when I was a kid. I remember you slamming doors and cursing Frank out. There was a shady deal.

Zack: Frank and I have been in on a lot of deals.

Ronald: I don't know all the details.

Zack: Good. It wasn't any of your business.

Ronald: Going to take everything to the grave, is that it?

(*Zack says nothing.*)

Mom has admitted that whatever it was messed up things between you and Frank ever since. Is that much true?

(*Zack remains silent.*)

Franklyn is my godfather, and I didn't see him for seven years because of what happened. Is that why your own political career stalled? You had as much promise as him. Everybody says so. You might have gone to Congress. Instead, you're in the background. Why?

ZACK: Maybe it's all for the best. This cancer I got would've curtailed my political career, anyway.

RONALD: And maybe you're sick because of Frank. All the years you've spent shielding him and keeping his secrets and taking the heat for him. Who knows?

ZACK: Precisely. So forget it.

RONALD: I can't, Dad. It stays in the back of my mind whenever I see him. It was there when I shook his hand and said yes to running for Mayor. And it was there years ago, when Frank wrote that letter that helped me win my scholarship to Yale. When he asked me to represent him at the State Party Dinner, and my speech had all those big shots shaking my hand and talking to me about running for office, all I could think of was my dad, seated at a table so far back you needed a telescope to find him, and how at that great moment in my life, my father, the man who helped put Frank on the map, was forgotten and ignored. Franklyn Longley has done a lot of good things for a lot of people; a lot of good things for me. But he also played a role in bringing my father down. I can't forget that.

ZACK: What happened to me happened because I made the decision, not Frank. For good or ill, you're going to want the same kind of loyalty from the people around you, and the only way you're going to maintain it is by letting them know, when the time comes, you are not afraid to be ruthless.

RONALD: How ruthless is ruthless?

ZACK: That's up to you. Your conscience, your decision.

RONALD: Yes, sir.

RONALD: Back in those days nobody likes much to talk about, an African man and an African woman walked quietly down the gangplank of a slave ship in chains and stood in the hot sun and breathed a sigh of relief. Right behind them another African man and woman had to be dragged down that gangplank, kicking and screaming, and they stood in that same hot sun, plotting how they were going to break those chains. You'll know which ancestors you come from when you stand on a plank looking down at whatever chains life has decided to put around your wrists. Remember that.

Ronald: I will, Dad. I promise.

Lights. End of Scene Six.

Scene Seven

The Mayor's office. Franklyn *and* Ronald.

Franklyn: What are you doing in town? I thought your committee had a big vote coming up.

Ronald: The State Capitol's not that far, Mr. Mayor. I can get down there in time.

Franklyn: Seeing me is that important?

Ronald: Yes, sir. It is.

Franklyn: Should I be flattered, or worried?

Ronald: That's up to you, sir.

Franklyn: (*Looks at* Ronald.) What's on your mind, Ron?

Ronald: Clarence Johnson, Jr.

Franklyn: Clarence? What's he got to do with anything?

Ronald: He made a donation to my campaign.

Franklyn: Good for you. People think a lot of Clarence around here.

Ronald: I didn't solicit anything from him. I barely have an operation going.

Franklyn: You've got a famous name. Everybody looks up to your dad. If Clarence Thompson wants to help you out, I don't see how that's a bad thing.

Ronald: That was a pretty fat check he sent me.

Franklyn: So? That community nonprofit is not his only source of income. He has a restaurant that's doing real well. Maybe that's where the check came from, if that's what's worrying you.

Ronald: I don't like money that suddenly appears out of nowhere.

Franklyn: Then how the hell did you ever get elected?

Ronald: What's that supposed to mean?

Franklyn: Can you really stand there and say for sure that you've got a line on every dollar that comes to you through your campaign committee?

Ronald: Most of my money doesn't come from the likes of Clarence Thompson, Jr., I can promise you that.

Franklyn: You're getting a little too high and mighty, you know that?

Ronald: He's not as popular on the street as you think, Frank.

Franklyn: Then some people don't know what they're talking about.

Ronald: Frank, haven't you been paying any attention to some of the bad news that's been coming out about his group? The job training that never leads to anything, the instructors who can't keep their hands off the girls—and some of the boys?

Franklyn: That stuff's been looked into, and no evidence was found to—

Ronald: People have been bought off!

Franklyn: Oh, Jeez. Come on, Ron—

Ronald: Did you know Clarence picked up a sizable charitable contribution the other day from the Tri-State Construction Company?

Franklyn: Good for them.

Ronald: That's Jeffrey Calabrese, isn't it? He's one of the guys bidding to put up those office towers downtown?

Franklyn: So what?

Ronald: You're not concerned by how that looks?

Franklyn: How do you know about all of this, and what the hell are you doing looking into Clarence Thompson's private affairs?

Ronald: Intelligence gathering, Frank. Something I learned from you.

Franklyn: Well, I hope you also learned another lesson from me : A *little* intelligence can be a bad thing. If you don't have the whole picture you don't know the whole story.

Ronald: I don't like that he's so close to you, Frank.

Franklyn: I don't apologize for that, either. He worked with your dad, in case you didn't know.

Ronald: My father never trusted him.

Franklyn: Zack never had to. I was the one doing the heavy lifting. If there was any beef, I settled it. You got a problem with Clarence Johnson, you come to me; that's how it works.

Ronald: No, Frank. This is my campaign.

Franklyn: And this is my city.

RONALD: As you like to remind everyone.

FRANKLYN: I'm trying to say I know this kind of campaigning is new to you. It's not long distance, like running for the Assembly. Campaigning for City Hall is much more personal. Here, you get to look your opponent in the eye practically every day, and you damn sure better be prepared to hurt him, 'cause he's out to hurt you. That's my kind of world, Ron. And Clarence Johnson is a weapon at your disposal.

RONALD: If he has to be around, I want a wall ten feet thick between him and me.

FRANKLYN: Fine.

RONALD: I don't want to see him. Ever.

FRANKLYN: Sure. I understand.

RONALD: I want to be sure you do, Frank. I want a clean campaign. The people need to know I'm someone different.

FRANKLYN: Different from me, is that it?

RONALD: That's not what I mean.

FRANKLYN: "Clean campaign," you said. "Someone different." Seems pretty clear.

RONALD: You've drawn the wrong conclusion.

FRANKLYN: Enlighten me.

RONALD: You run things from the top down, Frank. You sit in your office and the people never see you. They only see the results of your decisions. Some good, some bad. I'm just saying.

FRANKLYN: Go on.

RONALD: I want to be a hands-on Mayor. The people will see me. I'll be out in the local precincts, visiting the churches, playgrounds, talking to the people, being where they can talk to me. What I was in the campaign, that's what I'll be in City Hall, if I win.

FRANKLYN: *When* you win. I can tell you this, though: You give the people that kind of access, you'll never get anything done. And stop idealizing "the people." "The people" don't care about a damn thing except taking care of themselves.

RONALD: I can't think like that and run for office.

FRANKLYN: You'd better. "The people"—yeah, that sounds great when you're a young "seeker after truth" out there leading a march, or making a speech promising to make their lives better. But "the people" are fickle and selfish, and will turn on you in a minute. Wait until the day comes when you decide to do the "right thing," the "moral thing," and it means "the people" have to step outside their own comfort zones or make a sacrifice. Hope you know how to teach a course in political science at the community college, because that's exactly what you'll be doing after the next election. "The people." Shit.

RONALD: And from your point of view I should be thinking about—

FRANKLYN: Doing what's necessary.

RONALD: I don't want to be Mayor for the sake of being Mayor.

FRANKLYN: But here you are, talking to me and listening. You're ambitious, you're intelligent, and you have talent. You're a young black man, and in this America that is still a liability.

RONALD: I don't believe that.

FRANKLYN: Really? Read the papers, kid.

RONALD: No, you read them! Our people are everywhere, Frank. Astronauts, CEOs of Fortune 500 companies; we even had ourselves a black President!

FRANKLYN: If that's what you're going to hang your hat on, then you're going to be disappointed every time. None of that black CEOs or Negroes in the White House means a goddamned thing, Ron.

RONALD: It does, because if enough of it keeps happening year after year—

FRANKLYN: (*Interrupting.*) Those are all *individual* achievements, Ronald. In the broad scheme of things their success doesn't mean shit because in this country no individual is stronger than the ethnic group from which he comes. That's why all this talk of "the people" is so meaningless. Collectively, our people have no money. And if you don't have money, you don't have power. And power talks in America.

RONALD: If this is the way you feel, I don't understand why you—

FRANKLYN: (*Interrupting.*) I'm a lonely shepherd leading a wayward flock across a wilderness we don't control. I've had to learn to make do with what I have. And what do I have? I have my body and my mind. You're a smart young man, Ron. You have to learn how to turn this black powerlessness into black power that works for you. You have to learn to be the brother who makes a way out of no way. That's what black politicians do: we shape, we manipulate, we cajole, we harangue, we pester, we scratch, and we claw until we create something out of nothing, like this dead city. Who knew it could be a platform into the governorship? Now it's your turn. You can either climb up on this platform, or you can stay down there on the ground looking up at whoever grabs the brass ring you pushed away. Either way, the choice is yours. And you'd better be damned sure you make the right one. There ain't no second act in black life.

Lights. End of Scene Seven.

Scene Eight

Lights up on TRICIA JOHNSON. *We hear the offstage voices of children. There appears to be disorder, a frenzied chaos somewhere in the darkness, including a baby's cries.*

TRICIA JOHNSON: Ebonie? Ebonie! Make sure the kids have dinner!...What? No. Your homework can wait. Do like I tell you!...You seen Maleek? He said he'd be in by now....Well, where is he?

(To herself.)

Hmph. As if I didn't know....Lord have mercy—Ebonie! Tell LaRhonda to keep out of Maleek's room. Alla y'all kids stay outa there, or you gonna get it from me. You hear? Stay out!...Ebonie, I got to take this phone call. Keep an eye on the children....When Maleek get in here, tell him not to go nowhere. I need to talk to him....I don't care. *Tell him!*

(She dials her cell phone.)

Cherice?...Yea, it's me....Girl, Maleek got himself a gun....No, I *saw* it....I knew it was gonna happen, sooner or later, but I just hoped—...I can tell him he shouldn't have one, but we both know he ain't gonna get rid of it....Whatchu mean your boy ain't got one? They both work for King Supreme. If Maleek got one, you can be damned sure your son got one, too....They *got* to have one. That's just how it is....Girl, everybody got a gun. I know I ain't got to tell you that. These people out here is crazy; got guns 'cause they sellin' drugs, got guns 'cause dealers scared of other drug dealers, got guns 'cause they scared of their husbands, others 'cause they scared of their kids. Everybody got a gun, Cherice....I told Maleek don't be bringing no guns in the house....Yes, you know one of the younger kids'll get their hands on it thinking it's a toy....Yes, it happens every day. Donchu read the papers?...These boys is grown before their time. They ain't listening to us. Your boy listen to you?...There. See?...I do what I can with him, but Maleek got his own mind now. He too big for a beatin'.....Last time I hit with a strap he just laughed at me. *Laughed*. Said, "Mama come on with that mess. I ain't no baby." He was eleven, and already as tall as me. And now he fifteen and got a gun.... I thought so too, till he pistol-whipped some crazy fool tried to grab Ebonie on the street.... Yes, he watches over all of us, and don't nobody mess with us neither. They know Maleek is always somewhere, nearby. You right. That is a helluva lot more than his damned daddy ever did.... Girl, I'm scared for Maleek, and yet I ain't scared at the same time. You know what I mean?... Yea, I know. But I can only fight so many battles, Cherice.... Maleek has made his choices. His life is what it is now. I still got Ebonie, LaRhonda, and Jamil, plus my sister's two and my cousin's two. I'm gonna do the best I can to get each of them to eighteen years old in one piece. How they turn out after that is up to them. That's all I can ask, that's all I can do.

Lights. End of Scene Eight.

Scene Nine

Lights up on FRANKLYN *and the* GOVERNOR.

FRANKLYN: We had a deal!

GOVERNOR: I made no commitment, Frank. I only said, we would talk. Listen, this is not an easy conversation to have.

FRANKLYN: But you're having it.

GOVERNOR: I just think it's time we moved in another direction.

FRANKLYN: There is no other "direction." I'm the strongest candidate out there. We both know that.

GOVERNOR: It's not the kind of strength this state needs. Not anymore.

FRANKLYN: That's rich as hell coming from the likes of you.

GOVERNOR: I'm just as old school as you. Sure, I'll admit it. And, maybe, under a different set of circumstances you'd have been Governor long before me. But the past is the past. And that's where the both of us belong.

FRANKLYN: You, maybe; but this is my turn.

GOVERNOR: You're out, Frank. I'm sorry.

FRANKLYN: I've done everything this party has asked of me. I've taken shit with a smile on my face for sixteen years, running a city you people tried your best to drain the life out of; waiting for this moment. And now, you have the nerve to stand there and tell me—

Governor: Oh, why the hell don't you get over yourself? You're not the only one in this room who's been kicked in the face by the old boy's club.

Franklyn: *You're not the kingmaker in this state anymore! This isn't over! I'll be damned if I let you mess over me!* (Franklyn *starts out.*)

Governor: Don't try anything stupid, Frank.

Franklyn: That nomination belongs to me, and I will have it!

Governor: What're you going to do? Go to the press? Hold rallies on the steps of City Hall? Get some of those pastors you keep in your hip pocket to preach sermons about how you are a victim of the State Capitol? The Great Black Voice unjustly stilled by the cruel hand of White Political Caprice? You really think that's going to get you into the Governor's Mansion?

Franklyn: I'm going to win this, and it will be all the sweeter because I'll do it in spite of you. So you go right ahead: Put your hand on Shannon's shoulder. Or Swanson. It doesn't matter. They don't scare me. I'm going to erase them, and I'm going to erase you.

Governor: Those are not the men I'm endorsing.

Franklyn: Then, who—?

Governor: I'm going with Ronald Drayton.

Franklyn: Drayton?! He's one of mine.

Governor: Not after I've given him the one thing you couldn't.

Franklyn: You just killed that kid's political future. My people won't throw me over for the likes of him.

Governor: Maybe that's what they'll think, at first. But eventually they're going to look at that squeaky-clean kid and then they'll take a second look at you. And maybe people will begin to think Drayton's not so bad after all; a handsome young black man, with a beautiful wife and pretty young kids. The media is going to love him. You should see the look on your face. You know I'm telling the truth.

Franklyn: That little punk doesn't scare me. I've forgotten more about politics than he'll ever learn.

Governor: And that's why you'll accept this deal, Frank: Because you're a smart politician. The times are changing. Look: Search your heart on this one. If you can't do that, then make some calls. See how much support remains once word gets out I've gone for Ronnie Drayton.

FRANKLYN: I'll see you in hell first. I'll see all of you in hell!

(FRANK *turns and walks out.*)

Lights. End of Scene Nine.

Scene Ten

Lights up on the Mayor's office. FRANKLYN *and* RONALD.

RONALD: I didn't stab you in the back. The Governor made me an offer. I accepted.

FRANKLYN: You don't have the apparatus or the connections I have. How do you expect to—

RONALD: I've got the Governor and his people; even the National Party Headquarters wants to get in on this.

FRANKLYN: For you.

RONALD: I guess they love my dirty drawers now.

FRANKLYN: Boy, you got your head so far up they ass you couldn't see straight if somebody lit a match and pointed the way out for you.

RONALD: You want to challenge the Governor's decision, you go right ahead. But I don't have to stand here and listen to your bullshit; not anymore.

FRANKLYN: You're not one of us. You're one of those high and mighty Ivy League Negroes who don't know shit. You've never had to run anything in your whole life. You've never had to be responsible, or make a decision that amounted to anything. People like me are the ones who had to do the heavy lifting; we're the ones who had to get shot, spit on, and pushed back. We parted the goddamned clouds so you kids could bask in the sun. And this is our payback: Watching you hitch your star to some of the very people we've been fighting all our lives.

RONALD: You got violins to go with that speech?

FRANKLYN: You little—

(FRANKLYN *starts at* RONALD, *who quickly steps back, his fists clenched, fire in his eyes. With one hand,* FRANKLYN *grabs one of the chairs near his desk, lifts and holds it at his side like a club. He fixes* RONALD *with his own glare.*)

Find something else to do with those hands or I swear you'll be dead before God gets the news.

Ronald: It figures: When all else fails, the thug comes out.

Franklyn: Please don't tell me you're just finding that out?

Ronald: I can't be like you, Frank.

Franklyn: Right. So you betrayed me.

Ronald: My dad told me that Melissa asked you if you knew what kind of governor you wanted to be. And either you couldn't, or wouldn't, answer her question. That stayed with me, Frank. If you couldn't answer the question, was there ever a time when you could? And if you wouldn't answer the question, then what kind of man have we been admiring all of these years? There has to be a better way.

Franklyn: And that way is you?

Ronald: It sure as hell ain't you.

Franklyn: We'll see what all that is going to come to, Ron. Everything you'll have won't belong to you. Your political apparatus, the staff that goes to work for you, your media people—they'll all come from the Governor. Oh, yes. Don't even think otherwise.

Ronald: And things would have been different if I had stayed with you? After all, as you reminded me more than once, this is your city.

Franklyn: Where you were born and raised. Where everybody knows your father. Where everybody knows the people who will vouch for you. I gave you a center of power.

Ronald: I need my own center of power, Frank, however imperfect.

Franklyn: That question Melissa asked: You think my reaction to it reveals some kind of lack of understanding, or conviction. But I've always understood how power really works, and that's the only thing that matters. I spent years in the struggle and I helped bring our people to political relevance in this state. That's something I am very proud of. Martin Luther King had the dream, but it's my generation that had the responsibility to make those dreams work for our people. That's what I did, and I stand by that.

Ronald: No, Frank. No. Something's been lost. There's a coarseness that has overtaken our community and it's choking the life out of us. And our leadership is floundering. What do we stand for? What's our vision? Something has to matter beyond clinging to power? You don't know what to do, anymore, except cling to power. You tell yourself you're doing it for the people, but it doesn't matter because somehow at the end of the day, you no longer remember precisely what the ideas were that originally drove you.

Franklyn: I want to see how your vision keeps members of your own party in line when they decide to test you. See how far your righteousness gets you when the Governor shows up to collect that pound of flesh you most definitely will owe.

Ronald: Talk to Efrain Rodriguez about being Mayor. Get him on your side. More black folks are moving out of the city every year. It's the Latinos turn now. Efrain is solid and he's earned a shot. Helping him to move up would be good for your legacy.

Franklyn: You're not going to change your mind about running for Governor.

Ronald: Not a chance. There's nothing you can do, Franklyn. No one you can talk to. Good-bye.

Lights. End of Scene Ten.

Scene Eleven

Lights come up on Zack Drayton, *an African-American senior citizen. He is not in the best of health, and rests quietly.* Franklyn *enters.* Zack *looks up.*

Zack: Well, I'll be damned.

Franklyn: How are you, Zack?

Zack: Still kickin'. Sit yourself down.

(Franklyn *sits.*)

Melissa alright?

Franklyn: She sends her love.

Zack: Thank her for me.

Franklyn: I miss you, my man.

Zack: You're here about Ron, eh?

Franklyn: He won't listen to me, Zack. I'm hoping you might talk some sense into him.

Zack: I don't talk sense to my son anymore, Frank. He's a grown man who makes his own sense.

FRANKLYN: How can you let him do this to me?

ZACK: Now, wait just a minute—

FRANKLYN: Ron is about to undo everything I've built—everything we've built. Can you see that? Everything we've stood for is put in jeopardy by that young man's rash actions. I know he's your son, Zack, but you've got to see that he's stepping out too far, too soon, and with the wrong people!

ZACK: There was a time when people were saying the same things about us.

FRANKLYN: They were wrong then, but I'm right now.

ZACK: Ronald senses something, Frank. It may even make him as uncomfortable as hell. But he knows this is something he's got to do.

FRANKLYN: What the hell could he *possibly* know? His whole political career he's been guided along—what to do, what to think, when to act, when to keep his mouth shut, who's ass to kiss, who's ass to kick. He's only known what we wanted him to know. And now suddenly we are supposed to sit back and accept that Ron can think for himself?!

ZACK: If that's the only way you've ever viewed my son, then you're the one with the mistaken ideas, Frank. Not my son.

FRANKLYN: I'll break him, Zack. I swear to God. I'll break him.

ZACK: You're not going to touch him.

FRANKLYN: You better think again! I'm fighting for my political life here.

ZACK: You're in the autumn of your life, Frank. And I'm nearing the end of mine. Things begin to get real clear if you let them.

FRANKLYN: I was with you in the hospital when that boy first came into the world. I'm his godfather.

ZACK: Then let him grow. Don't get in his way.

FRANKLYN: You're saying these things because he's your flesh and blood. I understand that. But that doesn't make any of it any truer, or right.

ZACK: Frank, I did not raise my boy to be like you, or me. Sure, I wallowed in the gutter, and even had your back on some pretty tough deals we dished out. But I knew what I was getting into, and I knew why. I did a lot of shit in my time, and maybe that's why my body is rotting from the inside now. But I want better for Ron.

FRANKLYN: Talk him out of this, Zack. This is a fight our people don't need right now.

ZACK: Oh, now suddenly this is about us being race men.

FRANKLYN: Everything we do is about the Race.

ZACK: Then accept this moment for what it is.

FRANKLYN: No! Help Ron?! I'll be through, and you know it! I'll be done in this state! I may as well go home and blow my goddamn brains out!

ZACK: Stop, Frank. Just stop. Take a step back. *Think* about what you're saying.

FRANKLYN: I'm not going to be a punk. And I'm not going to let the Governor, or Ron, or you, play me for a fool.

ZACK: No, you're doing a pretty good job of that on your own.

FRANKLYN: Fine. I came to you as a friend, more than that even. And you won't help me. I'm sorry about that. I truly am.

(FRANKLYN *starts to leave. Suddenly:*)

ZACK: You remember Quentin Gaffney?

(FRANKLYN *turns. He remembers Gaffney, but is incredulous* ZACK *would bring such irrelevancy into this conversation.*)

He just flashed into my mind. I don't know, that's been happening a lot lately. Bits and pieces of my life.

FRANKLYN: Yea, I remember him. Linebacker. Played for South District. Used to call him Frankenstein, 'cause his forehead was so big.

ZACK: Yea.

FRANKLYN: What's he got to do with anything?

ZACK: That night at Jean Phillips's party on Morton Street; you punched him out.

FRANKLYN: We were knuckleheads. All of us. We're lucky we all didn't wind up in jail.

ZACK: Gaffney got drunk and tried to feel Jean up. I got pissed and got in his face. I must have done a good job, 'cause he backed off. But then I turned my back to see if Jean was alright and his fist went straight up the side of my head. That big foot of his would have crashed down on my neck if you hadn't been there.

FRANKLYN: I wasn't gonna let him coldcock you.

ZACK: I remember how everyone congratulated you for standing up to Gaffney, 'cause no one ever did before.

FRANKLYN: That was forty-some years ago. We were kids.

Zack: When we were walking to the bus stop, looking over our shoulders every five steps to see if Gaffney and his boys might be coming after us, you said something to me that stuck in my mind: You said, "As long as we're out here fighting each other, we'll never get anywhere as a people."

Franklyn: I was trippin'. I had just finished reading *The Autobiography of Malcolm X.*

Zack: What you said then is just as true today, Frank.

Franklyn: Save the trip down memory lane, Zack. It's not going to stop me from doing what I have to do.

Zack: We used to live by those words. You and me built our whole political lives around those words.

Franklyn: We didn't always agree.

Zack: We fought like cats and dogs, sometimes.

Franklyn: I remember.

Zack: They were some wild times. I thought they'd never end.

Franklyn: We had to grow up, grow wiser.

Zack: And now we've grown apart.

Franklyn: That's what you think?

Zack: Yes.

Franklyn: I'm through asking, Zack. And I'll never beg. Even if I want to.

Zack: That's too bad.

Franklyn: You've always been the righteous one. That pisses me off to no end.

Zack: I loved being with you, Frank. It was a helluva ride.

(Franklyn *clasps* Zack's *hand. Neither says anything further. No words are needed. Their hands remained closed around each other as the lights fade.*)

Lights. End of Scene Eleven.

Scene Twelve

The Mayor's Office. Tricia Johnson *is at it again.*

Franklyn: Ms. Johnson, why are you in here bothering me again?

Tricia Johnson: You know why, dammit. I need a place to live.

Franklyn: We found an apartment for you.

Tricia Johnson: Me and my kids is back on the streets!

Franklyn: Your son is a known felon, engaged in illegal activity.

Tricia Johnson: I tried to make him stop!

Franklyn: I guess you didn't try hard enough.

Tricia Johnson: I need help. I pay taxes for?

Franklyn: You're on welfare; you don't pay taxes.

Tricia Johnson: Oh, now you think you better than me.

Franklyn: No, I'm not going to be gamed by you.

Tricia Johnson: It was people like me put your black ass in office, and we can take you out just as quick.

Franklyn: Ms. Johnson, I don't have the time—

Tricia Johnson: Oh, hell no! Don't you dare say that "I ain't got no time" shit to me! You better find a way to make some time. I'm a citizen in this city. I was born in this city, grew up on these streets, and been strugglin' from sunup to sundown to keep some food on my table. Telling me you ain't got no time. You're supposed to help me!

Franklyn: Help yourself! Get a goddamned job! Keep your kids in school! Most of all, keep your fucking legs closed!

Tricia Johnson: Who the hell you think you is, tellin' me how to live? Judging me, you hypocrite!

Franklyn: Now, you listen to me: I grew up on the same streets as you and went to the same schools as you. Life is about choices, Ms. Johnson, and every choice you've ever made has messed up not only your life, but also the lives of your children, and instead of taking any kind of responsibility for it, you want somebody else to cover for you. What? You think you're going to embarrass me into helping you like last time? All those pictures of you and your kids camped out on the steps of my City Hall, like this was Charles Dickens or some shit, getting all the white liberals in a froth about the insensitive black mayor unwilling to take care of his own people. You played that card pretty well. I had to take low for you that time, but not now. You better find someplace for your family to live, or you can pitch that pup tent back up. In fact, I hope that's exactly what you do. I been looking for a way to have your crazy ass declared unfit. Keep those babies in the streets, and see how fast I have every city agency I can muster, coming down on you like hellfire. Before the night is over, I'll have you under arrest and every one of those kids in foster care. Have I gotten through to you, Ms. Johnson? Are we finally on the same page?

Tricia Johnson: You just a cold bastard.

Franklyn: One more reason to be absolutely sure you understand me.

Tricia Johnson: No! You been out here for years, you and all your friends, grabbin', gettin', keepin', and reachin' to your heart's content. Waxin' fat off our sweat and sufferin', stayin' in office an' runnin' your mouths on TV. You act like we so dumb, we can't see what's goin' on.

Franklyn: So you decided to scam the city government to get even, is that it?

Tricia Johnson: Why shouldn't I pull a hustle to get something better for myself?

Hell, you doin' it! Why the little people gotta obey the rules, when you big shots be breakin' them every day? Imma get mine, just like you gettin' yours.

Franklyn: You don't know a damned thing about me, or what I do. Now, get out of here before I call Security.

Tricia Johnson: You can't grow, Mr. Mayor. You may get by, but you can't never grow, 'cause in the end you won't do right by your people. And that's your curse. That's what's gonna bring you down to your knees every time.

Lights. End of Scene Twelve.

Scene Thirteen

Lights up on Zack. *He holds a zip drive and a folder.*

Zack: There was this boy—let's call him Hannibal—who had a talent with computers. Loved the damned things. His family couldn't afford to buy him one, but he always found a way to get on a keyboard somewhere: A friends' home, or at school, or at the local library. He was obsessed. Barely a C student, that same boy with hardly any social skills and the handwriting of a six-year-old had somehow got to the point where he was taking computers apart and then putting them back together again. And somehow, I don't know how because I don't know a damned thing about computers, Hannibal learned to hack. And Frank found out. So he gave Hannibal a job and put him down in a windowless old storage room in the basement of City Hall and gave him a title, Special Assistant, Community Relations. And he was answerable only to Franklyn. It looked like just one more patronage job from a Mayor who knew how to spread those things around.

Frank caught heat about that, but he didn't mind because all those complaints about Hannibal being a "patronage baby" only served to obscure his actual role: Every day, sometimes for up to twelve hours, Hannibal sat in that room with no windows and hacked his way into the e-mails of every member of the City Council. Frank knew everything about all of them. What they were thinking, who they lunched with, who they were sleeping with, and, most importantly, where they were getting their money. Frank blackmailed one Councilman into resigning. He got the top donor of another to switch his support to a candidate more to Frank's liking. He was always one step ahead of the Council because he had Hannibal. And he kept him happy. Bought him a new computer every year. Gave his mom a job with the city and she soon qualified to buy a small house in the city under the city's "sweat equity " program, and just like that they were comfortably middle class.

I can give you a list of names—five, ten other officials with stories of their own, who owe everything to Frank. And will do anything he asks. And that's how, across sixteen years, Franklyn Longley created a new middle class to replace the old one that had abandoned the city long ago. He instilled loyalty in the population and created a smoke screen that effectively obscured the money he skimmed off the top on various city contracts, hid the purchase of properties in the Caribbean, or the further shifting of campaign contributions to his private accounts.

Hannibal always wanted to go to college. He used to talk to me of maybe doing something really important in his life. Then he met Franklyn. We all met Franklyn.

(*Holding the zip drive and folder forward.*)

My name is Zachary Drayton. I am Chief of Staff to the Mayor, and these documents, Mr. District Attorney, will allow you to meet Frank Longley, too.

Lights. End of Scene Thirteen.

Scene Fourteen

FRANKLYN *and* MELISSA.

FRANKLYN: That was Harold MacMannis on the phone. There was a meeting of the Big Four. They told the Governor they're going to support Ronald. They're going to go ahead with him and finish my project downtown. That construction is going forward without me. I'll be forgotten. It was my idea, and when it's finished it will be as though I never lived at all.

MELISSA: I'm sorry, Frank. But at least the city will grow. Isn't that what you wanted?

FRANKLYN: To hell with them all: They'll find they can't do this to me. They'll—

(FRANKLYN *does not finish the sentence.*)

MELISSA: "They" didn't do anything to you, Frank. Zack did. You underestimated him.

FRANKLYN: I sure did.

MELISSA: You were going after his son.

FRANKLYN: That was politics. That doesn't give Zack the right to rat me out to the Attorney General. We were *friends*.

MELISSA: The things y'all did... God, Frank.

FRANKLYN: We didn't hurt anybody who didn't have it coming. You forget, some of those people were trying to hurt me. It's all going to come out in the papers now. Chaka and Tamara are going to find out.

(*Pause. He composes himself a bit... or tries to.*)

I haven't said anything to them about a divorce. Have you?

MELISSA: They're adults with lives of their own. They'll handle it.

FRANKLYN: I kept hoping you'd change your mind.

MELISSA: I kept hoping you'd change yours.

FRANKLYN: Just remember, you're the one who wanted to end this marriage. Not me.

MELISSA: And *you're* the one who *caused* it to end.

(FRANKLYN *looks away. Then:*)

FRANKLYN: The Attorney General will come after you to get to me.

MELISSA: I don't know anything.

FRANKLYN: You know enough.

MELISSA: They'll be wasting their time.

FRANKLYN: You wouldn't have to say anything if we're still married.

MELISSA: What?

FRANKLYN: Don't underestimate me, Mel. I'm too smart not to make this go away.

MELISSA: The graveyard of black political careers is filled with the names of people who thought they were "too smart." I told you, years ago, when you first started down this path, there was only so much I was going to take; only so much I'd do. And one thing I was not going to do was wash up your blood, figuratively or literally, because there is nothing—*nothing*—in all this worth your family, your reputation, or your life. And if you're so deluded with hubris, or whatever, to see that, then I don't need to be around you.

FRANKLYN: Melissa, please—

MELISSA: I've got to get away, Franklyn.

FRANKLYN: I'm fighting for my life here. I need you, Melissa. Just until I get through this. Afterward…

MELISSA: No.

FRANKLYN: Alright then! But I'm going to win this. Let them drag me into court. All that evidence Zack gave the State Attorney—the letters, the e-mails, the memos, the receipts, alla that stuff, has other people's names attached to them, not just mine. There's only so much I knew, or was responsible for, and a lot of what I knew Zack also knew. Sure, Zack wants to confess to a lot of stuff, now that he's at death's door and suddenly discovered heaven. But, funny he should get an attack of conscience at the same time his son is running for Governor. There's *always* a price to doing business with anybody. This is capitalism we're talking about. Just because something looks unethical doesn't mean it's illegal. I can point to politicians all over the state who got question marks hanging over their heads and no one is pressing charges against them, so why is this big hammer over my head? I'll have my lawyers throwing so many balls up in the air the jury will grow dizzy trying to keep up. Over and over again, day after day, till by the time they get the case, no one will know which way is up, and there'll be as much going for me as against. When it's all said and done, when all the howling stops, I'll still be the big dog holding the bone.

MELISSA: For the sake of our grandchildren, I shouldn't want you to go to prison. But to stand here and listen to you not once acknowledge the harm you've caused, I can't believe we have so little to hold on to, that our people are so starved of any pride that we are content to make you a bigger hero than ever, with few of us even bothering to ask what it means for our community.

FRANKLYN: I still matter, Melissa. *I still matter!*

(FRANKLYN *looks off. There is silence.* MELISSA *looks at him. Then:*)

MELISSA: All this time and you still don't get it. It's not whether you matter, Frank. It's whom you matter to.

Lights. End of Scene Fourteen.

Scene Fifteen

Lights up on TRICIA JOHNSON.

TRICIA JOHNSON: Ebonie, you call your uncle Henry about that suit he said he had?...God...No, he won't mind. It's too small for him, and it fits Maleek perfect....Suddenly, I'm thinking about my mother....Yes, it's a shame you never knew her. You might have liked her....Yes, that day I remember being surprised at how brown her eyes were. I never had noticed, I don't think. Never truly appreciated just how brown her eyes were. Just surprised the hell out of me. I just stood there looking into my mother's beautiful brown eyes. Before I closed them. That was my first time in a morgue. Been there a lot since: my sister, two uncles, a nephew, and a great aunt. Cancer, heart disease, alcoholism, diabetes, auto accident, and Alzheimer's. We don't go quietly in my family....But Mama was in a hospital morgue. This here is the County Morgue. All business here; no time to be trying to soothe you with soft voices and kind words. Here, they usher you in, sit you down, then come get you when you when it's time for you to view the body. That's how it's going to be with Maleek....No, I don't know who shot him....Does it really matter who did it? My baby's dead. Can't nothing bring him back to me. So I don't think about who did it, or why....People put up a little memorial for him where he died. The flowers and the candles are real nice. It went up so fast....I didn't know he had so many friends. So many people who cared...No, you ain't going in there with me to see his body....Yes, baby, I know you loved him, and he was your brother. But, no...The people from the funeral home will come get him, clean him up, and lay him out proper. You and the children can see him then. In his uncle's suit, looking his best. I don't want you seeing him the way them hoodlums left him....You go on home, be with the children till I get home. There're some cold cuts in the fridge. Fix some sandwiches and make sure they eat....Get the little ones ready for bed. Don't say nothing to them about Maleek. I'll do that. I'm gonna need you now more than ever, Ebonie.... Your brother tried his best, honey, but he just didn't make it.... Maleek was never mine to hold. In this world, a black woman rolls the dice when she births a baby boy.... Put all this in a special place in your heart, and lock it away, girl. Just lock it away. You got to live.... Tonight, we going to sit with Pastor and say a prayer for Maleek. Then tomorrow morning we going to get up and make sure the children get to live one more day.... Sit up straight, Ebonie. That's right. Straighten up your back. You a woman, now.

Lights dim on TRICIA JOHNSON. *End of Scene Fifteen.*

Scene Sixteen

Lights up on FRANKLYN. *Alone.*

FRANKLYN: I stood on the platform, waving to the crowd, with a grin on my face so wide I could literally feel my skin stretching to a breaking point. The election was over, and I'd won. It was the most exhilarating and fantastic night of my life. The cheering, the shouting, the camera lights in my eyes; everything I could have possibly wanted. Melissa was standing next to me, waving to the people, smiling just as broadly. Our kids were there and they had the grandkids with them.

I looked over, and my father was there, staring at me with that serious look he always had when he thought I was getting too far ahead of myself, and he said, "Wake up, Frank. You're dreaming." And so I was. My father had died long before I was ever elected to anything. I opened my eyes and just lay there, staring at the ceiling. Then, after awhile, I got up out of bed, went to the kitchen, drank myself some warm milk, got back in the bed, and drifted off to sleep. I never had that dream again.

(FRANKLYN *stares off for the longest time, then...*)

Lights fade to black.